Transgression and the Inexistent

Suspensions: Contemporary Middle Eastern and Islamicate Thought

Series editors: Jason Bahbak Mohaghegh and Lucian Stone

This series interrupts standardized discourses involving the Middle East and the Islamicate world by introducing creative and emerging ideas. The incisive works included in this series provide a counterpoint to the reigning canons of theory, theology, philosophy, literature, and criticism through investigations of vast experiential typologies – such as violence, mourning, vulnerability, tension, and humour – in light of contemporary Middle Eastern and Islamicate thought.

Transgression and the Inexistent:

A Philosophical Vocabulary

Mehdi Belhaj Kacem

Translated by P. Burcu Yalim

Bloomsbury Academic
An imprint of Bloomsbury Publishing Plc

B L O O M S B U R Y
LONDON · OXFORD · NEW YORK · NEW DELHI · SYDNEY

Bloomsbury Academic

An imprint of Bloomsbury Publishing Plc

50 Bedford Square	1385 Broadway
London	New York
WC1B 3DP	NY 10018
UK	USA

www.bloomsbury.com

BLOOMSBURY and the Diana logo are trademarks of Bloomsbury Publishing Plc

First published 2014
Paperback edition published 2017

British Library Cataloguing-in-Publication Data

A catalogue record for this book is available from the British Library.

ISBN: HB: 9781472534934
PB: 9781350021433
ePDF: 9781472526021
ePub: 9781472528629

Library of Congress Cataloging-in-Publication Data

A catalog record for this book is available from the Library of Congress.

Suspensions: Contemporary Middle Eastern and Islamicate Thought

Typeset by Fakenham Prepress Solutions, Fakenham, Norfolk NR21 8NN
Printed and bound in Great Britain

Contents

Translator's Note

While the translation of *être* as "being" poses no particular problem, the translation of *étant* (originally with reference to Heidegger), which is the substantive from the present participle of *être*, presents more difficulty. I have adopted the translation of Alan Bass in *Writing and Difference* and rendered this term as "the being" (slightly modifying Bass's translation as simply "being") or "beings," according to context (rather than the alternative translation as "entity" or "entities," or as "existent" in other cases). However, in order to avoid all confusion, I have provided the French word in parentheses in most cases. For a detailed explanation on this term and its translation, I refer the reader to "Translator's Introduction," in *Writing and Difference* (Jacques Derrida, trans. Alan Bass, London: Routledge & Kegan Paul, 1978, p. xvii–xviii). For the term "being," in the sense of being in general, since the context is not strictly Heideggerian, I have written it each time with a lower-case initial.

Le vide is translated as "the void." MBK also makes frequent use of its different forms, such as *vidé*, *évidé* and *évidement*. I have translated these terms respectively as "emptied" (from *vider*, "to empty" or "empty out"), "voided" (from *évider*, "to hollow out" or "scoop out"), and "voiding." I have translated *évidant*, the present participle of *évider* as adjective, also as "voiding." In most cases, I have provided the French term in parentheses.

I have translated *s'approprier*, which ordinarily means "to appropriate" as "to (self-)appropriate," adding the "self-" in parenthesis, because MBK plays on the reflexive prefix *se* or "self." This is also the case with *se posséder* which, instead of "to be in possession of oneself," I have translated as "to be in (self-)possession of oneself."

Foreword

The anti-scholastic that therefore I was

In a sense, this book is a testament; in a sense that is perhaps only parodic, and to me, all the more so.

When a number of my readers suggested to me the idea of writing this book, I could not then foresee the premonitory aspect the project itself had: to recapitulate eight years of intellectual construction work sedimented into a system, and disseminated in an academic fashion in the five volumes of *L'esprit du nihilisme*: *Ironie et vérité* (Nous, 2009), *Manifeste antiscolastique* (Nous, 2005), *Ontologique de l'histoire* (Fayard, 2009), *Être et sexuation* (Léo Scheer, to be published in 2013), and *Le sinthome politique* which became under the pressure of circumstances, *Après Badiou* (Grasset, 2011). To these I must add the two "phantom" volumes: *Inesthétique et mimêsis*, published by Nouvelles Editions Lignes in 2010, and *La conjuration des Tartuffes*, by Léo Scheer in 2011. These will still be followed, as two addenda, by two books as yet unpublished in French: a book on a major philosophical contemporary, Quentin Meillassoux, and another on the Father of philosophical modernity, Rousseau. I often allude to these in the following abecedary, and I mention them especially since it is very likely that the first will be published in English before it is published in France, not long after the publication of the present book.

After considerable hesitation about what form to give to such a book, once again upon many suggestions by the readers, I opted for the form of a lexicon. However my initial reaction was reluctance, since this "abecedary" form smelt somewhat too much of Deleuze, and my offended modesty reckoned it was somewhat premature, pre-forties, to opt for a form with such strong connotations of consecration, maturity, if not the end of the reign and embalming. At first, I wanted to content myself with a little synthetic "account" of the five and a half volumes. In spite of this, the idea of a lexicon kept on making its way like an insidious worm in the ripening fruit. In my head I could not help writing it in that form. So I ended up admitting defeat and complied. In the end, to constitute a kind of pleiade of my conceptual syntax, by taking a score of keywords with their intertwined, introductory definitions, was the best means of making the reader *see* the organic interaction of the concepts and the systematic character of the entire undertaking. Furthermore, since the École Normale Supérieure in the rue d'Ulm, upon Martin Fortier and Nicolas Nely's initiative, had convened an important colloquium on my work on 22, 23 and 24 of March, 2013, I would see this work through to the end in order to present all participants with a "bestiary" as complete as possible of all my concepts. It is indeed a matter of drawing a systematics. And therefore, a philosophy.

Thus, this systematics was not given beforehand. The research was carried out as if on demand; there was nothing systematized that pre-existed it and so it is after the fact that its organicity revealed itself to me: not even "as I went along," but rather in a revealing flash of lightning which all of a sudden shed light on the whole undertaking. But how? As a matter of fact, the essential text of the entire undertaking is *Algèbre de la Tragédie,* which concludes *Ontologique de l'Histoire.* It is in there that was revealed—as if at the crucial moment of an analytic cure—the extent to which my thought, while I had been developing it, was architectured without even me being aware of it. All I had written before, perhaps even including the literary works of my youth, and which seemed to my own eyes like a vast, non-systematic construction site, appeared as if relentlessly striated after the fact. And all I wrote afterwards was merely an "unfolding" of everything the said text had conquered: the consequences which, although implicit, went without saying for those who can read. All this to say that the system was not preconceived when I proceeded to write my cycle, and that it is exposed entirely neither in the *Algèbre* nor in the texts that followed. Thus all this goes to underline the significance of the present book, which is all the more strategic as it is after the fact—the trick being also to make it as tight as possible, because it was initially meant to clarify the "system" of the SoN[1] for not more than a score of people; but in the end, it turned out to be the clearest of all my books, and therefore the most pertinent for a beginner to get familiarized with my work. On that point, when Bloomsbury Publishing approached me for the translation of a first book into English, I deemed the *kairos* particularly ideal, and the present book the best to introduce my entire philosophical endeavor, in the form of a retroactive catalogue.

§§§

One of the signs which subjectively marked my philosophical path was the violent break with a philosopher well-known by the Anglo-Saxon and inter-national public: Alain Badiou. My reading of *Being and Event* in 2000–1 was a genuine shock for me. Because of it, not only my work, but entire chapters of my biography turned out to be irremediably transformed, for better or for worse. In the end, the worse prevailed. I had a long lasting and vast collaboration with Badiou; my work obviously bears witness to it, but the reverse—necessarily dissymmetrical—was not less true, as laid bare by the note dedicated to me at the end of *Logics of Worlds*.[2] Yet it is in 2005, during my presentation of his seminar to the audience that Badiou proved to be the most prophetic, by presenting me as his "best enemy." I am afraid that what followed forever keeps proving him right …

And therefore upon Bloomsbury's proposition, I added several passages that did not exist in the first version of this abecedary, and which, for the Anglophile neophyte, elaborates more in depth the reasons for this very violent break, which had immense polemical repercussions in France, with the book that announced it: the above-cited *Après Badiou*. Needless to say, it is the conceptual and technical details that count; but if I open my heart about it already in this foreword, this is for two reasons. First, it is in order to stress well enough from which position I engaged in a parricidal war: in France, I have been much reproached for using in *Après Badiou* the recurring, paradigmatic comparison with Nietzsche's break with Wagner. I have of course been accused of megalomania and of taking myself for Nietzsche (something Nietzsche said, and which he wrote on the edge of his so-called madness, has always made me laugh a great deal: "I would much rather be a Basel professor than God; but I have not ventured to carry my private egoism so far." It is in the next paragraph that the reader will understand the motive for this parenthesis…). The accusation is unfair. My work, following Schürmann's,[3] is a total and ruthless war engaged against the root of all psychological megalomania, which is the almost *automatically* megalomaniac essence of metaphysics, from its origins to the present day. It is Badiou and Badiou alone that is the proper name of this megalomania today. In these pages, we will find out why and how. Yet what the French accusers did not get about my gesture is that the comparison was not on the side of Nietzsche: I have too much admiration for the latter's heroic saintliness in order not to think that even if I obtained a tenth of the historical outcomes that he obtained in philosophy, I would conclude that my life and work will not have been too much in vain. No: it is the second term of the comparison that is intended here. Yes, my relationship to Badiou, admiring for a long time, would appear to be similar to Nietzsche's long submission to the Wagnerian project. And even if, following the second Nietzsche, Adorno and Lacoue-Labarthe, one became, like myself, the most radical of *philosophical* anti-Wagnerians—for instance against Badiou and Žižek's recent attempts to redeem Wagner—one would have to recognize that, if one is hardly a committed music-lover and connoisseur of the History of western music, Wagner is at the very least one of the twenty most important and creative musicians in all the said History. As for metaphysical genius, I am not far from thinking, *still today*, exactly the same thing about Badiou. His is very likely the vastest conceptual construction to emerge in Europe since Heidegger. Yet, exactly like Wagner's case, the question that arises is the question of what *envelops* the core of genius: the one musical, the other metaphysico-conceptual. Now, Wagner's idea of art was very specific. He took himself for a great dramaturgist (alas, this is what Žižek and Badiou think). He had an idea of politics, which historically proved to be very specific as well (hence the true horror inspired in me by Žižek and Badiou's matching of Wagner with Stalin and Mao, and which, if I may say so, has been the drop to overflow the glass of an apostasy that had been in turmoil for a long time). There was even a Wagnerian *philosophy* ("Art and Revolution": an entire program, literally and in every sense). In short: even if the composer Wagner was as an indubitable genius (although quite belated... like Badiou himself peaked towards his forties), everything he understood by theory, philosophy, art, politics turned out to be disastrous. I ended up thinking exactly the same thing about Badiou. Not only what he *makes* of his metaphysical genius, in terms of a *"grande politique"* inspired by Asian mass massacres of the twentieth century, in terms of art (necessarily "oeuvral" and "monumental": Wagnerian), in terms of his rather regressive views on the division of sexes ("woman semi-exists, or exists me,"[4] he still writes in full in *Logics of Worlds*), in terms of philosophy of science, not only all this but also, quite simply, what he calls *philosophy* on the basis of his tremendous metaphysical constructions, finally appeared to me as calamitous as what Wagner made of his uniquely musical genius, in terms of art. Badiou is to metaphysical virtuosity what Wagner was to solmisation; but he is also to philosophy, and his relationship is to "truths," what Wagner was to the always indivisible suture of aesthetics and politics. Thus all of these come under the first reason, whose ramifications will be argued in the following pages. The second reason is very important to me: it is that I am not even remotely academic.

When I tell people that I have never had university education, that I have never taught, and that my most distinguished qualification is the baccalauréat, they blink and do not believe me. Yet it is the truth, and a crucial truth to understand, with insight, the very meaning of my undertaking. This is why I deemed it appropriate to mention this second reason in the foreword: because it is more closely related to the first than it would seem at first sight. Indeed, among the numerous foreclosures it should have on consciousness, the notion of "anti-philosopher" coined by Badiou is not the lesser one. He *does not even* realize that the *elementary* feature common to all those he slams as "anti-philosophers" is to have worked *outside* the walls of the university. But I have observed only too well that there is none so blind as the Platonist blinded by the bedazzling exit from the Cave... Let us suppose for a moment that the most spectacular academic animal we have ever seen (a kind of Normalian Mao-Wagner) is right, in this foreclosure itself: since Kant, the philosopher is necessarily a professor. Hegel, Husserl, Bergson, Heidegger, Deleuze, Derrida, Badiou ... therefore, the question posed by my own path, after so many others—and a very serious question since, by definition, nobody would be in a position to answer—is:[5] how does the fact of being inalienably academic affect philosophy it*self*? Its weight is all the more crushing since no one would be in a position to put into perspective how this (all the same moderately glorious) condition of the "functionaries of humanity" is poisonous for their own presuppositions, if we accept Badiou's foreclosed postulate: whoever articulates a conceptual systematics outside the university is *ipso facto* an "anti-philosopher." This is the consequence I do not allow for. I call "philosophy," in a very precise sense, closer to Hegel than to anyone else, the conceptual system I have created over a decade with my own hands, so to speak. This had to be said once and for all; therefore, I say thank you to the quasi-providential circumstances which finally let me.

Let us put it differently. I gave up the idea of becoming a professor for—in a way—"selfish" reasons: I was too attached to my "difficult freedom." However painful certain episodes might have been in my life, however half-crippled my life might have often become due to my sometimes Dickensian material precariousness, nothing will make me regret having always lived as an absolutely free man. This is a luxury that has become much rarer than our democratic false consciousness tends to delude us into believing. Yet with the distance, the long way I have come, the many material and psychological difficulties I have had because of the fact of philosophizing outside the walls of the academy, I realized that there was also something eminently *altruistic* about this decision—besides, the poverty in which I lived could serve as a good enough proof of this. Yes, there was something sacrificial about this decision. In a way, it is for philosophy's own sake that I refrained from teaching for a such a long time, including even the unbelievable deliberate mistakes I probably made subconsciously: in fact, since philosophy has been practically monopolized by professors for two centuries, are we not entitled to put on trial the gigantic *professional deformation* that this quasi-exclusive background imposes on what is said explicitly in 90 percent of all that is written in this noble discipline? Without going as far as wishing that a mechanic or a farmer be philosophers, even if in a perfect world it would be desirable, are we not entitled to hope for a little more *sociological diversity* among philosophy's representatives? With all this, I finally saw, very late, that my decision in the negative had something sacrificial about it: *there had to be at least one such philosopher.* And even though for two centuries, all attempts to extract philosophy from the sole professorial coterie had failed, mine included—at least in the existential sense of the term,[6] since furthermore we cannot say that Marx or Nietzsche did not produce some effect, the question still being at what price *to them,* and why—it had to be tried, at least one more time. There had to be, in my time, at least one contribution to philosophy that was not professorial.

One day a friend of mine told me she admired my "ability to (self-)manipulate (myself)." I replied it was because I loathed all propensity to manipulate others—you know what I mean. With the slight clumsiness of its expression, and said in a Maghrebian accent, this remark was still exquisitely accurate: I also added that it was an integral part of my philosophy, to consider oneself as one's own toy, one's own automaton, one's own actor-instrument. Oneself as an other. Yet, to be exact, the reason was actually far from selfish: ten years of social happiness cheerfully sacrificed in a spirit of perfect self-abnegation, so that the innervation of the philosophical circuit is not made solely through academic channels. I repeat that this says nothing against the eminent dignity of this occupation; but it is obviously a question addressed to the strict sociological exclusivity of those who in general relentlessly prescribe miracle-answers to all imaginable problems in any domain whatsoever.

For all these reasons, the present book obeys the Epicurean principle of rejecting the cumulative conception of philosophy which is typical of academic practice. All in all, who, better than myself, could put himself in the position of resuscitating practical self-education, invented by those who philosophized not in the Academy nor at the Lycée but in their own garden? A true philosophy should fit in a corpus of maxims as short as *possible,* which you should later be able to recall at any moment, and put to use in all circumstances, without the need to open a book, whether you are in jail or on a desert island. A structural Epicureanism, all in all. So I set an example of myself, and forced myself not to open *any* volume of *The Spirit of Nihilism* in order to draw up the present conceptual "breviary." Thus, everything in this book has been written "from memory" so to speak. I contented myself with defining in this way, without any books to serve as rear-view mirror, the principal concepts I created along the way, such as they are sedimented *in me*—in my most ordinarily psychological and everyday person—since the time I discovered them while I wrote the different volumes of the SoN. I threw them on paper such as they serve me in my "daily life" so to speak. We *know*, and I remember that time very well, that one has fully become a philosopher when the concepts one has created oneself become like a *second nature*, and even a quasi-literal *sixth sense*, which allows you to detect, in the most trivial phenomena of day-to-day life, things not yet perceived by anyone—and I am certain that my readers will perceive them, just as a philosopher I admire is always someone who has functioned like a perceptual "graft" on my intellectual "body."

I hope the present summary does not blunt the reader's curiosity: the volumes recapitulated in a "testamentary" fashion contain countless further subtleties, if not entire continents (an entire *literal* philosophy of History that the present breviary does not even touch upon), that are not broached here. The appendix at the end of the treatise recapitulates it all: it is a protreptic. Yet the protreptic justifies itself retroactively, for being sedimented in a mnemonic "depot" of concepts that can be summoned and efficiently put to use at any moment.

I hope the "abecedary" tree that can be taken anywhere does not however hide the forest that gave birth to it, but that in it, the new reader feels warmly *welcome*.

Affect

This functionary, however, has been thoroughly mystified; and the remote source of his defeat lies in the supposition that the Minister is a fool, because he has acquired renown as a poet. All fools are poets; this how the Prefect feels; and he is merely guilty of a non distributio medii in thence inferring that all poets are fools. (…) I know him well; he is both. As poet and mathematician, he would reason well; as mere mathematician, he could not have reasoned at all, and thus would have been at the mercy of the Prefect. (…) The mathematical reason has long been regarded as the reason par excellence. (…) The mathematicians, I grant you, have done their best to promulgate the popular error to which you allude, and which is none the less an error for its promulgation as truth. (…) The great error lies in supposing that even the truths of what is called pure algebra are abstract or general truths. And this error is so egregious that I am confounded at the universality with which it has been received.

Edgar Allan Poe, *The Purloined Letter*[1]

AFFECT: "Mathematical," i.e. always very exactly *proportioned*, sign of appropriation (see below). It is possible to talk about a form of "affect" in plants, which appropriate water and light for themselves, and are thus literally affected. Yet it is with animal appropriation that we can talk of affect in the strict sense.

The soul is the body of sensation, Aristotle *dixit*. And sensation emerges only by an evental *power* of appropriation, a *dunamis*, which the mineral realm lacks absolutely, and which the vegetable is endowed with rather ridiculously compared to the specifically animal, and then even more singularly (in yet other words: eventally), human, appropriation.

Human affects, that is to say, affects of the technological, i.e. metaphysical animal, are all "perverted"—we will see how—in relation to animal affects: technological appropriation aims at an exponentiation of jouissances, a supernumerary excess that is well and truly obtained. However, this appropriation also produces a lack, a deflation, all kinds of affectual *voidings* [*évidements*], which will have the heaviest consequences on the destinal constitution of what we call "humanity." Hence this counterbalancing, which is at the ethical core of what *The Spirit of Nihilism* investigates, produces just as well a reversal and a torsion: an ontological perversion.

Would this mean that Spinoza is null and void? Everything in his system comes down to the increase or decrease in power quantified by the affect in every living being [*étant*]. I do not intend to play tricks with the indisputable "prince of philosophers," an undying pleasure to read for anyone in love with philosophy. However, does he account for the fundamental torsion which the philosophy of Evil called *The Spirit of Nihilism* points at? When a cat cuts a lizard in half and enjoys the show, it is not for the pleasure of making it suffer. It is because the cat is amazed by this unprognostic faculty that it has not come across in other prey, and this derogation from the usual Laws, which makes the lizard keep moving even after what should have caused its immediate death. Predatory cruelty obeys a necessary Law which overhangs the predator; its jouissance consists of the one and only increase in power caused by ingestion, and not in the noetic delight at the victim's supposed suffering. There is no torture in animals, because torture is a *technical* practice, in the most trivial sense of the adjective. Technical, i.e. metaphysical; that is why only the human animal practises metaphysical torture *as well*, literally and in every sense.

The presence of all these affects perverted by technomimetics, and their detailed phenomenological description in the SoN, show well enough that this latter is a philosophy of Evil which, in this respect, puts on trial the classico-dogmatic metaphysics, whose pinnacle is probably Spinoza. What is the always renewed presupposition of this metaphysics, or yet again of "dogmatic" philosophy caesured historically by Kant, which will finally allow, as we will see, a thought of Evil? It is that the being [*l'étant*], whatever it may be, *cannot not* want the Good. Spinoza's *conatus*, universal Desire, recapitulates this point historically with excellence. And hence, from Plato to Spinoza to Badiou, *Evil* is nothing but an erroneous—and as such rectifiable—access to the Good (see *Nihilism*).

Everything is decided here. Classico-dogmatic philosophy, since its origins, has been a perversion itself. Since Good, as defined by classico-dogmatic philosophy, is *conatus*, the hierarchization of *eros* since its origins, philosophy obliterates the fact that already in its envoi it is a discipline measuring appropriative *ferocity*. It spiritualizes, sublimates this ferocity; philo-sophy which also means: appropriation of knowledge [*savoir*]. It has its driving force specifically in what constitutes the root of all Evil for religion (again see *Nihilism*).

Spinozism would thus *apply* to the animal in us, if *conatus* could want nothing but the Good. Only the animal can "innocently" want the destruction of an other being [*étant*], the rational satisfaction of *conatus*. And yet, since Schelling, man is well and truly the one who perverts *conatus*, literally and in every sense, in technomimetic astuteness: he is the one who can *want* Evil *as such*.

The non-Spinozist torsion of human "affectology" is that technology, i.e. *mimesis* (see below) is what conditions the appearance of noumenal phenomena such as jouissance before the spectacle of the other's suffering (originary aesthetic voyeurism, see *Art*), and even of the suffering one inflicts on another (sadism, torture precisely), jouissance as a torsion of one's own suffering (masochism), but also the appearance of *voided* affects ("depression" in all its historical forms) or else affects that are much "fuller" than those resulting from mere animal instinctuality (philosophical beatitude, mystical ecstasy). See also *Desire*.

Man, from the very beginning, is the animal of technological affects. Predatory animal cruelty becomes torturing perversion; the affectual binarity of all other mammals, in the Nietzschean-Spinozist mode, where every being [*étant*] aims at an increase of power and avoids its deterioration (in short, joy and suffering) producing phenomena like masochism. This perversion obeys strictly *logical* laws, but their logic is not that of "pure" or "formal" logic: a strictly philosophical logic. In Nature, animal nature included, affirmations and negations obey the "pure" and "formal" transcendental logic; in the anthropological closure, affirmations and negations function in a perverted manner, and all the "nerve" of the conceptual syntax developed in terms of "general affectology" by *The Spirit of Nihilism* lies in there. The avowed stake being the creation of an entirely novel type of dialectics, the guiding sentence of the whole undertaking is the following sentence by Adorno: "Dialectical thought is an attempt to break through the coercion of logic by its own means."[2]

Because of *mimesis* (see below) and repetition, human affect most often functions in the mode of "the more it is less, the less it is more" [*plus c'est moins, moins c'est plus*]. But why? Because, primordially, everything turns around the fundamental affect of sexual jouissance (see below). The mimetic appropriation of this jouissance, the fact of repeating it beyond reproductive necessity, aims precisely at obtaining a *more*, a kind of an originary "affectual surplus value," an intensification. It obtains, in an unprognostic way, a whole avalanche of *less*: the catalogue of these subtractions, in the yet again mathematical sense of the term, constitutes the phenomenology that runs through the entire *Spirit of Nihilisim*. We would recognize the question of *Evil* (see below).

Double negation for instance, or apagoge, do not lead to the same results as those of "pure" and "formal" logic. We will see how as we examine each and every fundamental concept of the SoN.

Suffice it to remember the simple but essential innovation which constitutes the fundamental perspective from which *The Spirit of Nihilism* tackles the question of affect: there is no affect other than appropriative. Yet because man is the being [*l'étant*] of *maximally* appropriative affects, he is then immediately the being of maximally *expropriating* affects.

On this subject, I borrow an adjective quite brilliantly formed by an excellent scholar, Pascal Taranto, in a not less excellent collection of philosophical texts, gathered around the notion of ressentiment:[3] pleonectic [*pléonectique*].

> In fact, for all the passions where it is actually a matter of prevailing over the other, it induces a fundamental perversion of the rule, owing to the pleasure provided by the exception of self. We could call these passions "pleonectic," after the Greek noun *Pleonexia*, itself formed after the verbal group *pleon echein*, and whose literal signification is "to have more." If this Greek term originarily designates the immoderate desire for riches, and especially jealousy of the other's wealth (but also of honours and power). Locke gives a more general signification which justifies this usage: "*Pleonexia*, 'covetousness' [*convoitise*], in the common sense of the term, signifies that we let ourselves desire that to which, according to the law of justice, we have no right."

My work provides an even further, ontological extension to the signification of "pleonexia": it demonstrates that the analytic of being as event cannot underestimate—as did the entire metaphysical tradition up to Heidegger-Schürmann, who disrupted it—the importance of the "appropriative-expropriative" play in all evental occurings. It will show just as well that the "fundamental perversion" is as originary as man itself, as the animal of technomimetic appropriation.

As Reiner Schürmann writes on the non-fortiutous subject of Luther: "He will be saved who confesses that he is rotten to the core with egotism."[4] The metaphysico-theological tradition which recently thought to have concealed its stench of sacristy by replacing the religious with the "laicity" of the word "political," has always reckoned that to be done with the efflorescence of Evil, one had to cut off its roots, which is the ego subordinated immediately by technomimetic appropriation. In other words, by doing exactly what appropriation has been doing, from the very beginning: expropriating animal egoity in a "superior" subjectivation. We will see that the ethical outcome proposed by the SoN differentiates itself from the entire tradition, doubtless with the exception of Epicurus and Nietzsche, although in an entirely different mode from theirs.

It is a matter of taking Luther literally, but how? It is through an unconditioned *formal* assumption of the indivisible pleonectic egoism, a figuration we will call *play* (see below).

Finally, my singular definition of affect, based on appropriation, would not be semantically complete if it did not refer to the other terms of the present lexicon (see below: *Appropriation, Desire, Expropriation, Jouissance, Sexuation…*) that echo it, affirming its full extent. Affect, since its emergence, which constitutes the animal stage, is an appropriation of *space* which becomes *time*. We will see right away how.

Appropriation

APPROPRIATION: The sign that decisively marks the advent of humanity as event is the sign of *appropriation*. For us, this appropriation is what is designated, very broadly, by the syntagm of "Science." Man is an ultra-appropriative animal because he is the animal of protoscientific astuteness: of technics and imitation (see below, Techne, Mimesis). But the animal is already an appropriative being [*étant*] with respect to other beings, namely vegetables: whereas plants merely receive and absorb light and water in order to grow before they wither (and all forms of withering are the trait of expoptiation which inevitably sanctions all appropriation, as we will see), the animal, by moving about in every direction and the supernumerary assimilation of the purely vegetable but also "alter-animal" stage,[1] *wastes* its being-there to achieve an over-appropriation of time and *space*. The mineral persists in much more extensive portions of time, because it does not come out of itself or does so rarely: because it does not make time and space its *own*.

Indeed this is what *The Spirit of Nihilism* contributes to the great German metaphysics of time and space, especially Kant and Heidegger: time is nothing other than the *factual* oxymoron of an appropriation of space which is an expropriation (see below). According to Heidegger, with sovereign insight, "The abyss is the originary unit of space and time."[2] This unity, which qualifies the "normal" being-there of the mineral cosmos, is broken by the—at first vital, then techno-mimetic—event of appropriation. The living is a *gratuitous* appropriation of space, which is time and temporalization. Yet this temporalization is also a *jeopardizing* [*précarisation*] of being-there.

The intensification of this process, that is the aim of purely animal appropriation, ends in a regime of expropriations, inexistent until then: suffering, withering, evanescence, death. Time is a Transgression (see below) of space, which is an appropriation-expropriation of time.

The cosmic mineral, planting itself placidly in its spatial being-there, dwells in a "time" which is not yet properly time—here, there are but germinal affects, while on such a planet there exist the molecular stammerings of this trans-statistical miracle called "life." In *transgressing* this being-there by an "ingestion" of space which was not provided for in the program, animality, *then* technology, exponentially digging the abyss that separates the two, *creates* temporality itself, that is to say, affect (see above): first, biological durations and cycles, and then History (see below) and the eras.

It is in here that consciousness is born, which we share with the entire animal kingdom: the soul, since Aristotle, is nothing other than Deleuze and Guattari's "Body without Organs," i.e. the body of pure affectual intensities: the incorporeal body of sensation. In order to cut short Deleuze and Guattari's temptations of hylozoism,[3] we will say that affect is inchoative with respect to the supernumerary appropriation of the animal kingdom, which consists of an appropriation of space and time: in what Heidegger called "motility." Compared to the mineral interstellar Empire, the vegetable kingdom is itself an evental regime of appropriation; which amounts to saying that the emergence of life on earth is the ultra-event on which all the others depend. This event depends on such an unprognostic intersection with countless factors that it may be considered as a laic "miracle."[4]

Every event (see below) has the structure of a pathology, of a becoming-monstrous: "monstruation." The animal stage of appropriation probably reached its highest point with the dinosaurs, the acme of the purely organic ability to (self-)appropriate things *materially*. This culmination was evidently a pathological becoming-monstrous of animal "pleonexia." The technomimetic, i.e. human stage of ontological "pleonexia" singularizes itself with respect to the other, helping itself to the entire materiality of things, by appropriating that which governs this matter yet itself is *not* material: its Laws. Whereas the animal and the dinosaur blindly devour whatever falls before their jaws, this human appropriation is a *transcendental* appropriation: literally, an ingestion of the pure void. Yet the "mask" of Science and rationality conceals nothing other than an exponential "monstruation," like in the animal stage and like a crazy maximization of the myth of Dorian Gray. Life-event is ontologically monstrous, but technology-event is even much more monstrous. Every event evidently consists of a becoming-(always)-more-monstrous of being.

Techne is a pathology of *physis*. But *physis* itself, planetary "biodiversity," indeed seems to be nothing short of a tremendous pathology—like mold on all things fresh—of the astrophysical impassivity revealed by Galileo's telescope. As I always say, everything was decided there, in the sense that: statistically, nothing forbade *de jure* that planets other than ours should be populated by countless life forms as well, which would prove that this "biodiversity" is Nature's norm, like we have always supposed it to be.

Nothing of the sort: Nature is itself pathological, statistically miraculous—or catastrophic, since it actually seems that the more we move towards appropriative "beingness" [*l'étantité*], the more ontological cruelty becomes the norm. To return to the first trace of an event is like investigating a crime—we will run into Edgar Allan Poe more than once during our conceptual mini-golf.

Being as event cannot be thought otherwise than as a huge pleonectic pathology of being. Besides, the venture of *The Spirit of Nihilism* is nothing other than the first *laicization* ever made of the religious doctrine of original sin. Its whole stake is to take back from religion what religion has stolen from philosophy for so long, subordinating it to itself for thousands of years.[5] On top of the Good that philosophy too readily tends to read in it, in what way is science Evil? And why, as the Bible suggests, is learned appropriation the fact of *sexuated*, singularly mammalian organisms? *The Spirit of Nihilism* responds to these questions soberly, that is to say, *technically*. It conveys original sin in the following terms: the more appropriation there is (and this is "Good"), the more there is expropriation (and this is Evil). The animal as a being [*étant*] is much more appropriative than the vegetable (carnivorous plants are the only trace of a possible "reversal of situation": the embryo of a counter-event,[6] when it is almost always the animal that (self-)appropriates the plant). Carnivorous animals are evidently more appropriative than the herbivorous; and the omnivorous are indeed the ones to prefigure the technomimetic animal. Yet man, because he (self-)appropriates the *empty* legislative *being* [*l'être*] of the beings [*étants*], is not only omnivorous *ontically*, he is the only omnivorous being *ontologically*.

To paraphrase the Heideggerian pathos: man incorporates only and uniquely nothingness. This is why it is only among this species that we come across phenomena such as *anorexia*, whose truth consists never in "not eating anything," but actually *eating nothing*. The anorexic is nothing other than the *overtly* pathological mirror of the pathological *in science itself*, which science wants to know nothing about, not more than philosophy which so often condones it spiritually and unconditonally. Science incorporates the legislative nothingness of things, and this *fact* then takes on a structural function for any anthropological subjectivity, including non-anorexic. The animal immediately devours whatever it finds in its need to feed itself; the technomimetic animal, by short-circuiting this instinct, produces both an exponential consuming excess, and a lack, a deflation, a kind of constitutive anorexia. Since feeding is no longer only a need, but a supernumerary luxury, it becomes a *choice*, which is also called, as everybody knows: freedom. Freedom is pleonastically human. And only a human being can from then on, for all sorts of reasons, *choose* not to eat: anorexia, hunger strike, "diet," etc.

Thus at the same time as the soul, the senses, pleasure, jouissance, and consciousness, emerge suffering, disease, cruelty, and death. Therefore man, through technological astuteness, *overbids* on animal appropriation and incites Evil *in the strict sense*: planetary expropriation, torture—and no longer the "simple" predatory cruelty of the strongest, endless agony as the ransom of "Good" that is medicine as such, war—and no longer just the territorial micro-conquests, etc.

In several instances of *The Spirit of Nihilism*, I jested about the manner in which Catherine Malabou[7] claims that capitalism has something "ontological" about it. Everything depends on what we call "ontology," and there is so much to say on the subject, from Heidegger to Deleuze and Malabou to Badiou, that we cannot go through each of them in here. But if we hold that the syntagm applies to the mineral cosmos, as well as to the evental reign of vegetable and animal life, there is certainly no capitalism in "being" [*l'être*] itself. The appropriation, of which these forms of being become capable, is not yet the *monstrous* form of appropriation-expropriation that should be called "capitalism." Capitalism does not just appear here or there in the history of humanity, with the end of monarchy or industrial revolution: it is the most distinctive functioning of the region of beings [*étants*] that has made itself responsible for *technological* appropriation. "Marking one's territory" is not "capitalism." It is a proto-expropriation, but capitalism is an expropriation allowed by technomimetic astuteness: a doubling [*dédoublement*] of the form of animal expropriation (see *Representation*). Hunting and then mass extermination double predation. Private property and contracutal legislation double animal and tribal territorialization.

Hence we must be clear about this. Capitalism *is* "ontological" as long as we agree—in Heidegger's wake rather than Badiou's—to think being *as* event. But then we must take the greatest care with the very term "ontology" and, there too, it is the later Heidegger's circumspection rather than Badiou's peremptory triumphalism that proves right. Why? We will drop more cartridges in the part on mathematics (see below), but this one concerns what we call "ontology." Heidegger, lucidly, renounced the term that he asserted so bluntly in his youth: "fundamental ontology" would give way to the "thought of being." The Nazi turn obviously played a crucial role in this "turning point." He very quickly realized that what he called "fundamental ontology," the existential phenomenology of *Sein und Zeit*, could not be what it claimed to be: a "science of the most general properties of all things." It concerned only one type of determined-undetermined being [*étant*], and that was man, despite everything he said about it (dismissing all "anthropologism" with contempt[8]). *Sein und Zeit* was nothing other than an anthropology. A brilliant one, but anthropology all the same. As Derrida would say quite aptly: Heideggerian *Dasein* both *is* and *is not* human being [*l'être humain*], which means that it is human being *all the same*: because only the human being [*l'étant humain*] has to such an extent the ability to be at once what it is and what it is not. This is what Heidegger would understand, even if only in embryo, after *Sein und Zeit*: the human being [*l'étant humain*] maximizes the cleavage between appropriation and expropriation that stigmatizes the grasp of being as event.

In order to think being [*l'être*] outside of the being [*l'étant*], "ontology," i.e. the science of the most general and "universal," i.e. subsumption as the most lethal weapon of metaphysics—mistaking mimetic astuteness (see *Mimesis*) for the identitarian "ground" of things—historically had to be dismissed. We might as well say that crime is quasi-genetically inscribed in the basic metaphysical grammar, in respect of the pleonectic-mimetic impulse maximized into a fully subsuming vocabulary.

And then what? And then! Well, there is *no* science of the most general properties of all things, and this is what *The Spirit of Nihilism* demonstrates. The Kanto-Nietzscheo-Heideggerian envoi was correct: we must criticize relentlessly the claims of metaphysics in this light. Badiou, in identifying ontology with logico-mathematics, would only essentiate metaphysics in its minimal framework. It is true that identification is "eternal," in other words, as old as metaphysics itself; and it is this eternity that is decomposed before our eyes, assigning to the animal of identitarian fiduciarism the same fate as his ancestors in pleonectic fury, the dinosaurs ...

What is in literal terms the Achilles' heel of metaphysics, which would lead it to its point of no return? It is that metaphysics explicitly undifferentiates the known cosmic universe from the *exception* that is terrestrial life. In Badiou's work this undifferentiation is entirely explicit, hence his by all means exceptional status as the belated "last metaphysician." To cap it all, this metaphysics claims to speak of "event," while *excepting* the event, or the events, which make of us what we are here and now: life and technology. It is not pointless to mention incidentally that this assimilation of everything into mathematical equivalence, this suspension of evental exception that is terrestrial life with respect to mathematical universalism which delivers the *empty* form of all there is, is at the root of contemporary planetary suicide, as Heidegger's greatest and least well-known "son" Reiner Schürmann has shown. A little bit further on, I collect a few stones for the stoning (see *Logic, Mathematics*). A contemporary work of metaphysics must not cease to take a *critical* look at itself at all times; its "basic banality" consists in not excluding the two events that overdetermined it, before speaking of "event."

Therefore, against a whole contemporary tendency of philosophy (the "speculative turning point"[9]), the decision to renounce—at the very root of the philosophical gesture—every claim to ontological flattening, which only leads to the undifferentiation of everything, starting from the total suspension of the emergence of terrestrial life as event, is a more cautious and lucid decision. The philosophical twentieth century thus shot itself up with "anti-humanism" to the point of becoming a caricature. After Lacan and Lévi-Strauss, for whom the order-word was still backed up with excellent reasons, anti-humanism becomes affectation in Foucault, who never produced anything other than a critical anthropology, and in the case of Althusser, who held that in Marx's *Capital* there was not the slightest trace of human being, a vesanic fit before sinking into actual dementia—we might as well say that the road was open for some to uphold that capitalism is, para-hylozoically, inscribed in the very genes of mineral matter.[10]

Deleuze defined the resolution—and the gamble—to play a philosophy of immanence against a philosophy of transcendence by the following criterion: never to have the conceptual pretense to treat of anything other than the earth, and people. While today's program congratulates itself for "snatching the event from life in order to give it back to the stars," the parallel, *underground*[11] program of the SoN makes it a point of honor to snatch the event from logico-mathematical isomorphism, which sees absolutely no difference between our planet with those who populate it and the others, in order to give it back to Deleuze's inalienable categorical imperative: to life on earth, this miraculous pleonasm; so long as we add that the SoN is not—in the manner of Spinoza, Nietzsche, and Deleuze—a *vitalist* philosophy. Because it considers life as an anomaly, i.e. an event of appropriation, it does not close its eyes to the outrageous cost of *expropriations* that sanction its appearance, first in animal cruelty, then in the even more outrageous sadistic price that life is made to pay by the technomimetic stage of appropriation.

Spinoza said that philosophy is a meditation of life and not death, that the wise man worries about nothing as little as he worries about death. This is what has ethically become *impossible* for us to grant him: indeed, it is not his greatest contemporary disciple Deleuze who did it, meditating on death with a profoundness equal to Heidegger's or Blanchot's, but Badiou, who would thus justify all literalizations that Lin Biao would bring to the sentence ("the fear of death is counter-revolutionary"), or Pol Pot ("death is nothing"). Spinoza himself, were he born "after Auschwitz," most certainly would have reconsidered this. Therefore, on the subject, the SoN does not give up on one of the essential gains of philosophical modernity since Hegel: it has the ethical *obligation* to meditate—at least as much as "life," if not more—on the manner in which death, in the technomimetic age of appropriation is *monstrously* modalized compared to its simple surgence at the animal stage.

Art

ART: The event that singularizes the human animal with respect to the rest of the realm of the living and the terrestrial, is the event of technomimetic appropriation, which is historically sedimented into what we connote by the name of "science." This appropriative regime, which just as well tallies with what philosophers ingenuously designate as "Good," ends almost immediately in a regime of *generalized expropriation*, which intersects with everything we designate by the term "politics." It is also here that appears what must be called—beyond predatory animal cruelty—Evil (see below) proper, in all its forms: "dreadful strategies" (Schürmann) authorized only by the event of scientific—and neither biological nor animal—appropriation. What exactly is the place of art in this constellation?

Art's envoi is always Attic tragedy. In other words: art is the public exposure of what politics overdetermined by science *does*, in an immanent way, to human animals; that is to say, art is the exposure of Evil. In modernity since Sade, this structure of what art *is* refined itself to extreme ends: the arts of the masses, allowed by technology itself, democratized all forms of what Artaud called the "theater of cruelty." From Goya to Bacon, from Schönberg to Ligeti, from the horror film to "Gonzo" journalism, from rock 'n' roll to rap, in short and at the end of the day: from Sade to the pornographic mega-industry, be it popular or exclusive, art became what it has always been in essence: an uncompromising, systematic, and complacent—it is sometimes said—exposure of pure Evil.

Art, as we know, is *mimesis*. However, the SoN demands taking a closer look at the question, and with new lorgnettes. What professional reflex could have so conditioned philosophy—whether it be in order to criticize (Plato) or to praise it (Aristotle)—that it originally identified what Adorno calls "mimetic impulse" with the sole domain of art, without even taking a second look?

In reality, the SoN shows that originary *mimesis* is nothing other than Science itself; i.e. *techne* in its infancy. Agriculture is nothing other than the imitation of food gathering. Hunting is nothing other than the imitation of predation. The SoN also shows that politics—at its most indivisible root—is nothing other than the imitation of Science. Art *as such* (as distinct from simple and identified *techne*, for instance, in drawing), when all is said and done, comes rather late. Moreover, and already with Lascaux and Chauvet, art itself already seems to do nothing other than what Sophocles, Christian art or Sade would do: *sublimate* Evil in its detached representation. The bulls were the ones to be slaughtered technically, the horses, those to be enslaved with no less technological excess-cruelty, up until the cold infamy of our horse races.[2] And as we see with tragedy, it is nothing other than an imitation of this imitation that is politics, which is itself an imitation of science, which is itself an imitation … of "nature." *Mimesis* of *mimesis* of *mimesis* of … it is in this infinite *but never reiterative* structure of mimetic doublings [*dédoublements*] that resides as it were in the "nerve" of my conceptual syntax: its *dialectical mechanism*.

We know that art is also *catharsis* (see below). From the gouged eyes of Oedipus to the Calvary of the Cross and the catalogues of Sade or Goya, to contemporary chain-saw massacres, art provides a jouissance from imitating that which—lived as direct experience—has got nothing to do with jouissance. Baudelaire, creator of modernity all by himself, resumed this situation with the simplicity of genius: "the flowers of Evil." Once again, the SoN fully elucidates how it comes about, this age-old structure tied to art itself: but also why in metaphysical tradition this structure is assigned solely to the aesthetic domain, and why this error. But it is not by way of "art" as such, figuration and music, poetry and narration, etc., that we can understand all this, but by going to the very bottom of the link which ties together *techne*, *mimesis*, and *catharsis* (see below).

In order to understand this, we must pose the issue in terms of the fundamental Hegelian concept of *Aufhebung* (see below). It is with Hegel that modernity itself begins; that is, from the French Revolution onwards, all that counts will constitute a *surpassing* [*dépassement*]. As we know only too well, this is the mainspring of the Hegelian system: not only must one surpass incessantly, but this surpassing must be surpassed, and this surpassing of the surpassing must be surpassed, etc. In philosophy this was obvious: if you try to find a philosopher of the Middle Ages, or the seventeenth century who presents himself as the terminal surpassing of all the others, you are not going to find any. From Kant onwards, all philosophers presented themselves as "surpassers," each more radical than the other: Fichte surpasses Kant; Schelling surpasses both of them; Hegel surpasses these surpassers; Marx will over-surpass Hegel, etc. Even Heideggerian deconstruction, despite its anti-Hegelianism and its anti-dialectic, will present itself as a gigantic surpassing of metaphysics; and Derridean deconstruction itself, as a surpassing of that surpassing. This philosophical moment of course served only to reflect what was happening in its time: and first and foremost, in politics. Politics lived on nothing but the concept of Revolution, for almost two centuries: from the French Revolution to May '68, which designates the parodic involution of surpassing in politics, and to China's Cultural Revolution, which counter-signed in blood and atrocity the saturation of the ideological scheme of Terminal Surpassing. In art, the modern, i.e. romantic program is the program of a revival of the entire tradition which would be a surpassing of the latter; in the twentieth century, avant-gardism would purify [*épurer*] romanticism, it would claim to surpass its surpassing, and the history of art in the twentieth century until the seventies will be nothing but the stenogram of the surpassings, and the surpassings of the surpassings, etc., each more radical than the others. For forty years now, this ideology is particularly involuted in parodic postmodernism (see *Irony*). As to customs and habits, it is just as obvious: the history of the last two centuries has been the history of overcoming old customs, the liberation of women, homosexuals, of "the" sexuality itself oppressed by the old metaphysico-religious collusion, etc. It is again with May '68 that this "long march" against the moralizing oppression of the metaphysico-religious comes to a head, before being involuted more than ever in *transgressive parody*: the *femen* are parodies of feminist transgressive heroism; *queer* is particularly a parody of transgressive heroism in sexualities, etc. Once again, all roads lead to Rome: from Sade to *Salò*, we have come full circle. Pasolini, in his *Teorema*, still believed in the "subversive" virtues of sexual liberation; from the seventies onwards, he realized that the age of transgressive heroism, in sexuality as elsewhere, was over, and that the becoming-commodity of sexual transgression as art could deliver, at worst, nothing but monsters, at best, nothing but parodies; if not *monstrous parodies*. We are still there. In philosophy, a precisely monstrous anachronism of Badiou's is to be the last and the most radical philosopher of perpetual "surpassing": for him, event designates the absolute surpassing of what precedes, without ever preserving [*conserver*] anything of it. It is entirely caught within the twentieth century avant-gardist ideology, of which he constitutes the most eminent philosophical reflection; without even *realizing* that this ideology has been stuck in its own parodic involution for forty years, and that this obstruction in its turn has absolutely no chance of being surpassed. We need to look elsewhere and otherwise.

In other words: not to *condemn* the post-revolutionary age of unlimited surpassings, which has brought about invaluable positive outcomes in all domains: in the philosophical domain of course, in the salutary liberation of daily customs, the innumerable productions of masterpieces in romantic and then avant-gardist art, in popular uprisings,[3] and finally in the Promethean achievements of Science (in which case we can simply no longer ignore that they give birth to just as many abominations). It is a matter of showing the fact that this sequence is over, well over for almost half a century now; and not, as in Badiouian philosophy, of dreaming of restoring what preceded this half of the century, that is to say, the heroism of perpetual surpassing, but precisely, of thinking this half century itself in its apparent "nihilism": to draw its *philosophical* consequences, according to the famous paradigm of the Owl of Minerva; to make its retrospective philosophy, which alone provides a viable forecast on the century opening before us; and therefore not attempts at a regressive *Restoration* suggested by the supposed Žižeko-Badiouian "Revolutionaries." And henceforth philosophy cannot but ask the one question not asked by Badiou and Žižek, who remain ideologically stuck at that point: *in what way* is the ideology of perpetual surpassing shipwrecked for fifty years?

Since then, art, emancipatory politics, but at bottom even science—until then very poorly regarded by religious authorities, precisely for suggesting unprognostic "surpassings"—and finally sexuality, for almost a century and a half have lived on surpassings, each more radical than the other. Hegel has triumphed; he was truly the very great philosopher of that period and, for not coming across a philosopher to match him since, we are still there. In other words: "heroic" philosophies which will have attempted a radical surpassing of the Hegelian moment of perpetual surpassing, like Deleuze and Badiou, will have been defeated for good in assuring a hegemony comparable to Hegel's in his time. What is the reason for this failure? What is the reason for the "victory" of those philosophemes that are apparently so opposed to the "affirmationist" philosophemes of our two heroic French philosophers? Why will the concepts of "nihilism," Nietzsche and Heidegger, or of "postmodernism," Lyotard and Baudrillard, have qualified modernity with infinitely greater pertinence than these two "positive" and "affirmationist" philosophers? It is this question that *The Spirit of Nihilism* tackles.

Aufhebung is the word Hegel chooses, for all sorts of reasons, in order to translate the word that would later become "event" (see below). One would have to wait for Lacoue-Labarthe (whose work I merely extend *systematically*) to understand that *Aufhebung* designates such a solid conceptual *complex* that, as soon as it is enunciated, it abandons the domain of the pure concept, in order to get infused, as it were, "to the naked eye" into reality: the *mimesis-techne-catharsis* complex, at work since the dawn of humanity, but displaying its planetary triumph in our age alone. Very plainly Aristotle, rather than Plato. The *system* of *The Spirit of Nihilism* wrestles with nothing other than this complex: *aufhebung=mimesis-techne-catharsis*.

Therefore Hegel, with the concept of *Aufhebung*, made a breakthrough, and perhaps delivered *the* essential concept not only to *understand* modernity born with the French Revolution, but also to *act* on this modernity. It is impossible to grasp it without getting to the bottom of the archeological inquiry into this concept. It is precisely because for almost fifty years the concept has exhausted all its practical-speculative resources that philosophy *can* finally give an exhaustive account of it.

In actual fact, I think the influence of Hegelian dialectics, through this concept, has gone well beyond all possible evaluation. The dialectic of *Aufhebung* is the dialectic of surpassing. And, after Hegel, all modernity has in fact lived on the fuel of the categorical imperative of surpassing, and the surpassing of surpassing, etc. The entire history of art from the beginning of the nineteenth century onwards, but also all the history of the sciences and philosophy, all the history of the modern subversion of daily customs and sexuality gives itself to be read as the history of biddings, overbiddings and over-overbiddings on the most appropriated surpassing in a given historical moment.

This acceleration, like all acceleration, comes to saturation at a given moment, in other words, to a precocious exhaustion. After a century and a half of surpassings, some more so than others, things involuted in less time than what was needed to say it: the dynamics of perpetual surpassing began turning to no avail, proving to be *parodic*. I date this turning point back to the sixties and especially the seventies. Some will qualify this turning point as "postmodern": these best of the thinking heads will be Debord, Baudrillard (see *Irony*), and Lyotard.

Should a motive be needed throw light, other than ethical, on my violent break with Badiou, it is based on the fact that his philosophy is an off-beat philosophy of perpetually compulsory surpassing, more brutal even than Hegel's: it is a philosophy of an absolute and fanatically puritan *aufhebung*, which suppresses *all* that precedes it, and preserves *nothing* of it, in whatever domain it is applied. This is the absolutely *truncated* aspect of the Badiouian conception of the event.

And it should go without saying, but is better to say, that the long ideology of perpetual surpassing has also been a fanaticism of the *perpetuated* event: Avant-garde in art, mass political party, or enlightened groupuscule in politics, Promethean upheavals of the world by science. Starting with the sixties, the avant-garde is exhausted in art and goes round in circles in the postmodern blink.

The politics of emancipation is exhausted by totalitarian planning and media-parliamentary resignation.[4] And, for the first time in the history of philosophy, the doubt cast on scientific positivity by people like Rousseau, Nietzsche, or Heidegger begins to be heard: scientific Prometheism could indeed lead us to the catastrophe. Postmodern melancholia consisted in witnessing the spectacle of reflex surpassings in their involution, their turning around on themselves to no avail. The becoming of art showed it with a nihilism more frank than any other. This is why art constitutes the key point for understanding what all this is about, provided that we really agree on what is called *art*. And I maintain that the supreme form in which art is historically destined to accomplish itself, is *play* (see below).

Hence the SoN's entire ethical stake consists in taking note of the *accomplished decline of all ideologies of surpassing as categorical imperative of modernity.* Postmodern means: the surpassing is terminally surpassed, without ending in a superior dialectical "outcome" in the operation of doubled auto-negation. I grant this point to the postmodern diagnostics without reservation. But this philosophy—mine!—does not concede point to postmodern *melancholia*, which shares a latent Platonism with what it fights, that is to say, an implicitly *eidetic* conception of the being [*l'étant*]; which deems that there actually is an original, and that its generalized parody or simulacrum is parody and simulacrum. The SoN *proves* that there is no such thing, or rather, that one has to overturn all accepted orders of metaphysical precedence, including those reversals that praise the reversed precedence of simulacrum, mime, and parody, like in the works of Baudrillard and Lyotard but also, on an altogether different level, Deleuze. It was good to start with. But I go a bit further than that, showing that in our *singular* post-evental situation as technomimetic animals, original and parody are *one and the same thing*: For us, everything *starts* with the parodic, which is the only original. This is what art will have always *told* us.

Once again, it is the domain of art and the domain of art alone, in its modern deflationary nihilism, that indicates the life-saving avenue for us, which is, very simply, an unconditioned assumption of the parodic *as our most originary condition*. There is no eidetic archetype that holds, other than the archetype of *mimesis*. The whole life of the technological animal takes place, by definition, under the sign of parody. This implies that one should dismiss equally the obscene (and most fortunately for us, obsolete) philosophical prometheisms that condone the criminal prometheisms of science and politics; and postmodern melancholia, which in fact grieves for something that has *never seriously taken place*. There has never been a first degree with respect to which our time would constitute the irreversible decline into the second degree. Even the most criminal of Promethean metaphysical maximizations were parodic in their essence. For us, human animals, everything has always been *in the second degree*, as soon as a primate dared to repeat the rubbing together of two flints.

Philosophy's original sin (yet another one!) is well known: All regionalized forms of the City must be excluded as "art" in order to *establish* the perfect art of republican politics. Therefore philosophy, right from its envoi, is defined as that which suppresses art in favor of politics, through the intervention of science. Philosophy is that which presents science to politics, by sacrificing the bad scapegoat that is art's complacent presentation of Evil. Even art's postmodern deflationism is a manner of deploying this complacency: to ironically promote the null, the insignificant, the mediocre (see *Irony*) is a manner of promoting the "not Good," by making a *philosophically oriented*[5] long nose (see *Irony*).

Actually art could have never been done with avenging itself for the—criminal—error in diagnosis philosophy made on its subject right at its very origins. From Schelling and German Romanticism to Nietzsche and Heidegger to Deleuze and Derrida, philosophical modernity would make a few efforts to correct this originary error in diagnosis. *The Spirit of Nihilism* differentiates itself from all those philosophies, by not doing—as they did—with art what Plato and so many others did with Science: endow it with an inspiring precedence, the status of a paradigm. It merely examines how art is the *exponent* [*l'exposant*] of an error which dates back to the birth of metaphysics itself, and which is *not* the belated philosophy, but the technomimetic act as such.

Thus, this philosophy—of the SoN!—dreams of a relationship between art and philosophy which would be characterized neither by competition nor by a tag-along. That art cease to be, more or less consciously, a perpetual reprisal to the prescriptions of philosophers, from Plato to Kant; that philosophy be neither an originary condemnation of art, nor an archi-aesthetic which does with art what Plato did with Science (Nietzsche, Heidegger, Deleuze … each in their own way assigned to Art the status of an inspiring Paradigm which Plato assigned to Mathematics).

As a matter of fact, *The Spirit of Nihilism* is a method that holds art, science, politics, eroticism, law in its unthought grounds [*fondements*], history, etc., at *equal distance*. It produces a *critical* discourse, in the strict sense, on all these domains, which thus countersigns its autonomy *as* philosophy. It does not proclaim, in a dishonest reckoning, "being at the service of truth procedures" (Badiou). On the contrary, it asserts itself as a truth procedure in its own right, which consists in extracting from other processes (a word I prefer to "procedure," which is too bureaucratic for my liking) the truths which these processes want to know nothing about. As such, it is more originally useful to these processes—not only to politics, science, art, and love, but also, as we will see, to play, Law or the thought of sexuation and an erotic without love—than the philosopher, falsely modest and disinterested, "simply" pretending to hold the candle to truths that are external to him—logico-mathematical isomorphism, archaizing "love," politics of extermination in the name of "equality," and post-Romantic and post-avant-gardist ultra-elitist art.

Aufhebung

Aufhebung: As in all the literally crucial points of my work, it is to Philippe Lacoue-Labarthe that I owe the present conceptual elaboration. The much-lamented Lacoue-Labarthe's brilliant find is that the famous *aufhebung* of Hegelian dialectics, which we translated above as "surpassing" [*dépassement*], which I translated elsewhere,[1] with reference to the classical period in music history (Haydn, Mozart, and Beethoven), as "resolution" [*résolution*], and which Derrida also translated as "*relève*" (relief); this well-known concept of that which suppresses all the while preserving what is suppressed, which implies casting into the suppressed that which has become useless—*caduc*, Arafat would say—and preserving only that which feeds the progress of History and Idea—well yes!—this famous and very influential concept of our modernity in which originates for instance all of Marxism, whether speculative or real; this concept is in fact a pure and simple translation derived from Aristotle's *catharsis*. And *catharsis* is the no less famous artistic operator par excellence. This has tremendous consequences, since in that case mimesis itself, the originarily mimetic being of art, is the condition of purifying *catharsis*; *catharsis* which, in Tragedy, suppresses the negative affects such as terror or pity, and at the same time preserves them, sublimating them in a higher stage of the spirit, in the aesthetic jouissance of Tragedy precisely. It is the same principle with the two fundamental tragic affects pointed out by Aristotle, as with all directly lived painful affects of reality: if burglars take me hostage all night, beat me up and finally blow my brains out, none of it would be a pleasant experience (and let us keep in mind that this sort of situation is at once typically anthropological, *mimetically* amplifying simple predatory cruelty); if the same thing was represented to me in a movie, I would feel the sensual delight of what is called "suspense."[2] By eternalizing painful or dreadful situations in indefinite technological repetition, art in the broad sense removes the brute intensity in the affects of painfulness proper to technomimetic life, purging them from their very painfulness.

In reality, no one likes feeling Terror or Pity (see *Affect*); once art gets hold of an apparatus, History or an event which gives rise to Terror or Pity, once it *imitates* a situation that produces Terror and Pity, well then, Terror and Pity are at once suppressed, they cease to be the painful affects they usually are, they become absolutely liberating and pleasurable [*jouissifs*] affects, and at the same time they are preserved, since it is *nevertheless* Terror and Pity we feel in tragic imitation, before the fate of Oedipus or Antigone, and this is what *catharsis* is: the successful sublimation of completely negative affects, at once suppressed *in their negativity*, and preserved in their intensity through artistic *mimesis* in general. "Purified" ("purged") [*épuré*], is how Lacoue-Labarthe translates this on his own behalf. "Cathartic" alchemy suppresses the negativity of literally *deadly* affects in order to preserve nothing but their intensity, that is to say, it converts them into affects of *vitality*, as voluptuous as the vital affect par excellence: sexual jouissance. The connection between the transferential intensity of death and sexual intensity was not made yesterday.

Now, we saw what philosophy claimed to be in its originary envoi, and so many contemporary philosophers, whether consciously or not (as lesson-givers always in charge of the Good, although almost always in the greatest blindness) want to set the same table for us: philosophy is the *aufhebung* of art in politics, with a "good" comprehension of Science as mediator, that miraculous placidity that is the very definition of "philosophy." The philosopher is the one who, starting off from a superior comprehension of Science, suppresses art in favor of the "good" politics. Art is suppressed by this good understanding of science, yet preserved *as* politics: and this is the unfortunate originary definition of philosophy.

No doubt, everything proceeds from an erroneous understanding of the very notion of *mimesis*. Plato not only identifies art as bad *mimesis*, but *mimesis* itself as bad. This is to place the act of philosophizing, right in its envoi, in a sort of vicious circle of the autophagous Ouroboros. Nothing in philosophy that *can* not be mimetological, because nothing in science that *is* not mimetological, and as to politics, we can say that it is *by definition* the domain where *mimesis* spreads most severely its ravages. Moreover the proof should not cease to overwhelm the philosopher, whose function is to willingly set up models, and to set himself up even more willingly as a universal model. Not only does scientific, i.e. strictly technological *mimesis* precede by far properly artistic *mimesis*; not only is politics itself *immediately* the monstrous *mimesis* of Science; but moreover, it is actually *because* of the originary Platonic error in diagnosis that political *mimesis* appears historically, as if from very afar, the most devastating of all; in other words, because of philosophy. All in all, we will say that art is, from its tragic envoi to Sade, an absolutely *correct mimesis* of the mimetic *horror* that is politics with respect to science.

Morality of *aufhebung*: "after postmodernism," that is, after the archaic Prometheism that postmodernism will have surpassed, sometimes melancholically sometimes sarcastically: all surpassing *must* preserve what it suppresses. Postmodernism was merely the acknowledged receipt of a saturation of the model of perpetual surpassing: an involuted, parodic surpassing of surpassing. All in all, it was this, rather than the ideology of which postmodernism was the death certificate: the ideology of thoughtless surpassings, which preserve nothing of what they suppress, and which generally lead to nothing but this final "surpassing" which is, opportunely, death.[3] *Catharsis* does not make do with suppressing death in aesthetic spectacle; it preserves it as well, and this is how it is for the extended catharsis that is Hegelian *aufhebung*. Moreover, Hegel knew better in terms of phenomenological descriptions of the modes in which death persists in human life. Heidegger, Bataille, Blanchot, Derrida, Schürmann, Deleuze, Lacoue-Labarthe, Adorno ... modern philosophy will no longer act as if death, in the technomimetic closure, did not live a second life. The SoN not only remembers this, but renews the investigation. The first time I felt I had become a true "philosopher" was the day I *knew* that I had a concept of death, therefore of human life, which was entirely my "own." Every *modern* philosopher is *defined*, purely and simply, by the original concept he makes of specifically human death, without which it is impossible to understand anything about the life of the technomimetic species.

Because the operation of the extended *catharsis-mimesis-aufhebung* complex is fundamentally *techne*, the appearance of the technological beyond life, the "suppression" produced by the first forms of technomimetic event—such as agriculture or hunting—over *what* they "suppress"—natural efflorescence or biological natality—*must* be immediately parodic: always the parody of suppression. What is suppressed must always persist: without biological life that *mimesis-techne* has surpassed, no *mimesis-techne* at all; and the same goes absolutely for *all* domains where the specter of *aufhebung* extends its operations, that is, all domains of anthropological life.

Hence the programmatic *aufhebung* of our times consists of two points: to renounce the deadly ideologies of terminal surpassing; to turn the page of postmodernism—the depressive incorporation of these ideologies we know to be deadly—once and for all. And this is to be done by the assumption of what postmodernism only falsely assumes: the originarity of parody itself (see below, Play).

In short: not to propose an [n]th surpassing, but to *shift* the thought of surpassing.

Desire

DESIRE: Desire is the propensity of the being [*l'étant*] to appropriation. There is more desire in animals than in plants, and more desire in men than in other animals. But the difference between human desire and animal desire is not an intensive difference: man does not desire "more." In other words, he does not desire more "energetically" than animals. In this respect, it is easy to see that he rather desires *less*. This is because man is animal de-natured, or an *emptied* [*vidé*] animal. The evils that strike man, melancholia and depression, neurosis and psychosis, "the evils of the soul" as it were, result precisely from the innumerable advantages he has bestowed upon himself by techno-mimetic appropriation: by the fact of *dominating* animal life through the transcendental appropriation of the Laws of Nature which cause an infinity of *supernumerary* Laws to emerge, from politics to art, from daily customs to play.

Once again, I must recognize my immense debt to Rousseau-Lacoue-Labarthe with respect to this little breviary. Let us cite these noble men. Man, "compared to the 'Beasts,' is no less absolutely inferior for that. It is even precisely because he is inferior (in short, he is a sub-animal) that he can satisfy his properly animal or vital needs."[1] In other words (and here it is Rousseau speaking—I will emphasize): "living dispersed among other animals, and finding himself betimes in a situation to measure his strength with theirs (...), *and perceiving that he surpasses them more in adroitness than they surpass him in strength*, learns to be no longer afraid of them."[2]

Lacoue: "[He] *learns* to be no longer afraid of them. (...) *Techne*, in the sense of the art of tropes or polytropes, is the genius of the human, his naturally a-natural gift, since it 'supplements' the lack of instinct."[3] Among the infinite constellation of mammal faunas, almost *all* of which are physically stronger than him (elephants, great apes and even the small, tigers, wolves and dogs, bears ... whatever you like), man however gets the upper hand, and does so enduringly, by contracting the "supplementation" of "what has to be called survival, that is to say *metaphysical* life, or, it is the same, *technical* life" (still Lacoue). And *meta*-physical life is *mimetico*-physical life: Nature *parodied*.

Perhaps one of the ways in which the SoN intends to renew the thought of *aufhebung*, by proposing an entirely novel comprehension of the notion of parody, resides in the very *facticity* of the parodic such as it has been understood until now: the comic in general. In fact, what does parody understood in this sense, which is not the one I propose,[4] do? The opposite of what was understood for such a long time by the post-revolutionary ideology of perpetual surpassing. The parodist, the impersonator, the comic in general are those who openly *preserve* what they reproduce ... and who suppress it, as it were, *merely in passing*, as they undermine the imitated person. We know well that this is the comedian's whole motivation. This consideration is fairly rewarding for our purposes; provided that we insist on the fact that our construction of the concept of parody exceeds on all sides its simply comic understanding. But it had to be said in passing: if, after many other philosophers, from Aristotle to Bergson, we have to stress the fact that laughter is proper to man, we do this in an altogether different manner than theirs: comedy, whatever its mode or register, *always* reveals one and the same thing: the fundamental *incongruity* in which the animal seized by the technomimetic event finds itself. Parody in the strictly comical sense reveals simply, and with what notorious ease, to what extent *everything* is originally parodic, as far as we are concerned—one thing explaining another. What does the television impersonator of politicians do? He shows the fundamental incongruity of representational situations (see *Representation*) in which the technomimetic animal necessarily finds himself: we concentrate the bulk of power on ridiculous small bits of flesh and bone, with their manias and their purely *presentational* tics that have become profoundly incongruous under the exorbitant weight of the *representational* burdens and responsibilities with which these miserable little bodies are invested, because of technomimetic perversion alone: the sense-less excessiveness of technological appropriation and its terrifying effects of expropriation.

As Bataille knew well, laughter proceeds first from fear: it is perhaps nothing other than the *catharsis* of fear. The laughter provoked by the imitator at the expense of the politician, and by—*en abîme*—*mimesis* itself, is the exorcism of the ontological Terror in which he finds himself the animal of technological over-appropriation: the *excessive* concentration of force that technology has always allocated to an extreme minority, to the detriment of the extreme majority. Even an over-powerful animal such as the dinosaur, or today the whale or the elephant, have at their disposal not more than their "brute" force, localized in their strict being-there. They are unaware of the representational *excess* which becomes the over-appropriative prerogative of a unique species, which is the technomimetic species, and, within this species, the monopoly of only a few, still today, and still in our democracies. The dinosaur, the elephant, or Moby Dick terrorize, almost pleonastically, nothing more than the surroundings of their territory; whereas the ascendency of technomimetic "Monsters," sometimes concentrated *representatively* in only two hands, can spread to entire continents.

As to purely alimentary Desire, we can settle the matter quickly enough (even though ...): through technology, man can satisfy his needs, cutting himself off entirely from the predatory instinct. He thinks he suppressed the latter completely; and so he preserves it in the form of monstrous *waste*. But this is also what has taken the form of industrialization today, and makes man, more than need be, perfectly *destitute* in so many situations (a "sub-animal"): Deprived of all predatory instinct for having become the machine-animal of *techne*, the incredible number of famines that have always struck the human community explain why, "given the level of productive forces, the earth could here and now be paradise" (Adorno), and yet is a massive hell. It is because man is the only one to have provided himself with this presentational-representational over-shelter that is habitat ("in embryo" in animals' nests or territorial markings), that he is also the only one to find himself literally *on the street*: there are no tramps among mammals. Stray dogs become stray dogs because, just as literally, we *domesticated* them first: inclined them to the rules of technological over-power. And a stray dog always shows astonishing survival resources, of which man and woman, since their fall "into nature," that is to say, into the urban technological hell thousands of years ago, no longer show.

As we know, it all seems a bit more complicated with so-called libidinal Desire. Although ... It is that in reality the "deferred/differed" [*différé*] that *techne* produces on alimentary needs and the one it produces on libidinal "needs" communicate. Here I will not go into the details presented in the entire *Spirit of Nihilism*, and in particular *Being and Sexuation* (all the same, see Appendix), but I will only cite the following passage by Lacan, who summarizes it all in an excellent as well as amusing manner: "On one side, Freud puts the partial drives and on the other love. He says—*They're not the same*. The drives necessitate us in the sexual order—they come from the heart. To our great surprise, he tells us that love, on the other hand, comes from the belly, from the world of yum-yum."[5]

First, this is because of what concerns the whole disrupted economy of *affects* (see above) to which technomimetic appropriation leads. This is because, against the overwhelming majority of ambient philosophical yes-manism, the SoN maintains that the being-for-event [*l'être-à-l'événement*] of the human animal is essentially due to the manner in which technomimetic appropriation is *overdetermined* by a relation to jouissance that is fundamentally "perverted" by this appropriation. Therefore, the two are, as they say in philosophical jargon, inchoative: which means "co-begin", not in the strictly synchronic sense. Philosophy is often taunted for asking only questions of the following type: "which comes first, the chicken or the egg?" Philosophy pleads guilty here, without fear of ridicule (death by laughter, as everybody knows). It is even because philosophy asks this "type" of question that it elaborates concepts such as the concept of event: perhaps science will one day discover, empirically, which one, the chicken or the egg, precedes the other. Philosophy *takes the lead* in this matter, by thinking of the essential co-originarity of phenomena such as sexual chicken and technological egg. For instance, things as improbable, and yet literally crucial, as the co-originarity of being and event, event and repetition, *techne* and *mimesis*, etc.

From this point of view, it must be said that the most advanced thought on the question is not philosophy, including Spinozist philosophy, but psychoanalysis. There would be no technomimetic event if the event, for the most part, was not identified, and most often unconsciously, with sexual jouissance, which is the *fundamental affect*[6]

It is the typical yes-manism of philosophers: "event and philosophy have nothing to do with jouissance." It is the opposite that has proved absolutely right: the *specifically* anthropological being-for-event has everything to do with the *singular* libidinal economy overdetermined by the technomimetic impulse. Lacan liked to say that, for the Chinese, science was originally nothing other than a sexual technique; for once, I feel Chinese. But already, vital, animal and superlatively mammalian appropriation manifestly goes hand in hand with the appearance of sexuality as such. It is not because we are sexuated that we are maximally prone to appropriation; it is because, through an evolutionism of millions of years buried in the past, we have been destined for appropriation that we are sexuated. Through the technomimetic impulse, we maximize the "pleonexia" prefigured by the mammalian kingdom. All being-for-event is proportionate to being-for-jouissance [*l'être-à-la-jouissance*], this latter having become exponential through the technomimetic impulse; no affect without "pleonexia." And the fundamentally evental affect is jouissance. This is exactly why the non-sexuated affects most related to jouissance are always linked to some event: some pleonectic triumph.

For reasons meticulously explored by *The Spirit of Nihilism* and recapitulated in the present opuscule: today all aesthetics (see *Art*) is null and void if it does not take account of this point; and it must be said that the majority of contemporary philosophical aesthetics smacks of rococo, for obliterating the fact that our "aesthetic nihilism" has the same root as plain and simple "nihilism," which is the technomimetic mammal's biased relation to sexual jouissance.

For instance, the "nihilism" of so-called "contemporary" art is often incriminated to what Duchamp[7] did, based on which art is not only done "with whatever," but becomes literally "whatever" (see *Irony*). For my part, I think this "nihilism" does not date back (only) to Duchamp, but to the sixties and the advent of sexual liberty. Here I can only refer to the third edition of *Ontologique de l'Histoire*, which is *La forclusion, le vide et le mal*. But suffice it to say that psychoanalysis, before the aforesaid liberation, made the ruthless discovery that the overwhelming majority of our "negative" affects were tied to strictly libidinal reasons. And the lucid realization that it is not with sexual liberation, the achievements of which cannot be denied, that things would simply go on improving. And the reason is: from the very moment the human animal repeats *to no avail* [*à vide*] the reproductive "event," he wears it out in repetition and wears himself out by the same token. The curse that metaphysics and religion have always cast on sexual avidity is based on a slightly more clinical fact: we obviously need to get rid of the fairly corny "moral line" which continues to affect most philosophers: we have to make do with sexual liberty, and not give it up. We even need to go further—and this is what I do without the slightest hesitation—and claim that obvious "nihilism"—reductionist cynicism, what's-the-use-ism, etc.[8]—this nihilism is preferable to the splendid *petitiones principii* that are generally put up against it. This is a much more interesting philosophical problem than the "problem philosophers" who agree upon eternal truths, immortal greatness, etc. It has the merit of examining closely that which metaphysical maximizations not only make it a point of honor to foreclose, but actually overdetermine by galvanizing, in the name of an irresponsible responsibility, the "pleonexia" inchoative with respect first to animal, then to technomimetic being-for-appropriation.

Therefore, it is no to the "moral line" of philosophers and priests. But it is no as well to the reverse yes-manism of those who think sexuality is just great, and do not go on to find out why—since times as immemorial as archi-transgression (see *Transgression*) itself—humanity has always had more than a *problem* with sexuality, today more than ever. And why does sexual jouissance lies at the root of all our troubles? The historial "superiority" of religion over philosophy is due to the fact that religion is *always* a singular, decentered and critical discourse of the knot—un-thought everywhere else (especially by philosophers …)—between the libidinal and the political: moreover this is the case not only in Judeo-Christian culture, but in all others as well. I repeat: in this respect, the stake of *The Spirit of Nihilism* is to give back to philosophy what philosophy has left to religion for so long, without understanding much about the underlying reasons for this counter-monopolization. The SoN urges to leave the immemorial yes-manism of the functionaries of humanity, to break the spell of metaphysical maximizations that are as promising as they are not only deceiving, but also the blind instigators of the worst evils, in order to look into the otherwise fascinating investigation—itself *singularly* proper to the concept— of the most trivial, technical origins of these maximizations that are at the same time emphatic, and so curiously, systematically, devastating in their effects.

Concerning jouissance, the originality of *The Spirit of Nihilism* is also to show that, on the subject, we need to make a radical distinction between the masculine position and the feminine position (see *Woman, Man, Sexuation,* and *Appendix*).

Like I said to Valentin Husson,[9] in response to the admirable remarks on Rousseau with which he supplements Lacoue-Labarthe's work on the same subject, the "dangerous supplement," i.e. masturbation, because of which Rousseau torments himself in order to refrain from practising it in his *Confessions*, could actually not be a stranger at all to the intuition with which Rousseau *founded* our philosophical origin: *auto*-affection, tautology *en abîme* of the transappropriation of his "own" affect, and the exponentiation of this transappropriation, as technological expropriation: origin and basis of inequality between men.

That Rousseau should be the first ever not only to consider masturbation as the "dangerous supplement," but that he should also be, well before Sacher-Masoch, the first to speak of the masculine *masochistic* drive in a western text, does more than point out the eventually blinding way: between *erotic* supple-mentation of which, by definition, only the prehensile animal is capable (he/she who does not have hands cannot masturbate *at will*—and will, subjective ipseity, is born perhaps nowhere else than there), and *technological* supplementation which then constitutes the properly anthropological *event*, there can only be a simple relation of familiarity. It is not a fortuitous "family resemblance" but rather a congenitality, I must say.

Subjective will, erotic repetition, and prehension would be inchoative: they would predispose to the appropriative, metaphysical, and mimetic archi-event as such: to the pleonectic animal that is *redoubled* [*redoublé*], and thus exponentialized in tentacular technology. Erotic supplementation is indeed a *mimetico*-erotic supplementation: ceaselessly repetitive. And technological supplementation is a mimetic supplementation, period: owing to the *voiding* [*l'évidement*] he inflicted on his instincts, the human animal thus becomes the weakest of physical mammals, in order to eventually "surpass his congeners more in adroitness [in technological astuteness] than they surpass him in strength."

Now, everyone can try it out *again* here and now: erotic auto-affection is evidently what *empties* the simio-anthropological mammal of its instincts, *because it* ties together two phenomena which, raised to their (intelligible) "metaphysical" square, will hallmark the "exit" of the human animal from his environment; that is *prehension* and (erotic) *repetition*. Like Freud would discover much later: it is by way of this pretechnological void of repetition that instinct turns into *drive*. Drive is mimetically *voided* instinct.

In turn, the affectual force of the drives (the "violence of drives") stems only from the deferred/differed void through which we modulate, and even "mathematize" our affects. If our drives are "violent," this is because the technological deferred/differed is the very name of this violence, which has become global today: psychopathic killers are not beings of uncontrolled drives, but on the contrary, beings who command their instinctual "surges" with extreme mastery and coldness. The same goes for the great heads of state: one does not become a dictator by being "simply" a trembling neuropath. Hitler or Stalin were "crazy," but they are so due to excess of mastery over their affects, and not lacking anything.

Manual prehension (still "simply" physical, as it moreover seems to have already existed in dinosaurs) becomes scientific appropriation; and erotic repetition (in the *strict* sense of at least *possible* auto-affection), *mimesis*.

There are several obvious conclusions to this.

- Every event is connected with jouissance, because the ability to (self-) appropriate jouissance is immediately a *trans*appropriation, which is allowed by the simple fact of having a hand. We would not be technomimetic animals if we did not have organs of prehension: all other mammals and simians were right from the very start disqualified for the technomimetic stage of appropriation. Language [*le langage*] itself was probably nothing more than a sublimation of manual prehension, just as the logico-mathematical is merely the belated sublimation of the most archaic techniques.
- This transappropriation of jouissance *empties* us, affectually and physically. Contemporary "depressionism," which sanctions the excess of sexual

consumerism and related frustrations and/or exhaustions, in reality, merely displays, as Rousseau was the first to see, a process at work since the "simiform" dawn of humanity. Consequence: at this time Rousseau only caught a glimpse of it because he did not make the connection between the transappropriation of the "dangerous supplement" and the fact that man is the *exhausted* animal, it is precisely this primary ability for auto-affection, an affectual exponentiation which is equally a voiding, and therefore a de-instinctualization. In short, this dialectic between the *excess* obtained by repetition and the depressive *lack* which is its almost immediate price, is the reason why man becomes, *in order to compensate,* the animal of technological astuteness. Here as well, the Evil denounced by the philosophers and Church Fathers is the manifest condition of all Good. As a Derridean would say: empirical auto-affection is the transcendental of the scientific transcendental (of the empirical).

- The structure of the event, which is self-belonging in Badiou's mathematized lexicon, is therefore so familiar to the anthropological structure of jouissance, which is the logic of transappropriation commanding thereby *all the rest,* that it conditions it entirely, by its very foreclosure. The prohibition of self-belonging means: to be in fact faithful to the structure of things (in the cosmic material world, nothing self-belongs; and in the biological, i.e. animal and then human world, self-belonging is never *phenomenalized*), but to ignore the *logic* that departs from this structure, by introducing unprognostic events to it, which are precisely vanishing and asymptotic logics of always greater transappropriations (starting with ABC: the appropriation of the vegetable by agriculture, of the animal by hunting …). The human animal, through sexual compulsion, becomes what he is by exhausting himself "uselessly": he *then* has to compensate the resulting physical weakness, by racking his brain in order to simply live on. It is quite possible that auto-affection preceded even the flint and applied botany; that, in short, in the beginning was masturbation, which is mimetic transappropriation of sexual jouissance. With the same compulsion, he aims at an "eternalized transappropriation" which fails all the more to reach its purpose since it repeats itself compulsively. This transappropriation is revealed in its fundamentally expropriatory outcomes; its "successes" are due to its fundamental failure to persist, its "failures," to the original "success" of its astuteness, unknown to other animals. I will not beat around the bush: as it is confirmed still today with the apes, notably the bonobos, the phenomenon of manual prehension is immediately what makes the simians our closest "cousins," i.e. our ancestors in evolution—for being capable of what the good people call by the very fitting name of *pignole*:[10] namely masturbation, auto-affection. Whoever has seen a mammalian cousin of ours, other than a simian, literally thrashing about only to reach jouissance—for instance a male poodle struggling for hours to masturbate against his favorite toy, *in other words, making a physical effort which he would not even make in actual coitus*—will understand even better what I am getting at, and how the *exhaustion* of baroque repetition that the technomimetic animal makes of the sexual act is at the very root of his being-for-science: religion's original sin. If mathematics, and philosophy with its unconditional oath to it, want to know nothing of jouissance by which they are so manifestly conditioned, then too bad for them. This means that the philosophy which knows what it is conditioned by is superior to mathematics and to the philosophy which takes it as a model, precisely because it is less "pure", like poker (see *Play*) is superior to chess precisely because it is much more impure as a game, which means it mobilizes a much more extensive range of properties in order to shine. Let us sum up: Badiou marks self-belonging as the impossible proper to mathematics, i.e. rationality. In Lacanian terms, impossible means: real. Therefore self-belonging, as the impossible-real of rationality, designates the event for Badiou. Then what my work in its entirety shows is that the principle of identity, the supreme principle of metaphysics, *sublimates* this impossible self-belonging into the *last* referent of the discourse. And what it also shows, this time more frontally against Badiou, is that, by the same token, it sublimates the *fact* of appropriation. We will see (see *Mimesis*) how one of the at least speculative innovations of the SoN is to envisage the principle of identity not as the ground of being [*l'être*], as the quasi-totality of the metaphysical tradition, but as a particularly *singular event*. Here, suffice it to say that the anthropological archi-event, technomimetic appropriation, has everything to do with sexual jouissance, rather than nothing. Religion, with its conception of "original sin," saw this quite well (see *Nihilism*).

- As Kojève noticed, turning Lacan to his advantage, anthropological Desire is fundamentally mimetic (needless to wait for Girard).

Let us make a final consideration: the being-for-event, being-for-appropriation of the human animal, that is to say, of the mimetic Desire directed towards a repetitive jouissance which is transappropriated *because* repeated, and repeated *because* manually appropriated; this structure holds only for the *masculine* side of the technomimetic animal. Once again, this is a great Evil, what I shall call "originary rape," for the sake of a "Good." For we will see how the feminine side originarily knows nothing about this cleavage between desire and jouissance on man's side: this is the fundamental inquiry of my *Being and Sexuation* (therefore see *Affect, Man, Woman, Jouissance, Sexuation,* and *Appendix*). And hence I call "masculine metaphysics" the metaphysics which accordingly discriminates between being and event; and "feminine metaphysics" those which "bring closer" being and event to the point where they can no longer be distinguished. Philosophy, overdetermined by what Derrida called "phallogocentrism," and owing to its own foreclosed libidinal extraction, blinded to the truths that disappear as soon as they appear, and persisting in the world only by clinging to all the variants of the ascetic ideal, therefore put somewhat too much emphasis on the elective and rare event, like phallic jouissance itself, only to later on hypostasize all the better "ontology," that is, the hallucination of a universal which is *on principle* positive. As *The Spirit of Nihilism* shows, nothing is less obviously "positive" than universalism, i.e. scientific appropriation.

So perhaps the time has come for counter-ontologies not uniformly "feminine," which tend to confuse purely and simply being and event, but with more impure, tangential metaphysics that do not claim univocal ontological positions, but *pluralize* the study of the regions of articulation between being and event; in other words, a philosophy faithful to the plurivocity[11] of these regions themselves, without failing to be what all philosophy must be: systematic.

A philosophy, metaphysically *switch* and *queer*, but nevertheless dressed to the nines and a trifle dandy.

Ontological differend

ONTOLOGICAL DIFFEREND: designates a polemical doctrine of truth, with respect to the philosophical prejudices that seem to be unsinkable throughout the ages. It thinks that there is an inadequacy *in principle* between the universal, i.e. universal*izing* statements of science, and the *singularities* to which this universality applies, which are thus purely and simply *scored out* by scientific isomorphism. It serves as one of the spearheads of *The Spirit of Nihilism*; the one which strikes at the heart of the philosophical myth par excellence, today more than ever, the myth of an innate equivalence between universality and positivity. I truly hope that this conceptual specter will go on haunting the philosophical world for a long time: and for a long time will go on twisting the knife in that wound. It is *blatantly obvious* that the appearance of the universal on earth, the sublimation of technomimetic astuteness, is at the source of all horrifying evils. Even the "Good," evidently incited by "the positive universal" of Science, has something of an ill repute: something always greedy, omnipotent, utterly peremptory, in short: ultra-appropriative, doubly pleonectic.

The more a science is "pure" (at the extreme end lies the logico-mathematical, see below), the more it is isomorphic. Singularity then appears as a *monstrous* incongruity in view of the empty transcendentalization that science produces by leveling things out based on their common form, devised in principle. Besides, in this sense, in my lexicon there is no singularity *except* subject to capture by science (see below). When the singular is made into the simple particularity of a universal that is valid, "eternal" always and everywhere, singularity is *mortified* by scientific appropriation: expropriated. The appropriation of the eternity of laws merely *expropriates it* towards a *transgressive* precariousness.

Therefore, the ontological differend is "my" doctrine of truth. It particularly specifies the *singular* task of philosophy, which is precisely the extreme *care* taken in the study of political singularizations incited by the isomorphic universal of science. It is a hypercritical doctrine, which *shifts* (and above all does not "surpass"!) Heidegger's aletheiology just as well as Badiou's doctrine of indiscernibles: every truth is conflictual, expropriative, bloodthirsty, torturing. Every positive truth conceals its bloody aspect. This is obvious with art which "remains content" to "cathartically" expose and sublimate Evil. Yet, as I show in *Being and Sexuation*, the "positive truths" of love follow from an originary violence, more precisely, from a kind of rape, immemorial and archaic: masculine violence precedes all amorous sublimation, all family, all City, all civilization. Radical Evil and Wrong always precede Good. To forget this systematically, as did the metaphysical tradition itself in its envoi (and the thousand-year-old "superiority" of religions over philosophy because of this[1]), is in turn to condone the unprognostic avalanches of evil.

Science is in its ground violence and expropriation. *2001: A Space Odyssey* is for me the movie which, in terms of philosophical inspiration, is the richest of all time, and the most illustrative of my purposes: simians get hold of bones and make weapons out of them, with which they bring down other simian tribes and become the species that takes hold of power over the planet by slaughtering the others, and gallantly killing each other until "Law" and "Civilization" temper as much as possible the expropriatory apocalypse that coincides with the advent of technomimetics on earth. This means (see below): Transgression precedes Legislation, the touchstone of the SoN's entire philosophical edifice. In Kubrick's film, we pass directly from the apes—who, having discovered *techne* as means of trans-predatory violence never before seen on earth, become humans *ipso facto*—to spacecrafts: the ellipsis is exactly what the SoN brings to light, after—it must be rendered unto Caesar—Heidegger. The most advanced forms of Science, and especially "pure" Sciences, will never be anything other than *sublimations* (*catharsis-aufhebung*) of the most archaic techniques: hunting, war, agriculture, drawing, rape. Everything that metaphysics praises as sublimated maximizations is accomplished by technology in monstrous form, thus coming full circle. Initiatory "telepathy" becomes the Internet and the imminent neurotechnological paths, meta-physical immortality is on its way to being biogenetically realized. Monstrosity is the maintaining of that which was supposed to be surpassed, essentially animal singularity, in the form of sickly incongruity. As George A. Romero, one of the most lucid artists of our times, showed in his absolute masterpiece *Diary of the Dead*, the resurrection of the dead, promised to all by St. Paul, is *concretely* fulfilled in the waste of Science that is the Zombie. The latter is the body which, having abolished death, which also means having "surpassed" life, and preserving both as eternal *parodic waste*, achieves immortality.

Singularity (see below) is what Science (see below) has always *traumatized*, and it is this traumatism that metaphysical functionaries enjoy sublimating.

What the ontological differend indicates is this always more sickly—and to say it all, dreadful—disruption between the peaceful isomorphism of the universal and the living singularity is captured by subsumption.

Following Artaud, the situationists, Lacoue-Labarthe and Schürmann among others, the system deployed by the SoN is fundamentally *anarchic*. It is the oxymoron of a system of anarchy, of generalized singularization: its concepts describe only the mechanism of what the concept cannot subsume. They conceptualize the *adjusted* [*réglé*] failure of the very function taken on by the concept: subsumption. Schürmann alone made the connection between political anarchism and the metaphysical concept that reinforces it: an-archy signifies the lucid thought of a caesured, tragic, literally *disruptive* origin. In Schürmann's work, "the principle of anarchy" designates the characteristic of our age: the oxymoron of a principle of the absence of any driving principle whatsoever to guide our acts. On the other hand, Badiou is the archi-principial[2] philosopher of our times: hence the hyper-normative (in his words, "prescriptive") character of his philosophy. Which means that, were it enacted, it will not fail to create, in droves, countless *monstrous singularities* that satisfy neither principial ideality nor prescriptive legislation. Whatever Promethean efforts we make in order to try and stop it, our age will witness either way the principial triumph of the absence of principle: of anarchy, literally and in every sense.

Ontoligical differend, once again following the path cleared by Schürmann, indicates an *an-archist doctrine of truth*.

Event

EVENT: *Manifeste antiscolastique* was an impeded, confused book, betrayed by the semi-affectation of its style. In it you feel the moroseness of the disciple who would like to break his chains, find the means to have done with the Master, but cannot and carries on. The bitterness that struggles not to suppurate from these pages is due to the fact that 2005 was a very difficult year for me, and that the text in question builds up on a lecture I gave at the seminar of a certain Alain Badiou. I described elsewhere the infamous events that followed, and which stuck in my craw for a long time. The writing of the book suffered from it, yet not everything in it is to be thrown away, far from it. I am even happy to be able to bring back up to date a work which would reach its systematic maturity only a few years later.

Here is the diagram by way of which I recapitulate, "au Lacan" (it is my most Lacanian book, including in its bookish structure very much inspired by *Television*), the dialectic set out in this manual, and which will subsequently show all its resources.

As the arrows show, this schematization describes a process, which is the very process of the being-historical [*l'être-historique*] (see *History*), which equally means that it should be read in such a way as to connect, with an ultimate arrow, the symbol subtitled "event" to the first one subtitled "impossibility." So it is a question of a cycle, a motivity. Joyce said of History that it was a nightmare from which he tried to awake. If we understand this schematization, we see that it is not happening anytime soon—barring this negative "awakening" which would be the self-suppression of the human species on earth.

The first graph, ε ◊ R (read: ε lozenge R), signifies: it is impossible for the event, as such, to repeat. Here Badiou's influence marks the conception of the event I was looking for with its own pre-suppositions. I should have asked myself, already at that point, why an ultra-positivist position of the event, Badiou's, aroused in me nothing but gloomy rumination, despite the puffing efforts I made to sound enthusiastic (for instance, and I will come back to it, about the word "equality"). Conversely, it is after a great period of soul-searching which led me to elaborate a completely original concept of event,

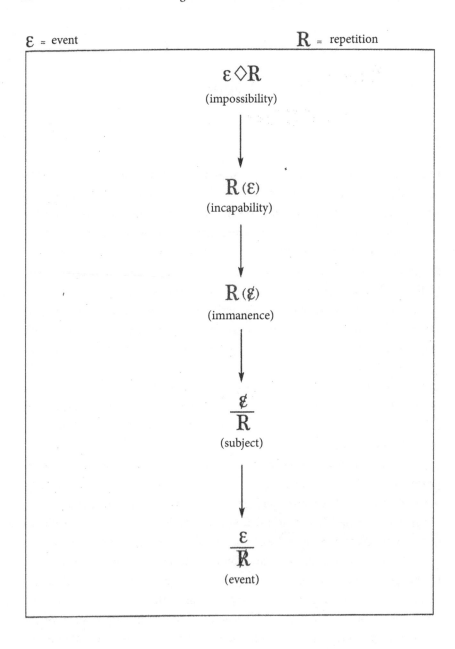

ε = event   R = repetition

ε ◇ R
(impossibility)

↓

R (ε)
(incapability)

↓

R (ε̸)
(immanence)

↓

$$\frac{ε̸}{R}$$
(subject)

↓

$$\frac{ε}{R̸}$$
(event)

with rather disquieting foundations, that I reached a minimum of philosophical quietism—not to say happiness: that would be rude.

However, it is perhaps this point itself that led me to the first symbol. The event, as positivity,—mathematical eureka, love at first sight, political revolt and so on (in a word, Badiou)—never repeats as such. The Subjects of May '68 live with the nostalgia of those few weeks all their lives. Whoever has been madly in love would give everything, assuming even the sufferings, to be in that state again. The eternalization of the event in repetition is an impossible motor of all human existence (see *History*). This impossibility is retained as impossible; it is what we call archive or memory. The lozenge indicates the deep cleavage that "separates" event and repetition. Yet of course, repetition, even in the tiniest detail of our everyday life, is what has long since surpassed the event, and yet preserves something of it, despite its suppression. One should never be afraid to forge again the fundamental stuff.

Then we arrive at the second graph. The impossible repetition of the event becomes the repetition of this impossibility *itself*: the rejected lover who still wants to believe, the scientist or the artist who has run out of inspiration and who slips into madness trying to get it back, the gifted player who burns in his struggle to regain the state of grace that made him win, etc. Incapability designates the *realization* of the impossibility that cleaves the positive originary event from a full repetition.

This realization, in the third graph, becomes *immanence*. Here we already find a little bit of solid Kacemian good sense, far from the positivist bravados of abstract ascetic ideals that are renewed at the expense of each new age in order to spread the anointing. Immanence, in the anthropological closure and common everyday life, is essentially negative because the *territorialization* of the event's "transcendence" consists in a kind of becoming-striated of the pathetic incapability to repeat the event. This incapability is made of the tissue of the repetitions themselves, which are concrete, "second natures" that we perform every day without even thinking about it: the set of social chores that we count as our "lives." Behind this constellation of *habitus*, such as enumerated by sociology for instance, there is the fundamental *fact* of an impossible repetition of the event. Let us call this, in the manner of Lacoue-Labarthe, "the caesura of the origin."

The fourth graph once again concedes important points to Badiou. The Subject is he who adopts the mourning for the impossible repetition of the event, but also the mourning for this impossibility, in working to prepare a *new* event: what Badiou, in his Pauline vocabulary, would call "Resurrection", later than when all this was uttered. But what would separate me from him, and which we summed up in one of our last exchanges, was already there in embryo: He said, "my" Subject was too "structural." And indeed, once again in Hegelian rather than Cartesian or Badiouian mode, it is entire humanity that I treat as Subject, in other words, as the animal seized by technomimetology.

In the end, when a *new* event, a new love at first sight or, at the poker table, a new martingale comes about, repetition is scored out and the event regains the upper hand over repetition. This is called the state of grace. But it is a very particular state. As I keep saying in these pages (of *Manifeste antiscolastique*), it is in fact a very sophisticated art of repetition that prepares the positive "event," the state of grace. We will see this with the concept of Play (see below).

Yet we should not fool ourselves: every new event is bound to "fall back" into the first graph. Love at first sight, scientific or artistic inspiration, but also, for all I know, philosophical inspiration, proves to be an impossibility: a kind of fleeting spark, which then virtually clings to us all our lives. A Subject, for instance a philosopher, is someone who creates a shell and a hygiene of repetition, in order to capture again these states of grace, whenever they brush against him like the Muse. The rest of the time, he lives on. Summed up somewhat funkily, this is where my wild imaginings led me.

Where, in this book, did the shoe pinch? Well, always in the same foolish superegoistic constraint, which is the constraint of the entire metaphysics itself, putting the philosopher in the obligatory service of Goods: I considered repetition as a form of "decadence" of the event. Love "becomes" sexual compulsion, politics "becomes" administrative or tyrannical violence, science "becomes" technology, etc. Always the schema of Platonic "decadence," which even the self-declared anti-Platonist Nietzsche failed to escape. We will see this with the question of parody (see *Irony*), etc. Each time we *maximize* a given mimetological operation, which is the Platonic gesture par excellence, and most of the time it is a matter of science, all that seems to *follow* from this mimetic appropriation seems, in its turn, a failed *mimesis* of ... that which is itself *nothing but* a poor imitation of an always much "richer" singularity (otherwise, there would be *nothing* to appropriate, ever: there would be no event[1]). Such is the metaphysical operation par excellence, relentlessly indicted by the SoN: to maximize *mimesis*; to pass off the (for instance mathematical) copy as the original; to pass off as a copy the *singular* original from which *mimesis* has simply *removed* an abstract archetype; and to discover suddenly that it is the original that fails to imitate the copy *correctly*, because of its *singular* incongruity. And finally, to blindly traumatize and torture this singularity by the age-old outcomes of the entire operation (see *Ontological Differend; Politics, Singularity,* and *Science*).

Therefore my dialectic, as recapitulated in the above diagram, holds despite everything, provided that we drop the disastrous atavistic prejudice of the functionaries of humanity: which boils down to considering every event as "fallen from the sky," "miraculous," inscrutable, unanalyzable: like some simply unprognostic grace, in the face of which there is eventually nothing to do but "bear the consequences." The whole polemical aspect of my work consists in breaking into pieces the very presuppositions by which Badiou connotes the notion of event; and it is the less rowdy and less maximizing philosophers, who are much more cautious about the blinding negativity of the world of technomimetic appropriation that have shown me the right way: Schürmann and Lacoue-Labarthe are my two Masters and the main influences on what I am trying to do in philosophy. To my mind, Adorno, although his conceptual influence on my work is not as direct as the aforementioned two, represents the highest degree of lucidity and vigilance on the links between aesthetics and politics: "aesthethics,"[2] wrote Lacoue-Labarthe with stunning brilliance. And as for Badiou, one need not be a genius to see that he is my best enemy, in that he is the purest bearer of the oldest propensity of metaphysics, the propensity of "purifying" maximizations, in every figurative sense and also, alas, literally.

I *demonstrated* in what lies the error: the "mystery" of the "Badiouian" form of the event, the impossible-mathematical form of self-belonging is the *anthropological* but foreclosed sublimation of that which *allows* the very existence of mathematical transcendentalization: quite simply put, appropriation. And no other domain sublimates these transcendentalizations as blindly as mathematics: hence its devastating effects on philosophy itself which, knowing the terrain, often appears to me like a historical parade of Oedipuses and King Lears ignoring each other, or funny, pontificating Ubus. The mathematical "ghost" of self-belonging is nothing other than technomimetic *appropriation* which then enables the human animal—from sublimation to sublimation, from hunting to slaughterhouses and batteries, from tom-toms to the Internet, from carracks to spacecrafts, from drawings to algorithms—to extend his grip and blindly, tragically, *pay* for all appropriative overbidding through increasingly monstrous networks of expropriations: *execrations*.

This is why it was impossible for me to resist a very nasty play on words: cacatharsis. Indeed, all technomimetic appropriation ends up in a regime of expropriation that is an execration, a waste. Already, at the very stage of the emergence of animal life, predatory, alimentary appropriation ends in the occurrence of a phenomenon that inexists to the mineral or vegetable proto-appropriation: defecation. However, this phenomenon is reabsorbed harmoniously, as they say, in Nature. Sometimes, even excrements are "useful": to other animal species, to the dawning of new vegetable or animal species. We know this precisely because we no longer dwell in Nature in the strict sense:

besides we would not have the slightest notion of it, had we not surpassed-suppressed-preserved it. We know that animal waste is "recycled" in Nature precisely because we are born to ourselves through *mimesis* that has *suppressed* Nature all the while preserving it: *techne*.

Techne is therefore, quite simply, *catharsis* of Nature. When technology crossed the threshold of the industrial revolution, it arrived almost a century later at the "ecological problem": the snowballing production of waste, quite rightly qualified as *non-recyclable*. Technology becomes the "cacatharsis" of Nature; *mimesis* that food-gathering primates made by agriculture, and predatory primates by hunting, etc., in short: the *mimesis* of natural and biological (and therefore proto-pleonectic) processes—such as feeding (and therefore defecation)—made by *techne*, becomes millions of years later a *hideous parody* of ingestion/excretion. The only animal species to have become Subject, the scientific species, is also the only one to individually commit suicide for *unnatural* reasons: Kant brilliantly showed how suicide alone was the proof of the existence of rational will, as distinct from biological desires, and even opposed to them (Freud would merely pad it out). This is to say, if *arbitrary*—or aleatory—suicide, not overdetermined by intelligible causes (moral, psychological, and therefore transferentially rational and teleological) were possible, no biological order could persist on earth. At the moment of Promethean nuclear appropriation, not only does the collateral *mimesis* of predatory destructions make hell on earth, not only is waste not recyclable, but *they turn directly against us*; and the species which produced first the individual, and then the collective Subject is, for the first time, summoned to ask itself the question of suicide not only *individually* (as in Kant's time) but *collectively* (and this is the time of the SoN).

Incidentally: similar to the pomp which philosophy creates around the notion of the "universal," I have always been extremely cautious regarding the term "communism," which takes for granted that the more things are in common and shared, the more we move towards the Good. The reader has only to hold out and put his hand, so to speak, in the well of *The Spirit of Nihilism*, in order to pick up many arguments that ruthlessly go against this presupposition.[3] Being in common with one another has always been our case unfortunately, caesuring our blissfully solitary mammalian egoism; then this egoism appears to the eyes of metaphysical pomposity as Evil;[4] and the same metaphysical galvanization will be seen in Condorcet's "mathematizable society", i.e. in a being-in-common [*un être-en-commun*] organized as a stable or a battery, the maximization of the Good, once again turning truths upside down.

The individual Subject is the *catharsis* of the individuated animal; and the collective Subject—"humanity"—is the *catharsis* of the multiple species that serves as its medium. The latter, in surpassing itself as animal species, becomes the sickly, tortured, "atrocified" *waste* of this surpassing, and this is the only thing the unsurpassable Hegel did not realize: in the process of *aufhebung*, he neglected to mention something that is essential to the SoN: the *remainder*, the waste, the excrement of every suppression-preservation-sublation [*sursomption*]. This is the conceptual and *technical* definition of Evil.

Everything is thus clarified in the still erroneous gropings of the *Manifeste antiscolastique*. There is no need to whine, like the entire philosophical tradition, over the always regrettable degradation of the original into copy: today, the degradation of the event into unfaithful repetition. This "betrayal" is in reality inscribed in the very process of appropriation: the greater appropriation is, the more the reverse of expropriation is not only to be feared, but ought to be infallibly anticipated. Because appropriation is, *right from the outset*, an unconscious expropriation or an expropriation that *wants* to be unconscious of itself (will, no doubt, arising nowhere else but there): extraction and retrieval by violence, exploitation and torture when it comes to animal life, ours included of course. And because, for us humans, event is *primarily* repetition: meaning, *mimesis*. It is not the beings [*les étants*] that imitate algorithms, Ideas and Principles, but the latter that imitate the beings, by simplifying them for the sole trans-predatory purpose of appropriation.

In order to prove, all the same, the real social and endemic power of philosophy, I always say that it happens to anyone, even illiterate, on any point of the globe, to wake up one day, and say to himself: "I have an Idea!" Just as most people drive a car but only a tiny minority are mechanics, so does everyone use philosophical notions forged thousands of years ago, without having to do applied philosophy. The *concept* of Idea did not pre-exist Plato's invention, whose only mistake was to conceal the fact that it was a question of a mimetic avatar, an artifact actually, a construction; the overwhelming majority of humanity does not need to have philosophical knowledge in order to make daily use of the concept of Idea. An illiterate person who has an excellent concept of Idea lacks absolutely nothing, nothing more than what a Maserati driver lacks for want of a mechanic's knowledge.[5]

Perhaps when the day comes that the SoN's philosophy, like every philosophy, will have made children by taking the public domain from behind, we will avoid somewhat better the calamitous costs of appropriation, never forgetting that it is always already, first and foremost an expropriation, an injustice made to some region of the being [*étant*]: downstream as well as upstream. And perhaps the intrinsically metaphysical, that is, Platonic scales of nihilism will have fallen from our eyes for good, when we will learn to recognize that repetition does not degrade the event, but allows it. And then …

Finally, with these revisions and precisions made after the fact, this image shows the nerve of the dialectical war waged by the SoN (its most "Hegelian" trait, if you like): the coincidence *and* the non-coincidence of event and repetition. *Mimesis* hopes to eternalize what it takes over: the harvest, literally and in every sense, of technomimetic astuteness, is not eternalized as anticipated, and unprognostic famines break out to punish the pleonectic *hubris* of the technological animal. The slaves of the Old Testament are more familiar with times of destitution than of abundance. In the minds of some well-intentioned thinking heads, this impossible eternalization can trigger the dream of a return "to this side" of the event of appropriation: to the lost paradise of Nature. For us, there is no possible return to the pre-technomimetic age of appropriation, which would constitute a collectively agreed suicide. What we eventually have to think, in order to stand a small chance of pulling through this, is the very abyss that opens up between event and repetition, at the very point of their "miraculous" coincidence. For us, to begin with, event *is* repetition: *mimesis*. Agriculture imitates gathering. It is *afterwards*, in *instituted* repetition, that agriculture becomes a "second nature" of our daily life, and the troubles really begin.

The following is a somewhat colossal instance of this impossible return to the origin, clinically called "regression": in the 1930s, extremist vegetarians called "vegans" who deem it wrong to consume anything but plants, even animal products like eggs or milk, decided they had to go even further and even renounce *gathering*. This meant returning to the animal automatism of grazing. The experience did not last long and several of them died. The technomimetic animal is incapable of returning to what religion called "paradise lost," which is nothing other than the innocent nudity of appropriative animal automatism. Harvests are eventually followed by regular droughts, as described throughout the Bible. Technomimetic appropriation, repetition as event, not only does not freeze into eternalized event, original paradise raised to its square, but rushes the appropriative being [*l'étant*] headlong into the counter-cycles of catastrophic expropriative accelerations. The event that *is* originarily repetition for us, never again repeats as such: it is immediately modified into "fall from original grace." The whole supernumerary *habitus* contracted by technomimetic appropriation, these "second natures" as the many forms of enslavement and chores, are the failure of the repetition of the event. The event which *coincides* with repetition, technomimetic appropriation, is never eternalized as such, and it is this failure that constitutes the fabric of painful "repetitions" that organize our everyday life, from hygiene to work, from medicine to habits and customs, from taxes and bills to "civic duties," from formal greetings to unconsciously necessary collective leisure activities.

This impossible eternalization that sanctions technomimetic "eternalization" has itself strictly technical reasons. It is, however, this radical and stinging, originary failure of eternalization that metaphysics would sublimate and still sublimates on sight in most of contemporary philosophical production (this means, unfortunately, the one that counts).

Expropriation

EXPROPRIATION: Needless to say, the philosophy of *The Spirit of Nihilism* has the sole objective of denouncing everything that seems to provide us only with "Good" and of unmasking all the ways in which philosophers lie or lie *to themselves* (which is always worse) in order to universally condone this foolishness. Expropriation is not the deed of some vicious fellow who, in order to get something out of it, exploits his own sort, themselves morally immaculate for the fact of being on the wrong side of exploitation. This does not come down to condoning the somewhat crude maxim by Scutenaire: "The chiefs are powerful [*puissants*] bastards, the subjects, potential [*en puissance*] bastards."[1] It certainly does not come down to forgiving the adipose CEO, the Saudi Emir swimming in petrodollars, the Tyrant of any kind, and preferring them to my friend Tonio the mechanic, one of the finest characters I ever met, or to my friend Patrick the construction worker who committed suicide, or to Nicolas the alcoholic cleaning boy with the looks of James Dean. Of course one must always side with the expropriated against the tiny and infamous minority of obscene despoilers. The SoN even provides a metaphysical arsenal, more *disillusioned* than any other, in order to tackle the question again at its roots, and eventually anticipate the new issues for the new century. Of course, ideally, the final stake of politics must be the abolition of private property.

And yet, historically, we *no longer* have the possibility ("exterminations still alive in our memories and planetary asphyxiations already in our throats,"[2] says Schürmann) of not looking things in the face: "capitalism" thrusts its roots into causes much deeper than unfortunate but rectifiable historical contingencies. It begins already with animal "pleonexia." This archi-appropriative trait, which marks the manifestation of being an event like a stigma, becomes abyssal with the technomimetic turning point. The Luciferian play of appropriation-expropriation is the indelible stigma of Religion's original sin. And it is against all these excellent *petitiones principii* that philosophy "proper" remains fully religious, in the worst sense of the word, fancying about "final solutions" which would wipe out once and for all this stigma that is such an inextricable part of our condition.

For instance, what is "private property" or "Rights?"[3] A secondary mimetic astuteness: a collective agreement to *protect* the second-degree egoity consisting of anthropological individuation, which has joined the massive regime of expropriation through the primary appropriation of technomimetics.

Once again, ideally, money should be abolished. The only attempt in this sense (save for Christ's with the money changers of the temple, which was aborted as soon as it started), the one and only time, say I, when the abolition of money was *actually* carried out, was at Phnom Penh, around 1975. As Badiou would say with his usual humour: "It is the intention that counts ..." In short: philosophers like to go on telling themselves wonderful stories where the suppression of all traces of egoism, in the anthropological closure, would always be the meekness that will reunite us in the best of all possible worlds. "Communism" is the preferred word put to use in order to sell the most dubious Ideal of the entire metaphysical tradition. Ten years of such mediatico-academic agitprop in this sense has remained remarkably ineffective.

"Metaphysical Lutheranism" means: the roots of Evil go much deeper than philosophers think, up to the abyssal caesura opened up by Rousseau-Schelling (see *Nihilism*). The SoN wants to go even a bit further in their archaeology than they themselves did, but certainly owing to the foundations laid by them. It removes the last casts and pokes the wounds. The pleonectic affect is—no pun intended, except the obvious—a pleonasm: it is doubly consubstantial with our conditions: as mammalian species first, as Subjects of technomimetic hubris afterwards. Evil is inchoative with respect to the most "ontological" of causes: being as event.

The SoN asks all the same whether the hagiographic figures of the revolutionary left are worth *fundamentally* more, and function *fundamentally* in accordance with another schema than that—consubstantial with and inveterate in human nature—of the always more hungry strategy of tentacular appropriations, even if they are not monetary. In what sense does the Marxist-Leninist tyrant, who monstrously imitates the functioning of tsarism or the old Chinese imperialism, and carries out exterminations in order to reach his proclaimed ideality, or the leftist star of the campus, playing the violins of equality all the while continuously reveling in his worldly successes and networks of influence, prevail *in dignity* over the adipose CEO or the Saudi emir?

To stick to the last century, the figures of political "sanctity" are evidently to be sought rather on the side of Benjamins or Debords: poets, players, and rascals: the outsiders.[4] What do they want? The political ideal which must become ours: the *catharsis* of our monstrous regime of appropriation-expropriation; it is *play* (see below) and play alone that represents it. In other words, as we shall see, art that has *really* become politics, that has really become "regulation," literally and in every sense, of the whole City. The abolition of *every* propensity to appropriation is not only the metaphysical crime par excellence, but a *conscious* lie. Political tyrants, and the petty tyrants of metaphysics who envy them, drooling, boasting in concert in the name of the definitive abolition of every pleonectic propensity, do so in accordance with the most ferocious strategies of the most impudently rapacious appropriation. Blackmailing with the Good, with eternal truths, with equality, etc., is a raving madness that has lasted only too long. Without technical appropriation and without pleonectic individuation inchoative with respect to our envoi, therefore absolutely "consubstantial" with our substanceless condition, no mathematics, no philosophy, no love, no family nor libido, no art, no City, and no Civilization: nothing. We owe everything to the pleonectic, for better as well as for worse. A unique word will designate what *beauty* could be therein, in the most profoundly aesthetic sense of the term: *emulation*. We shall later come back to this (see *Play*).

That said, the metaphysical blackmailing with the perpetual Good would eventually confess outright to the purloined letter: the terminal ontological Ideal that shows the tip of its nose behind this blackmailing with "eternal life" and the "Good," is the *literalized* nothing.

The SoN plays for high stakes, but with the light-heartedness of historial responsibility: it intends to be done with the "final solutions" of metaphysicians, through the assumption of the *dominant* feature of expropriation which underlies all appropriative gesture. It sincerely hopes to contribute to the fact that, in a century or two, and if we are still present on earth, philosophical work will have done away with these sordid ravings once and for all. Especially, and less anecdotally, it shows that the play of appropriation/expropriation is not a contingent political model of anthropological functioning, but is unfortunately inchoative with respect to the very event that made of humanity exactly what it is. Even in the domain that should belong par excellence to those great and noble disinterested feelings, pleonectic ferocity is at work. In every love story, the logistic of appropriation/expropriation is, it must be said, most often relentless. And the solution to this violence does not lie in the soppy displays of misty emotions and complacent indulgences,[5] but, as usual, in a formal sublimation of this pleonectic ferocity *itself*: in *play*, the organized *catharsis* of love as war continued by other means—which was figured out by the courtly lovers and refined libertines, Kierkegaard and Nietzsche, sadomasochistic practices, or Sollers' lived accounts. Erotic masochism, for instance, rests on a ritual regulated like a *game*, and which makes it into a *parody* of suffering: a suffering in the second degree, which plays with its re-presentation, and becomes a sensual delight. SM's masochism is a *catharsis* of suffering, like in all art, and in its singular mode.

Even the most "innocent" drawing in a prehistorical cave repre-sents—"cathartically"—Crime and suffering. Appropriation *always* expropriates—according to a very precise mathematics of which only philosophy is capable—something other than itself: *that which* is expropriated with the obvious benefit cashed by the appropriative being [*l'étant*], what metaphysics in its foreclosed candor calls "Good," always "avenges" itself every bit as mathemat-ically, and this is the *concept* of Evil, as developed by the SoN.

Once again, the appropriated being always comes to "avenge" itself in the most technical manner: for instance, the animals we exterminate collectively have "spontaneously" picked up the recent habit of endowing us with devas-tating viruses. The "mad cow" disease (Creutzfeldt-Jakob disease) and the "bird flu" (H5N1 virus) phenomenon, animal diseases transmissible to man, which have already killed thousands of people, but which, we are told, could even wipe out millions if there were epidemic, incidentally and precisely arrive from the two animals we eat most, and whose industrial treatment, especially in slaughterhouses and batteries, is literally *atrocious*. These viruses do not come from animals we treat "well" and do not consume, such as dogs and cats, but from those we torture and devour.[6] Those we *appropriate* the most ... "bestially," we would say, had we not learned that Evil was actually not the proto-pleonectic predation of beasts, but the monstrous parody of this "pleonexia" in the tentacular extension of technics. Through these epidemics, would chickens, roosters, and cows be the "sites" which can "make event" only in the mode of an objective wrath, without "will," a both biological and supernumerary eye for an eye, responding to the horror of industrialization, i.e. the human *techne* applied to the animal body? Lévi-Strauss did not fail to react to this phenomenon: one of the fundamental taboos of all civilization, but one which *already* holds for every animal species without exception, is the taboo of cannibalism—the particularly primary form of impossible "transappropriation." By *forcing* animals to eat products made not only from the very flesh of their congeners, but sometimes from their own excrements, "Nature" dominated by technology avenges itself *eventually*.

Must we hope that these viruses become more powerful and exterminate us in our turn? We would rather wish that today's "bioethical" trend manages to probe the profound metaphysical reasons for its righteous quests.

Woman

WOMAN: Identity of desire and jouissance. Metaphysically: indiscernibility of being and event (see *Sexuation*, Appendix).

History

HISTORY: Philosophy, although functioning in an always different, shifted temporality than the temporality of social, cultural, or scientific events, has its trends as well. Over more than two centuries ago, one would rather declare oneself idealist; today, it is obligatory to declare oneself materialist. And so, yesterday's idealists are reinterpreted as raging materialists, who were so either unconsciously or because they were obliged to conceal their game; but since everybody is materialist, it is not clear how all this would make a difference. The philosophical life is sometimes made unbearable by this constant exchange of hollow words.

One of the philosophical trends of our time, appropriate for very numerous exchanges of the sort, is antihistoricism. Just as one thinks of distinguishing oneself from the golden age of German idealism by brandishing the "originality" of a materialism claimed by all one's colleagues, in the same way, in order to soothe the haemophiliac wounds of a leftism that has been making up for it merely by autosuggestive drip-feeding for forty years, a password has been found to discreetly conceal this historical dead-end: antihistoricism. Since the deaths of Schürmann and Lacoue-Labarthe, and of Debord and Blanchot as well, you will not find one philosopher "that counts" who claims that the historical question is the essential point of his work. It is this claim that I adopt without the least reservation, a point stressed often enough by the SoN's principal volume: *Ontologique de l'Histoire*. "Onto-logic" meaning: the logic of being, accomplished as event, yields the oxymoron of the catastrophic miracle that is History. As being accomplishes itself as event, History destroys the very possibility of all "ontology," in the ever-accelerating haste of a being [*un être*] revealed always more disruptively.

The following formula sums it all up: "History is the alchemy that converts contingency into necessity." Today, for reasons that can no longer escape the careful reader, I would put the word "necessity" in quotation marks. Why? Because these "necessities" are intrinsically parodic (see *Irony*). Through the evental and singularizing appropriation of the Laws of Nature and being [*l'être*], the appropriative, that is technomimetic being [*l'étant*] territorializes an infinity of *supernumerary*, i.e. conventional Laws. These Laws are most often delicate, for the obvious reason that they are "artificial." And so they are just as often transgressed, something we intuitively recognize as "Evil." But the deeper reason for which these Laws themselves "self-transgress themselves" in each generation, or in other words, change entirely from one generation to the next, is that the fundamental event is itself Transgressive: the appropriation of the Laws of being and Nature is their Transgression (see below). In turn, this yields the other primordial formula of an ontologic of History: Transgression precedes Legislation. The scansion of these supernumerary Laws that change constantly with the generations—likewise with trends and fashions, philosophical trends included—is what is called History, and this is why the rhythm of Transgressions accelerates as well, and has even reached a point of speed that presents, with respect to legislations, a new take on the fable of the Tortoise and the Hare.

Hence it is obviously not enough to place oneself arrogantly in the quasi-pleonastic wake of the great philosophies of History since Kant, Hegel, and Hölderlin, then Nietzsche and Heidegger (not forgetting Marx and Foucault), and finally Schürmann and Lacoue (not forgetting Blanchot and Debord). The adverb points of course to the conceptual caliber of the invocations, and also the fact of being epochally against the current. It is especially imperative that the proposed concept of History itself be entirely original with respect to those of the above-mentioned tutelary figures.

Man is self-evidently the historical-being[1] [*l'être-historique*], because he is the animal of technomimetic appropriation. Technics and archive are the one and same concept. A cat, observing that it was itself brought forth as a kitten, and bringing forth kittens in turn, by inference, can guess that it has had grandparents, great-grandparents, etc. But she will never know what they must have looked like. This is why animal cycles are repetitive: a herd of cows from a million years ago and the herd of cows that I see through the window of my house in Corrèze are as alike as two peas in a pod. Nature, although dependent on an event—the miraculous emergence of life on earth—sediments this event in its own mode into repetition cycles that remain unchanged for ages. The event of technomimetic appropriation is that which has *disrupted* this articulation of event/repetition (see *Event*), making the cyclical repetition of Nature abnormal, and supernumerary technological exception the "norm." This is history, and this is "culture." But these norms change from one generation to the next, "fissured," as Schürmann would say, at a rhythm that accelerates as History progresses, quite simply even, *scanned* by these ever more insane precipitations. This is what governs the set of priorities of a *modern* philosophical work, because the event of appropriation that condoned History, concealed, through two thousand years of metaphysical functionary work, the price to pay: monstrous, globally tentacular networks of expropriations of all kinds, for which we need the "political" neo-candor of the *new-look*[2] metaphysician in order to hold, precisely, that they are simply "political." The countless transgressions undermining these "norms," which make these innumerable networks look like gigantic porous pipings of nuclear waste in the former USSR, proceed also from what the standard functionary work of metaphysics did not realize: the primacy of Transgression over Legislation. The Mosaic gift of Law comes after the original sin; Kant's second critique is an abreaction to the unprecedented transgressive possibilities opened up by the French Revolution.

The other beings [*étants*], the other animals in particular, are incapable of *wanting* [*vouloir*] repetition, just as they are incapable of being capable [*pouvoir*] of it: of (self-)appropriating repetition. This is why they repeat *themselves* [*se répètent*] almost immutably, quasi-eternally, throughout the ages. Man is he who *wants* and *is capable* of repetition, and this is exactly why he repeats himself much *less*: he ceaselessly provokes the *new*, and with all his generational might, causes the expiration of that which was only yesterday considered the *nec plus ultra*. Derisory, and yet continually overexposed worldly phenomena, such as fashion, "hipness," or "hype," are in reality the microscopic reflection of an otherwise overdetermining processuality, that of History itself, once the scales of metaphysical maximizations fall from the eyes. Schürmann supremely asks: "What would happen if, instead of discrediting some single referent of beings so as to accredit another—instead of becoming tired of what is 'out' and getting excited over what is 'in' for the usual return to school this fall—our attention were to dwell on the tragic conflictuality that is being?"[3] Those who heard him, almost twenty years after his death, can still be counted on the fingers of a mutilated hand.

This is the key point of the SoN: it shows how it is the aptitude for the *doubling* of what the other beings [*étants*] merely undergo that characterizes our *singular* eventalness. The repetition of repetition gives everything except another repetition: the event that is *properly* ours. The *mimesis* of *mimesis*, the semblance of semblance, etc.: we will see how what I call appropriation, as technomimetic appropriation, is the same thing as this properly human faculty of doubling. To repeat repetition is not to iterate it for an nth time, like the opening of a flower or the birth of a bovid. It is, precisely, to do what no other being does: to *(self-) appropriate* repetition. This appropriative doubling *short-circuits* the simple iteration in which results every other repetition, outside the anthropological closure, and always provokes a radical novelty. We will see more exactly how.

History is the alchemy that converts evental contingencies into necessities, into *second natures* literally. This is also the philosophical name of freedom. How are we to understand this?

We should know since Kant that freedom is indiscernible from what is considered its exact opposite *in the common idiom*, i.e. *constraint*.[4] In other words: nobody obliges us to wear clothes, wash ourselves everyday, have an email address, etc. The only necessities of our biological lives are well known: eating, excretion, and sleeping. Through appropriation, we surround ourselves with entire constellations of supernumerary "necessities" which repeat the event by "eternalizing it." Culture is an infinite network of *parodies* of necessity. Nothing *obliges* me, physically speaking, to dress up in order to go out and have a cup of coffee; none of the *established* natural laws, because we (self-) appropriated them. And yet, if I went there in my simplest Adam outfit, and ordered bleach instead of an espresso—everything that would not come to the mind of any animal, but whose transgressive phenomenality exudes from all the pores of the anthropological-normative closure—I would get myself into serious trouble. Freedom, which is nothing other than everyday life, which is nothing other than the being-historical, is the unconsciously overwhelming *weight* of all the "categorical imperatives" with which the human animal is crippled because of his "own" fault, both appropriating and expropriated. The being-communitarian—"hell is other people"—to which nothing obliges us, is the very name of freedom, that is to say, the countless and striated implicit constraints that weigh upon our everyday life.

This is why man lives in "the upside-down world": every appropriation becomes expropriation, alienation in constraint, and every reappropriation which "puts the world back upright" appears, to the eyes of the post-evental conformism of man, as an anomaly. This is the purloined letter of the philosophical Sages—their most cunningly pleasant professional secret. Solitude is the *normal* state of the overwhelming majority of mammals. Man is the animal that puts itself in the insane situation of a henceforth global community ("communism" has always been there), in the consciousness of the existence of his six billion congeners. This insanity is that which passes off as "good sense." A Bengal tiger certainly does not have the slightest idea of the existence of the African tigers and vice versa. He is conscious only of his environment, and not of the continents, nor of the fact that the planet is round, etc. The technomimetic animal, under the crushing weight of the constraints he self-inflicts, hence undergoes a kind of unbearable psychic depressurization: the tragic condition that is being as event.

Science has therefore the structure of a *hallucinatory psychosis*, and this is why only the human animal can suffer from psychosis, paranoia, schizophrenia. *The Spirit of Nihilism* comes to overturn all the common prejudices of philosophy: for man, it is Evil that precedes Good (the Good is nothing but an invention meant to *compensate* the expropriatory atrocity resulting from the event of appropriation), madness that precedes reason (if we caught our domestic animals in an act equivalent to rubbing two flints together, sowing seeds or drawing, we would put them down, call the vet, or alert the media, shaking to the bone), Transgression (see below) that precedes legislation (every event has the structure of a *Transgression* of the given, and this is to convert (appropriative) contingency into (alienating, i.e. expropriative) necessity).

Let us come back to the philosopher's cunning secret. The Sage is he who "returns to normal": again the structure of apagogical doubling, the doubling of *mimesis* and parody, Irony (see below) and the impossible iteration of semblance. Where the ordinary mortal, ensnared by the "natural metaphysician in us," hurls himself into the exhausting social life and gregariousness with a forced smile (hell is Edith Wharton's world), passing off this supernumerary archi-constraint as "normality," the regular metaphysician, who is quite often he who has rushed his congeners into this voluntary plebeianization, cunningly withdraws from the game in order to return to the harmonious normality called "solitude." The hermit deceives his fellows by making them believe that his "ascetic ideal" is arid and painful, when it is the surest path to quietism and immaculate happiness. "Sooooolituuuuuudine amaaaataaaa...," sings Seneca from Monteverdi's wonderful opera, *L'Incoronazione di Poppea*.

Likewise, the Chastity of the Sage, who appears in the eyes of his congeners as a holy exception, is in fact a doubly perverse strategy of return to normality: for the overwhelming majority of mammals, with the exception of a few of our close simian cousins, "chastity" is the normal state, and rutting, the exceptional event. Through the event of appropriation, technomimetic astuteness, man converts the exceptional event, rutting and coitus, into the daily "necessity" of having sex. The Sage, by perverting the perversion that has become second nature in his congeners, by short-circuiting the sexual drive which in reality is a self-inflicted constraint and a worldly reflexive convention, obtains a pleasure unknown to sex compulsives: beatitude, that is to say, a kind of return to mammalian normality ... *in the second degree*, which is particularly parodic. His apparent idleness, solitude, and chastity, is no longer the pleasure of the cat that lies around in the grass all day long: it is the hard-earned victory over all the senseless constraints self-inflicted by humanity following technomimetic appropriation. Perhaps he then realizes Joyce's dream: he withdraws from History and its truncated "eternities" …

There is no eternity, and all the less so because one accedes to it: because one accedes to "eternal truths" through Science, and especially logico-mathematics (see below). The SoN relentlessly shatters all the great hollow words of philosophy such as "eternity," "Good," "positive truths," smug "universalism." There is only an *eternalization* of the event of appropriation in "second natures," in habits and customs, whose well-known cost is the exponentiation of expropriative pathologies that strike Nature's transgressor animal. This "eternalization" is the exact opposite of the eternity claimed to no avail by thirty generations of metaphysical functionaries. It is an acceleration and a *jeopardizing* of that which is accelerated, suppressed-preserved-sublated. It is the conceptual oxymoron of the fact that the more eternity (self-)appropriates, through the logico-mathematical, the more the *temporality* affecting the appropriative being expropriates it from its fixed being-there: vertiginously jeopardizing it. This was already maximally the case with Nature, with its extremely precarious harmony subjected to the uncertainties of the cosmos, and running the risk of vanishing from one day to the next, upon the impact of a comet for instance; and this is maximally the case with the event of which we are the *Subjects*, i.e. technomimetic appropriation, which, even before it culminates in a threat of destruction for all the terrestrial harmonies, consists of a *counter-cyclical precipitation* of Nature, and this is History. While the herd of cows unconsciously leaves it up to the multi-secular stability of the natural conditions in order to persist as such without even knowing it, the event of technoscientific appropriation destroys animal iteration which is (re)produced from generation to generation. The more History progresses, the greater are the upheavals that transform each successive generation, if not "apocalyptic."

The SoN hence destroys yet another one of the crudest prejudices of philosophers and common sense (the former quite often being the ideological *dealers*[5] of the latter): it is not memory that preserves and forgetting that destroys. It is the exact opposite. Other animals survive through thousands of years and beyond (dinosaurs survived for millions of years …) by forgetting the preceding generations. Being unconscious of the *laws* of repetition that make up their consistency maintains them therein. *(Self-)appropriating* these laws swerves our being-there on all sides, in a kind of "ontological depressurization" and expropriative dissemination. Once again, it may be that the movie *2001*, in its ending, *roughly* describes what awaits us, by dint of the blind and "Promethean" overbiddings on appropriation. Technomimetic retention, or in other words, archival inscription, destroys and transforms, and henceforth *literally* transmutes. Memory, the being-historical, is a precipitation of what is appropriated, a precipitation that is destruction *in continuous loop*. The more we accelerate the production of novelties, the more all kinds of appropriating events are multiplied because of the exponentiation of technological overpower, and the more we pile up a gigantic collection of waste with forever accelerating time constraints.

Up until the time constraint which could prove terminal: the SoN, like Schürmann, does not act as if we were not living the first ever century of our entire History in the knowledge that humanity, by its own fault, and by the very virtue of its metaphysico-Promethean hubris of the access to eternity and immortality, could die and vanish well before its time. If we had remained animal or primate, we could have lived for millions of years. The technologico-historical age, sublimated by metaphysics in the *normative* phantasm of the eternal and immortal, turns into the opposite of its promise: a vertiginous *jeopardizing* of our spatio-temporal life. The most gigantic *spatial* appropriation ever seen on earth, the appropriation of the complete technological stranglehold on the living, results in the most disastrous *temporal* expropriation ever seen (see *Appropriation/Expropriation*). Maximal appropriation through maximal expropriation, this is what we are *living* today.

The question is the following: the event, maximal intensive revelation of being, can it ever escape this fearsome proportional logic of appropriation/expropriation? This is one of the SoN's lateral contributions to Schürmann's tremendous undertaking: it *demonstrates* that the literal and always greater appropriation of eternity, infinity, and immortality results in the most sickly and pathetic expropriation ever borne on earth: due to a precariousness that could prove to be nothing but the most ridiculous evanescence, due to a finitude that is *aggravated* exponentially in pointless suffering, torture in all its forms and ceaseless exploitation, and finally due to the *sole* eternalization of death, in lieu of the "eternal life," the eternal dream of metaphysicians.

In this light, there is not the slightest "eternal truth," save for the pointless and hollow. The only genuinely interesting truths for a consistent, therefore atheist, in a word, contemporary philosopher is that the more interesting—i.e. evental—a truth is, the more it is jeopardizing, accelerating, and virtually devastating. Pending further information, expropriation always prevails over appropriation. It is by coming to know this one day, and assuming it politically that humanity will finally give itself the means to limit the damage, and—who knows?—finally enter the new age of a ludic and shared immanence, realizing here below what eschatologies of all kinds, including and especially "atheist" eschatologies, have promised in all kinds of the hereafter (see *Play*).

Man

MAN: Difference of desire and jouissance. Metaphysically: caesura of being and event (see *Sexuation*, Appendix).

Irony

IRONY: *Ironie et vérité* is the kind of book I somewhat regret having had published by a "small" publisher. The limpidity of its language, the reverberations it had in all those who had the good fortune of reading it, are such that it had everything to become a little "bestseller."

Everything began with a simple "sociological" observation. But philosophy is the putting into perspective of the obvious which, precisely because it is a "matter of course" as the behavioral "second nature" of a given period in time, is never questioned as such. As soon as it is, and often by philosophy, it ceases to be both obvious and "natural." We know the importance of the notion of "second nature" in my proposed thought.

This is why, if I had to invoke two key definitions of philosophy, by two illustrious colleagues, I would give equal share to both Reiner Schürmann's view that "Philosophy is the only literary genre which must not surprise. It must clarify a knowledge that all possess," and Deleuze's view that the measure of a philosophical talent is the number of concepts he has created. Here, as it is most often the case, it is especially Schürmann's requirement that I happen to fulfill. On the condition of adding that it is by answering to the German's criterion that I meet the condition set by the Frenchman: it is always by drawing a fundamental given, as blatant as it is nonanalyzed, from the dullest everyday life that I construct a novel concept of the situation, and thus pile up, like piles of poker chips, the "magic numbers" which for Deleuze should evaluate a philosopher based on the number of concepts he has created.

The "sociological" observation which was my starting point is, in a word, compulsory irony. For a—long!—time, from Socrates to Kierkegaard, irony was an elitist and aristocratic art, which was incidentally almost confused with the figure of the philosopher. Now for more than thirty years, irony has become, so to speak, a "*raison d'état.*"

What does this mean? The obvious "generational" fact which precisely would have us crippled: the derision, the disparaging perspective, the provocation of others as well as oneself, the mediatic omnipresence of comedy and sarcasm, imitation, and satire: irony is democratized. This irony is somewhat sad, especially when it is funny (televised comedians, whom I moreover like): it is in this democratization, this plebeianization of irony that I recognized the major symptom of "the spirit of nihilism." And thus I added "democratic nihilism" to my work—even though today I am more cautious about the name. The categorical imperative is: it is forbidden to take anything seriously.

The "political" scope of this diagnosis, blindingly evident, yet never recognized as such, did not escape even the usual apologists of the spirit of compulsory and omnivorous derision. A people who demeans itself by conditioned reflex, who laughs constantly at its own misery and mediocrity, still does not fail to acknowledge them. And hence, perhaps for the first time in History, entire populations self-proclaim themselves as mediocre, insignificant, miserable, etc., and pretend it is not so bad, that it is even a laughing matter. And as even one of the greatest living apologists of the ironic imperative pointed out to me, such a population would turn out to be more docile and manipulable than any other before. This is how I understand Lacan's wordplay: *"Les non-dupes errent"*;[1] which does not mean, he adds, that dupes do not err.

The *trait* of contemporary, i.e. ironic, subjectivity is to constantly demonstrate, through this spirit of omni-derision, that it can never be duped by anything. Henceforth it is the most likely to be fooled by absolutely everything. I have put it in a different wording in this small book: the *cogito* of the contemporary, ironic Subject is that it is perhaps the first subject of historical enunciation to *believe it does not think what it says*. Or, who does not believe it *thinks* what it says. This would attest, after all, to a lovely lucidity, in parallel with an entire portion of modern anti-subjectivist philosophy. From great linguists to Foucault, from Heidegger to Derrida, and including many others, this philosophy has truly shown us that there does not *properly* exist a subject of enunciation: that to be a metaphysical animal is, all in all, to be deprived of a proper voice; it is to be always-already "ventriloquized" by a language that precedes our individuated birth and succeeds our individuated death.

Joyce or Artaud, Cummings or the Lettrists, *Tel Quel* or Guyotat, all tried rather heroically to found a language that "comes from nowhere": the attempts, as such, failed. They failed in suppressing everything of the old language without preserving anything of it. But this is not what matters most with respect to the outcomes of the twentieth-century avant-gardist heroism. What matters is that these attempts would illustrate what the SoN conceptually and entirely brings up to date: all these attempts, rather than suppressing the old language, would manage—consciously or not—to preserve what ordinary language itself thought it did not preserve, that it suppressed entirely even: its *waste*. Guyotat, in *Prostitution*, manages to give an epic, drastic, traumatic form to the terminal waste-language of all the outcasts of the Earth: the *unspeakable* dialect of the streets of war-time Algiers, the dialect of the invalids and the prostitutes, the tortured and the raped.[2] Therein lay the greatness of "contemporary art": *to give form to waste*, and this is, as an instance of the most poignant paradox, *all* we must retain from it for the future. We must *preserve that which metaphysics deems irrecoverable*: I know of no other definition of an absolutely *modern* heroism.

Let us come back to another type of linguistic waste, the waste of compulsory contemporary self-derision. As we said, this obligation began to hurt in the chiasmus that is the enunciative position itself: in fact, by his own quasi-explicit reckoning, the contemporary subject of irony does not *really* believe in what he says. He does not *really* believe he is as null as that. He follows a convention: to show others that he "knows all about it" by taking nothing seriously, by turning everything into derision, starting with himself in order to well organize charity. Yet by the same token, he increases his standing and socializes. Irony has even become the archi-dominant asset of the feeling of wordly integration. There is no choice but to admit, following a remark by Jean-Luc Nancy, that "communism" is not something to be aimed at here or there; it constitutes our originary condition: first and foremost, because we are in common, self-constrained by technomimetic appropriation. And our contemporary way of being "communist" is *sarcastic communion*, disclosed wordly disillusionment, endless innuendo and wicked allusions, the half-smile of "all is derisory."

Hence the ironic subjet, seemingly depressing and nihilist, comes to present a face much more complex, not to say schizophrenic, than foreseen. I would like to make a remark here: perhaps I was lucky to grow up in a rather "weak" period. I bemoaned and cursed a lot in my youth, along with so many others, the mediocrity and insignificance of my period. But, after all, maybe it is a chance, if one knows how to seize it. In fact, if you are a twenty-year-old philosopher in the 1790s, or in the 1960s, you do not have to strain yourself to find "interesting subjects." In a way, everything is served up to you on a platter, whereas you have to dig deeper in lean times. You have to find in the apparent stagnation of the time that which, in this stagnation itself, is *revealing* of triumphal periods of evental emergences and spontaneous maximizations. You must find almost everything on your own, and ultimately this is perhaps more gratifying than being "spoilt" by a period considered fundamental in History; because you will have had to make the effort—the lucky generations being spared it—to

go seek out that which is interesting in an age that has self-proclaimed itself as
poor in the matter. Seemingly weak and uninteresting, there goes the subject
of compulsory irony, of "democratic nihilism," revealing itself as an extremely
curious beast, much more complex than it itself thinks to be.

Hence this "political" diagnosis asserts itself. What I wrote previously on
the subject was already not always without diatribes—which was to fall straight
into the trap of the time. "You won't take yourself too seriously, will you!" was
a reproach often made to me in my prime youth ... But today I would say that
this is not the essential point. I do not condone the categorical imperative of
systematic self-derision of course, whose everyday morbidity ends up being
a relentless fake laugh, its *real* psychological outcome being a notoriously
depressive and drifting population. But in order to grasp the essential aspect of
the symptom, it is the entire conceptual trajectory of *The Spirit of Nihilism* that
must be traversed.

For me, one name has summarized the debate better than any other: Jean
Baudrillard. He caused a scandal in the nineties with his article "The Conspiracy
of Art." Therein he attacked what had become what today they call "contemporary art." He was returning from a biennale in Venice and his first impression,
thrown in a sentence in one of his series (*Cool Memories*, I no longer know
which volume), was the following: "art's new function is conspiracy and insider-
dealing." In essence, the message of those artists was: "I am null! I am null!" [*Je
suis nul!*]. "And," Baudrillard concluded, "it truly is null."[3] It is difficult, at least
to a certain extent, to contest this diagnosis. I discussed this matter in private
with some of the most prominent personalities of "contemporary art," who had
publicly treated Baudrillard as an idiot, ignorant, or fascist, but who confessed
off the record that he was actually more than right in the things he wrote,
and that they had in fact loved the article. It is not a question of denying that
"contemporary art," in the last decades, has become too much like a huge enterprise of fashionable swindle: "insider-dealing" reminds us of what a magnificent
stylist Baudrillard was, when it is almost impossible to find an expression more
suitable for the issue, within the standard vocabulary of that day.

But what I find more interesting is precisely this age of the compulsory
parodic and the blackmailing with nullity and mediocrity. It is a true historial
originality, and, as we saw above, because I am one of the rare, if not the only
philosopher to still lay claim to the rather German tradition of a philosophy
of history, I preferred to question the conditions of possibility of such an
emergence which, in terms of aesthetics, is very closely connected with my
essential problem, "the spirit of nihilism," which I also could have called more or

less happily "democratic nihilism." In *Algèbre de la Tragédie* as well, I described this historical sequence as the aesthetic age of the *pathetico-parodic*. Let us finally add that my relationship with the said milieu of "contemporary art" has not always been easy, which alone could have justified my being quick on the draw. But this is not what counts most. And so the metaphysical functionary's conditioned reflex says, it is a question of art, *mimesis*; "postmodern" parody, imitations of trivial situations, etc.: *mimesis* of *mimesis*. In short, we are very close to the conceptual atmosphere which is already familiar to us. Here I quote a sentence from Lacoue-Labarthe which I think is canonical: "The *mimesis* of *nothing* is *play*."[4]

What does Baudrillard miss here, in his diagnosis which at least has the courage of the "first degree" and to "say out loud ..."? We must go a little back in Baudrillard's own trajectory. We know that he is the great theoretician of the generalized "simulacrum." I do not have the space here to explain why such a theory could only appear at a very precise moment in history; I made such an exhaustive explanation of it in *Ontologique de l'histoire* that I can only invite the reader to get hold of this little-known masterpiece. For the moment, suffice it to say that, starting with the eighties, with what would be called the "postmodern" (and which I provisionally called "democratic nihilism"), of which Baudrillard would be one of the greatest theoretical representatives (which probably led him to hate even more readily both the competitors and the artistic representatives, such as the "simulationists" who asked him for his support and whom he told to get lost), everything became "simulacrum." Simulacrum of art, of course; simulacrum of sex, with pornography or trans-sexualism; simulacrum of politics, with the dull media-parliamentary circus; simulacrum of war (since it was technologically won in advance), with the Gulf War, etc. As to the microcosm of the "radical chic of the left" to which Baudrillard, like myself, belonged in a paradoxal and conflictual way, the fact had been obvious for long decades: the diffuse sensation was clearly that there was no longer any radicality, but simulacra of radicality; no longer any events, but simulacra of events; finally, (and I will come back to this since here lies the heart of the matter) no longer any Transgressions, but simulacra and parodies of Transgression.

Baudrillard was a truly fascinating author who, owing to his quality and clarity of style, in addition to his numerous media appearances, attracted a much wider audience than the sole conventional professional philosophical ghetto. Let us quote a superb sentence of his: "To dissimulate is to pretend not to have what one has. To simulate is to feign to have what one doesn't have."[5]

I had turned my back on Baudrillard for some time when this scandalous article appeared in 1997. Today, I would say that Baudrillard, like all "critics of representation," was just an unconscious Platonist. Just like all conscious or unconscious Platonists, the purely *eidetic* conception of the being [*l'étant*] always gathers a discourse of decadent, nihilistic, etc. diagnosis of the hierarchical degradation and ineluctable deflation of the original into copy. Simulacrum: originary philosophical forgetting, which raised imitation to the rank of archetype, and singularities (see below) *without gender* to the rank of imitations of the archetype, could recognize nothing but monstrosity in the sudden incongruity of these singulars. I even coined an opportune neologism for this, which was picked up by my Master, Jean-Luc Nancy: *monstruation*.

But it is owing to this polemical, brave, and brilliant text that I realized the reason for Baudrillard's error, and the melancholia, or even "depressionism" of his generalized simulacrum theory, which brings him closer to so many other "critics" of decadence, from Spengler to Muray, including Debord and a part of Nietzsche, and so many others. It is always the same discourse: "There was a time when ... but henceforth we are finished, emptied out, damned. The best is gone: there is nothing left for us to do but pick up the remains."

Let us take a closer look at this. Art is always the mirror of its time, and of course vice versa. What does the "contemporary artist" wiped out by Baudrillard do? Does he pretend to be null, mediocre, insignificant, pathetic, ridiculous? Certainly not, since he lays his cards on the table. Does he pretend to have something he doesn't have? Nay, since he constantly makes worldly commerce of his nullity, mediocrity, insignificance, pathos, and ridicule. What is the operation here that is confused with the ironic operation itself?

Here is what I then found: the ironic subject does not pretend, *he pretends to pretend*. This is because—for reasons I will not explain to the reader since they strike at the very heart of our conceptual target—only the human being is capable of redoubling semblance in that way. This remark cuts across another, extremely profound remark made by Lacan: an animal, in the same way as the human being, can efface (cover) his traces and even make false traces. The only thing he cannot do *is to pass them off as false, when they are actually true*. Well then, in the ironic operation that does the same thing as what basically the Everyman does today, as exemplified by our "nihilist artists," the same process is at work. "And it truly is null!" However, we actually sense that the artist in question, like the average contemporary subject, does not really-really say he is null, insignificant, mediocre, etc. He increases his own standing for having *realized* that he is null, and therefore, by a very strange trick, for being "superior" for presenting himself as the low-water mark itself of artistic talent, like the average subject who likes to present himself as the harmless—but nice as anything—dreg of humanity. Is this a "politics of ressentiment" that Nietzsche prophesied, spun by the thick turf of the—probably democratic—"last men" in order to devalue all that is great, aristocratic, brilliant, and Promethean? It would be futile to deny that there is a lot of that. But the neo-aristocratism of the Nietzschean "overman" has hatched monsters, and is not a viable solution for us. The democratization of the world is inevitable, and if ressentiment, masked by the ironic imperative, must be the fundamental affect of such a future, so be it. Going against my own pubescent Nietzscheanism, I eventually deemed that it had to be sought elsewhere, and otherwise.

Irony is not to pretend, but to pretend to pretend.[6] I was very proud of what I had found … Alas! I come across a play by Marivaux, his last one, a masterpiece with a title that says it all: *The Constant Players* [*Les acteurs de bonne foi*]. The plot, very briefly, consists in a seemingly classical *mise en abîme* of the "theatre within theatre," whose reality lies elsewhere: the "amateur" play staged by the Don Juan of the village serves him, and a few other seducers and flirts, only as a means to confess their mutual love to each other, right under the nose of their "official" companions. It is a marvelous and very funny play, and in any case I will not say it all so as not to spoil your desire to buy *Ironie et vérité*. But it is in this play, on which I comment at length in my book, that I discovered the expression "to pretend to pretend." Grrr! Marivaux had said it before me, and said it clearly! Here is the line, which I write here in proper French (it is uttered by the village idiot, who talks with the peasant accent of the period one can cut with a knife): "And what's more, they mock my person in the cursed game of this diabolical play; our mistress, Colette, pretends to be soft on Monsieur Merlin, and Monsieur Merlin pretends to give her his heart, *yet despite the acting, it's all true! They're pretending to pretend, just to sell it to us.*"[7]

What does the "nihilist contemporary artist" do? What does the contemporary subject of compulsory self-derision do? They pretend … to pretend to be, as in this play, *what they really are*. Null, derisory, insignificant, pathetic, mediocre, etc. Yet, meanwhile, everything has changed.

I evoked earlier the conditioned reflex of the philosophical or literary moralist: this mediocrity is a characteristic feature of the time; you can only condemn it with no further ado, dreaming, more or less between the lines, of a golden age where all this never happened, or will no longer happen (Cicero or St. Augustine, always). Phenomena are then considered in the same way as you consider meteorological disasters: the catastrophe could have not taken place, but the tragedy is that it did, and all we can do is condemn the misfortune of being born at that moment, and eventually seek out the *single* culprits, CEOs, other intellectuals, pedophiles, or whatever. A philosophy of history, at least in the sense I mean it, never proceeds in this way. There has never been a golden age for its sagacity, situated, as it were, "beyond pessimism and optimism": the situation has been so radically corrupt from the start, since the original sin that, as Adorno says more or less, we are condemned to the decency that must be inspired by the sole fact of still being able to breathe in this hell. This philosophy fights all the variants of Platonism, including this form of Protestant, i.e. introverted Platonism we call Kantianism, because it fights all philosophy that says what *should* be, and not what *is*. In this respect, Epicureanism is the surest invocation to lucidity of the great philosophies of the future; for rather technical reasons, Aristotelianism as well. One must describe *how* things are, right at the origin. From then on we have every chance of discovering why they are *as* they are today, but also, against any form of Platonism, why they are *never* as they *should* be for the false candor of professional philosophers.

In this text of Baudrillard's, the shoe pinched, simply because in short it was a question of a self-refutation. What would the "postmodern" artists, blackmailers of insignificance, have done with mediocrity and uselessness? Were they simulating something, anything? Nay. Baudrillard says it himself: they confess, all cards on table, *being what they are*. "Truly null."

Then I entered a polemic with another adversary, the neo-Situationist collective *Tiqqun*, with which I was very involved at the time (1999–2000), whose leader Julien Coupat attracted a lot of attention in 2008, and whose *Theory of Bloom* made a great impact on the "plugged-in" crowd, which was captivated by the "Debord" trend, and so on the lookout for all that could come to represent a new Situationist International in our age of anorexic politico-intellectual cows. What was this theory about? It consisted in an operation miraculously close to the needs of our Subject, I must say. When Debord, rather platonically, denounced "the Empire of Evil" in the "Spectacle" as the industrialized realm of the fake and bloodless semblance, *Tiqqun* hammered it in. *Bloom* is the moment *when subjectivity itself becomes a spectacle*. We will call this the "*Star Academy* theorem." There were no more women, but *blooms* pretending to be women. No more "*cailleras*" from the suburbs, but *blooms* pretending to be "*cailleras*" from the suburbs. No more black people, but *blooms* pretending to be black, etc. This was the *Bloom* theory, the "democratic" generalization of the post-Cartesian bloodless subjectivity; and it was what you heard every day, at point blank, about everyone. No more substantial subject—all there is to say is *when* it seriously took place in history—just a bloodless subjectivity, feigning an inexistent substance. We would have to mention here the direct experience implicated by the theory, the everyday revolutionary-groupuscule atmosphere, fairly violent and negativist, psychodramatic, and actually stifling and depressive, because it of course spoke the truth of the theory itself. Things would end badly. Yet again, degraded Platonism: if every subjectivity is false and bloodless, all everyday existence must be incessantly sued for constant falsification.

The subtitle of this groupuscule's journal was: "critical metaphysics." When I think about it today, I tell myself we were actually far from it. In fact, what we have here is the essence of the age-old metaphysical sleight of hand. Is it possible, for a woman, to pretend to be anything else than what she is? Aside from a few novels and films relating an exceptional experience, such as *Victor Victoria*, I did not come across many such phenomena. It seems even harder for a black person, for instance in the United States of the slavery era, to pretend to be white. Yet even in our democratic and emancipated conditions, I met very few black people pretending to be white, and very few whites pretending to be black. There is of course Michael Jackson, who seems to have dreamed of "whitening" himself as much as his ridiculous means allowed him, or the trans-sexuals. But where is semblance here? A transsexual is not a man who *pretends* to be a woman, but who feels he *really* is one, and tries to *become* her if possible.[8] In the book consecrated to Meillassoux, I will furthermore expound the quite sophisticated *theory of becoming* proper to *The Spirit of Nihilism*. This is not the place to do it. Let us simply say, whatever harm MJ. did to himself to make us believe he was white, or a transsexual, to make us believe he was a woman, it still does not take up 99 percent of their time, and there are profound reasons for that.

This is the place to drive in a little bit further the nail that stigmatizes the metaphysical Christ. As usual, it is in the name of the eidetic conception of the being [*l'étant*] that one *denies* all real substance to a given singularity. This is pure metaphysical violence on behalf of the authors claiming to be its critics. Nobody pretends to be what they *are*. Most of the women in the world, for obvious socio-cultural reasons, are rather obliged, as *Tiqqun* would say, to be "*blooms* pretending to be women." We might just as well say that their whole lives are just evanescent masquerades, a conclusion any "critic of representation" would jump to countersign fiercely. It is this violence I have never been able to accept. Singularity *is*. And experience *is*, against all the "chic" philosophemes that always issue from the affluent and democratic West which deplores a hypothetical "end of direct experience."[9] That there is *no* "direct access" to the anthropological experience, that consequently there is always *representation* (see below) is what all our "critics" should have concluded, if they went all the way instead of darkening things more than they already are.

I open parentheses here. We see that this "critique of critique" called the SoN is consistent with the fact of having *localized*, clinically, the technical archeology of the appearance of Evil on earth. It is *never* the invariable metaphysical inter-pretation one makes of it; decadent *mimesis versus* lost authenticity or initiatorily accessible archetype. Yes, it happens, and even very often, that human subjects *overplay* the semblance they *originarily* are. It is at times wickedly efficient: see the feminists, militant gays, queers today (because playing on the ambivalence of "genders" is not pretending to be what one is not, it is playing, through provo-cation or overbidding, to be *what one really is*), the Black Panthers. Because, for me, perhaps this is the formula for the little happiness granted to us here below: when we succeed in *playing ourselves* with grace. I do not pretend to be who I am, I do not play something I do not have: otherwise I would have killed myself a long time ago. When I am happy, I *pretend to pretend* … to be who I really am, exactly in the same way as any subject of compulsory derision, or any "contemporary artist" overbidding on deflation does. This does not come down to taking oneself seriously. It simply comes down to sensing the *already concrete* utopia in which the world would be this immense, graceful theater it *can* become. Incessant game. And I close the pirantheses here.

Henceforth there is no need to go into the subtleties which the reader will find spelled out in *Ironie et vérité*. The "simulacrum," even in Deleuze (who, however, made its belated self-criticism in Jean-Clet Martin's book), has absolutely no chance of winning over what it presupposes: "the original" that philosophy dreams of, the so-called archetype, which is *in fact* the eidetic and empty, instrumental-appropriative imitation of the singular being [*l'étant singulier*]. For a detailed account on this point, see below, Representation.

Compulsory contemporary Nihilism in the second degree, of systematic irony, sarcasm as "second nature," etc., could then on turn out to be the *opposite* of Nihilism. Perhaps man learns in there, better late than never, that he is the archi-mimetic animal. That he is the (most) *playful* animal.

Play

PLAY: Humanity has always loved to play. Children, even before developing what will become their destiny as adults, aesthetic sensibility, or scientific mind, electively project themselves in all kinds of games they play. Even with mammals, as much as representational art or science traces insurmountable boundaries between us, they share with us the instinct of play. In fact, we cannot easily exclude the fact that the animals that play find in play nothing different from what we find in art in general (and of course, in games *very* particularly, as we will see very soon): a *catharsis* of predatory cruelty. Animal play is the proto-form of properly aesthetic *mimesis*; it is the only form of art that seems to be known by several animal species. Animal play has in common with human play and certain arts the *miming of death*: in other words, *acting death* [*jouer à mourir*]. But where animal play seems to take place according to *implicit* rules, a sort of instinctive consensus on the fact that one plays to fight and to fight for real, man defines his games according to the same criterion that differentiates him in general from the other animals: enacting the rules of nature everywhere, due to science, he also makes *explicit* the rules of his games. Because he alone (self-)appropriated the perennial rules of Nature and being, man alone can *enact* new rules: this is called politics (see below), for the worse, but it is also called play, for the better.

Play is one of the most revealing domains of the *being* [*l'être*] of man, and, for me, the only philosophical notion that still allows—"exterminations still alive in our memories and planetary asphyxiations already in our throats"[1]—to go on dreaming of a little bit of political utopia, when the essence of academic leftism fires blanks with its old slogans.

Man (self-)appropriates the laws of nature and this is called science (see below). He immediately reterritorializes his being-there by a set of rules that did not exist before, and this is called politics (see below). We always say, "the rules of the game" and not "the laws of the game." Just as politics is a parody of natural cruelty, and its laws, a parody which is the proper name of Evil (global "trusti-zation" is not the marking of territory; war is not fighting between tribes; murder and torture are not predation, etc.), play is always a parody of politics, i.e. most often of war, whether latent or declared. As is often the case, a parody that is, as it were, *secondary* to "originary parodies" turns out to be a "happy solution." The semblance of semblance is not a new semblance, but often a happy assumption of what was repressed, because of its evident toll of suffering, in the first degree. As much as anthropological libido seems to me to be based on an indubitable originary violence of the link between the sexes, what I call, following Adorno's idea, "archaic rape" [*viol archaïque*], violence which is *already* a parody of the "simple" mammalian reproductive "violence," and the introduction of Evil itself; *secondary* parodies, i.e. those forms as diverse, as historically dispersed as the archaic family or pornography, courtly love or sadomasochism, chivalrous or romantic love, are all to originary libidinal violence what play is to war. This is the subject of *Being and Sexuation*: while Hegel places the originary political link in the violence of the master-slave relationship, I base the originary amorous-libidinal situation on a no less negative envoi, which is a "violating" [*violante*] relation between man and woman. For a more detailed account, I refer you to the only volume of *The Spirit of Nihilism* that is as yet unpublished, *Being and Sexuation* [*Être et sexuation*]. Meanwhile, the reader can always refer to the Appendix at the end of this book.

Play is the *catharsis* (see below) of war. We can actually say that sports, with its obscene monetary millions, its stories about doping and oxygenated blood, its stupefying mass effect, etc., all in all, remains "just as violent" as originary war (a sociologist defended this view right in front of me); and that rugby and football, for instance, remain "as violent" as la soule which is considered their origin, in which players literally destroyed each other in order to send the archetype of the ball into the archetype of the goal.

Let us be serious. Play is really a surpassing of war. It is, superlatively, a suppression that is a preservation, a preservation that is a suppression. Jean-Luc Nancy called our attention to the fact that the etymological root of "cruelty" is the Latin word *cruor*, the color of blood, and that all aesthetic reflection should lean on this notion: play suppresses the atrocious cruelty of the bloodshed of war (or else, when libation is allowed, as in boxing, it is within tight limits set by strict rules), but preserves its *affect*. All art, even the most "innocent," is *catharsis* of cruelty: suspension of the bloodshed and the dying, but sublimation of pleonectic ferocity and the pleasure gained by the murder of the enemy.

Play is otherwise the only form—the only one—that humanity enjoys [*jouir*] the rule, while everywhere else—from education to taxation, from work to morals, from obligatory hygiene to military service, from religion to bills—the civic rules, all these *arbitrary* rules are lived *painfully*, and rightly so, by the overwhelming majority of their subjects. The fact that la soule or circus games have been the "intermediate" forms of the becoming-play of war says nothing against the obvious: play, as such, is one of the superior forms of civilization, in the same way as what is considered "art" in general. Rigorously speaking, play *is* an art form, sports included. As a matter of fact, the Greeks regarded neither Tragedy nor painting, neither sculpture nor music as the supreme art form: but the Olympics. Hegel had not failed to note this in an entire passage of the *Phenomenology of Spirit* dedicated to the "Religion of Art" that was the Greek moment. Must we remind ourselves that Pindar, the most underestimated of all great poets of antiquity today, wrote only on the Olympic Games? Why does a contemporary poet write so readily on porn actresses or Kurt Cobain, and never on the plebeian passion he so often shamefully shares with others, namely, football?

We can say what we please on the "corruption" of contemporary mass sports; in advanced capitalism what domain is immune from "corruption" anyway? The left-wing academic philosophy? Unions and parties? Alter-globalist groupuscules? Do not make me laugh. Humanity in its entirety is corrupted by original sin. It is *The Spirit of Nihilism*'s touch of indivisible "philosophical Lutheranism." Evil is primary, and profound. All the well-intentioned claims to *terminally* remedy evil have produced the opposite of what they promised. Classless society, global state of law as promise of the market economy, a Final Solution finally binding the earth and blood: each time a plan aspires to purge humanity of its originary vice *once and for all*, it provokes aggravated vice in return. The Nazi case is particularly interesting: I will not go into archaeological detail here,[2] but in German history, the National Socialist ideology, nourished by more or less well-digested Schellingism, Schopenhauerism, Wagnerism, and Nietzscheanism, marked a radical attempt of *caesura* with the Lutheran mould of this remarkable country. The Nazis fought everything that reminded them of Protestantism. We know the rest.

To be philosophically Lutheran simply means not giving up original sin. It is easy to cite the fundamental philosophical names in this family, the essential invocations of my work: Rousseau, half of Kant, Hegel. Modernity itself. The *Discourse on the Origin and Basis of Inequality Among Men* is *the* founding text of every philosophy to date, whether they know it or not (and even more when they do not, such as with Nietzsche and Heidegger, as Lacoue-Labarthe showed relentlessly, and as I demonstrate too in one of the two as yet unpublished books mentioned in the foreword, written in collaboration with Valentin Husson).

More recently: Schürmann and Lacoue-Labarthe were our great "metaphysical Protestants"—and the SoN is their continuation.

In terms of politics, it means the following: not to laicize metaphyiscal Catholicism; not to aspire to great purifications, purges nor great final redemptions, in the name of a Virtue so often much worse than what it claims to fight, and devoured by an always more fierce egoism than the one it denounces so readily in others. There is a saying of Christ—anti-Catholic, and therefore anti-Pauline, in advance—I particularly like, and which Luther cited regularly: "How is it that you see the mote in your brother's eye and not see the beam in your own eye?" And hence: to laicize a political utopia which makes do with the *indelible* given of what *The Spirit of Nihilism* laicizes as well: Evil is deep-rooted and co-substantial with the technomimetic animal. To claim to redeem humanity from this Evil once and for all is to always redouble or greatly increase it. I call this tendency "metaphysical Catholicism," and my finest professional rivals, Badiou and Meillassoux, come under it, but in very different ways. Badiou's passion is purification. Meillassoux's passion is redemption.

What more is there to say? One of the most senseless words dear to contemporary academic leftism is the word "equality." It is the word that has long exasperated me the most; it rings so hollow and never adds up to anything. It puts its upholders to the question on this point, and you will hear the same old stories.

The originary anthropological *fact* is indeed the radical introduction of exorbitant inequalities on earth. Inequality, first "by a short head," between the animal closure and the remainder of the being [*l'étant*]; then, the crushing of the remainder of the planetary being under the tyrannical yoke of just one miserable species, owing to the sole fact that it had the good fortune, the winning formula of "touching" the event of technomimetic appropriation; and finally, gaping inequalities within this same—anthropological—closure. There is absolutely no reason to be thrilled at it. But there is reason to open our eyes once and for all on the failure due to all the blank checks of metaphysics. What hastened the exponentiation of inequalities on earth? Precisely that which the metaphysician would like to "attain," in all these paradises, each more artificial than the other: technoscientific isomorphism; the principle of equality plated on things, for having (self-)appropriated the laws that governed them; the repetitive decalcomania that metaphysical functionaries often hope to realize, with science and politics. It is true that the latter is a repetition of science, but in the parodic sense (see *Politics*): therefore, not at all the same thing. And we do not have the slightest chance of seeing one day the arrival of a politics that would be "as harmonious" as a science.

Equality, before being a political notion at first entirely legitimate, in its native candor itself—I am thinking of the French Revolution—is first and foremost what I later call (see *Mathematics*) "the transcendental illusion *par excellence* of human consciousness." In other words, the *utilitarian*, technomimetic illusion of equality. It is the very form of appropriation. To sublate food gathering into agriculture is to appropriate the *empty*, transcendental law of the seed that grows to become a plant. Two plants only "of the same family," logically brought together by the animal to feed itself (the cow will recognize the grass, but avoid the nettle) become the *same* plant, in the *eyes* of architechnological inspection. This is how technical, i.e. metaphysical, isomorphism is set up right at the origin, with only all the time of History to ensure its expense reports are well in order. Mathematics, the belated sublimation of the most archaic techniques—hunting, agriculture, or drawing—wraps this up by what is probably the greatest crime ever committed against the mind, where Schelling saw, with good reason, the sufficient proof of the existence of God: x=x.

From this perspective, this should go without saying, but it goes better saying it: *The Spirit of Nihilism* does not forget one of the great conceptual conquests of the twentieth century, especially in France, the philosophies of difference. It goes all the better saying that we are currently witnessing a happy obliteration of their legacy, which should be mandatory: difference is an absolute transcendental, perhaps the transcendental of transcendentals.

Even in the prebiological world of inert matter, we can never say that a being [*un étant*], whether planet or dust particle, is ever perfectly equal to another. It is the same with two roses, etc. It is the opposite of Gertrude Stein's poem ("A rose is a rose is a rose ..."): a rose is *not* a rose is *not* a rose is *not* a rose ...[3] All things considered, it is at once *ontological* inequality that reigns in what was a long time called Creation. But one thing is certain: each time an event of appropriation takes place, and there is no event but that of appropriation, vital then animal then technological, inequality *evidently* becomes exponential. Hence inequality is ontological, it is a given; nothing is equal to anything, no meteor is equal to another, no atom, etc.

But if being [*l'être*] begins to think itself outside "ontology," as event, things become even worse. If event vouches for being, it dramatizes each time the inequality revealed in being itself. We are then swimming in troubled waters: and, yes, Heidegger's collusion with Nazism will disturb all those democratic and leftist beautiful souls. As Nancy bravely remarks in an interview, it must be admitted that it is no doubt for having strayed into the Nazi delusion, and without particularly attenuating circumstances, that Heidegger managed to touch something essential about politics, something that could not have occurred to a communist (alas, we are still there). Heidegger's Nazi turn had the dreadfully paradoxal "merit" of revealing, behind the inegalitarian "essence" of being he condoned therein (and this is what Lacoue-Labarthe called his "archi-fascism"), the until then unnoticed essence of this essence: the universal ontological *play* of appropriation-expropriation, growing vertiginously as being is accomplished as event.

A quick glance at the state of the contemporary philosophical scene makes you wonder whether, in this regard, we have progressed an inch. We are still dressing the wounds of our ravaged being-of-the-left, still unlikely to truly call into question all the theoretical presuppositions that are the real causes of the endless hemorrhage, and not the blows of the enemy, which only caused the injuries. A bleeding is cauterized if it is healed correctly. Whereas a hemorrhage that spreads over a period of four decades means we are bending over backwards to apply remedies that perpetuate the Evil, and it is not today's academic physicians that will put us back on our feet, since they are the ever so clever recyclers of the oldest tricks, which seemed "original" to a generation only because they had been long forgotten, and with good reason. Why did Heidegger understand "pleonexia," co-originary with being as event, owing to what Lacoue-Labarthe ruthlessly calls his "archi-fascism?" Because at least he could not close his eyes to what terrified the ingenuous leftists: that the pleonectic essence of man is ineradicable. It is constituted in all its historiality by the play of appropriation-expropriation, and cannot be brushed aside by a utopian stroke. That is why the "Badiou affair" is not less serious than the "Heidegger affair": the famous "passion for equality" had great consequences, in a perfectly constructed and "rational" discourse in Pol Pot ("our Robespierre," he recently suggested[4]), Mao, and Lin Biao. It is imperative that the smoke and mirrors metaphysical illusion that rules over this passion be deconstructed, if the politics of emancipation want to rise from their ashes. The assumption of this passion, even in its ultimate criminal consequences, and up to now, by a philosopher of Badiou's caliber, is a document of prime importance; not to put the person on a pyschological trial, which would be irrelevant, but to begin this deconstruction and understand to which major malfeasance is due "real communism," which has for the most part become as criminal as fascism or globalized capitalism. Exterminating doctors and teachers on the pretext that they were "petit-bourgeois" is not more forgivable than exterminating Jews on the pretext that they were the historial *éminence grise* of nihilism, as Badiou defends somewhat more than between the lines. I leave it for later, or to others, the task of showing how the SoN's dialectical apparatus enables deconstruction of the manner in which Badiou justifies the "communist" mass graves saying that they originate in the "void of the situation," and hence proceed from "true" events, whereas the fascist mass graves are unjustifiable, because they suppose a phantasmatic "fullness"; in other words, how the SoN pulverizes the speculative core enabling Badiouian reasoning, i.e. the argumentative criteria that allow discriminating an event of truth from a simulacrum of event. I will later on exemplify the complex torsion uniting the event and its presumed parodic "double" (see *Catharsis*).

Now here we have a fine kettle of fish. But on that point, tired of the depressive platitudes of the small leftist intellectual community, which was my non-disowned "family," no matter what people say, I preferred to shoulder my responsibilities. Yes to equity, justice, the gradual abolition of private property. But the *sincere* lovers of emancipation should renounce, and as soon as possible, a word as hollow as "equality," because if they keep it, it is the chances of their politics that will be mortgaged for a long time.

This is where the *thought* of play decisively steps in. Politically, it is much less aleatory than drawing blank checks on "equality." Because play, or sports, are the *catharsis* of the absolute sinews of humanity we call *emulation*. In *Inesthétique et mimêsis*, once again following Lacoue-Labarthe, I remind how Rousseau's "civic festival," an unintentional premonition of the French Revolution, was conceived as a gigantic *gratuitous* civic game of ceaseless and always renewed emulation. This theme has been haunting me for a long time; it is covered here in the section of Irony (see above): how to *play at being oneself*?

In short, a question of the *coming subjectivity* [*subjectivité à venir*]. Even more than in the French Revolution, is it forbidden to read in May '68 a premonition of such a *Society*[5] which would no longer be anything but play? The entire ethical stake, the "positivity" proposed—nevertheless and in the end—by the SoN's profoundly negative philosophy, lies therein.

And what if we surpassed the involute, deflationary surpassing of the ideology of incessant surpassing that would be the "postmodern?" And what if we discovered that the basis of this turning point was exactly what it was the de facto diagnosis of? And what if we realized that the parodic did not just happen here or there, unmasking and devaluing forever the grand ideals and grand narratives, condemning us to the sarcastic parodies of ideals and the "bonsai" versions of the narratives, but that it had *always been our condition*? And what if we took the man of compulsory derision *somewhat more at his word* than he himself takes himself? And what if, after all, this ironic categorical imperative remained complicit with what it fought, *still taking it somewhat too seriously*? And what if we showed him that he had *more reason for this than he thinks*, in other words, that in fact the metaphysical animal has for a long time *taken himself too seriously*? Meaning: he converted the imitations through which he appropriated things to pass them off as archetypes, the "second natures" he self-imposed in everyday life, as innate reflexes, the language by which he haunted things, as the things themselves, etc. And, on the other hand, he converted the *singular* originals subsumed by the technomimetic impulse, to pass them off as pale copies. And what if we learned, against secular metaphysical grandiloquence, *as well as* against the "last man" of compulsory derision, *to take seriously the one thing that deserves to be, and for this reason has never been, taken seriously*, that is to say, *precisely* parody? And what if, realizing that parody is our most surely originary condition, we therefore finally *lived*? In a word: *and what if we played the game*?

What I am saying here, and which I develop/argue at length in the entire *Spirit of Nihilism*, should be taken very seriously. For more than thirty years, what we call the "politics of emancipation" has been stuck in absolute stagnation, and will *never* rise from its ashes as long as its supporting intellectuals do not radically call into question the very notion of "equality." The brightest academic Stalinism is at least coherent: in Cambodia or North Korea, but already in the USSR and Romania, emulation was (and in Korea still is), de facto, rather looked down upon.

Who would want a society where the Lutheran *motor* of humanity, the pleonectic asymptote of being as event, appropriative emulation, is forbidden? Where the not-so-bright is put on an equal footing with the intelligent, the bad with the good, the incompetent with the gifted, etc.? Nobody. And here we touch upon one of the crucial aspects of the concept of play as an *entirely singular process of truth*, which no other domain is capable of, and especially not the other arts. In the latter, it happens most often that the most mediocre becomes well-established and that the best dies of hunger or madness. It is in the kingdoms of love and politics that the most excruciating and irremediable injustices triumph. Science is at the root of all the most poignant inequalities, in the very name of subsuming equality, even though there is no injustice in its own area of "professional competition" (a scientist, unlike an artist or a lover or a political rebel, is always "rewarded" in exact proportion to what he does), but it is precisely the *only* known anthropological domain where a great creator or actor is always recognized, more or less, at his true value.

The *only one… except for play*. This is why, in a Pindaresque accent, I consider play as the supreme art form. In play, there is no fraud possible, unlike in the market of plastic arts and literature, music and "philosophers," etc. I remember a long interview given by one of our greatest artists, Jean-Luc Godard, to the august French daily sports newspaper, *L'équipe*. One of the things he said will be our guiding line: "Cinema lies, but not sports." In a game or sport, it is impossible to pass the bad off as good, and the good as bad. In the other arts, very bad filmmakers are passed off as great, while the great filmmakers are for the most part pushing up daisies. In philosophy, the media is only after the counterfeit, whereas the great creators, at best, wallow in the academic ghetto, and if they do not have this professional lifesaver, they die precociously, become madmen, incognito, and live on in misery—only posterity redeems them from their abnegation.[6]

Therefore play, literally and in every sense, is *perhaps* the human production with the most *likeliness of truth*, with the exception, of course, of the somewhat too blatant paradigm of science. And this singular capability which play and all games possess should be—if the coming humanity hopes to make the least improvement—squared: the more play invades the City, the more we will be in truth. We can then say, paraphrasing Beckett: in any case we have our being in truth I have never heard anything to the contrary. Unbearable paradox: if we exclude the implacability of the scientific legitimation processes, it is only in play … *that we cannot cheat*. What is supposed to be the exclusive domain of cheating, paradoxically, turns out to be where there is much less cheating than in other arts, politics, love, etc.

We must return to the very grounds of all revolutionary thought, which is Rousseau. And he, as usual, had the following incipient, as well as decisive, intuition: we must leave the illusion of an "egalitarian" society to Condorcet; the true solution to the interference of radical inegalitarianism on earth, technomimetic appropriation, resides in the indivisible pleonectic essence *itself*, owing to which the being [*l'étant*] becomes the involuntary "agent" [*l'agent*] of being as event. We should *make do* with original sin, and not promise a truncated redemption, with all sorts of allowances and exemptions, invented only to satisfy the insatiable greed of the Roman Church: the pleonectic hypocrisy found in every "metaphysical Catholicism." There must be a *catharsis* of the ontological inegalitarianism of man, and as I show throughout my entire work that corrects Hegel and fights Badiou, the *aufhebung* which is *catharsis* is never a "simple" suppression of what it surpasses, but preservation in the form of waste.

If you claim that the event of appropriation, which always obeys the formal complex of *mimesis-catharsis-aufhebung,* merely suppresses what it surpasses without preserving anything of it, then waste will be exponential: the radical suppression of all inequality under Stalin, Mau, Ceausescu, and Pol Pot have spawned nothing but mass graves. By "eating" inequality in order to "produce" nothing but equality, they literally *messed themselves* with the latter. The industrial triumph of technomimetic isomorphism, in the post-production phase, produces megatons of non-recylable waste. "Egalitarian" societies have equalized nothing but the horror. And this does not boil down to supporting inegalitarian societies; we will see later how and why.

If, on the other hand, you *no longer* lose sight of the ineluctable price of decline, literally and in every sense, arising from every event of appropriation, you give yourself the chance to finally avoid the fatal trap par excellence of the oldest metaphysical reflex. Rousseau's "civic festival" suppresses inequality *while preserving it* in the form of incessant and organized *emulation.*

In short, the buried prototype of every revolutionary ideal, the Rousseauist civic festival, is nothing other than what I call *play.* All the history of revolutionary thought after Hegel consists of a huge "leftist deviation": *aufhebung* was squared: only *suppression* was preserved of this dialectical schema of surpassing. Therefore we need to learn again not only the essentially "conservative" dimension of all surpassing, in the non-reactionary sense, but very precisely the "chemical" dimension, which the SoN brings up to date: in every surpassing, what is surpassed is preserved in the form of waste. In order not to have to treat this waste shamefully, or even clandestinely, well this waste must appear in broad daylight: this is the civic festival, it is play. It is competition, but, like in the descriptions given by Rousseau, it is entirely made *visible*: it is both *mimicked* and *assumed.*

Ludic emulation is hence the *catharsis* of *pleonectic* ferocity. It is odd that the following remark is never made: games, and sports in particular, are the purest examples that can be found of aesthetic *catharsis,* much purer than in the other arts. I find it hard to believe that Aristotle did not devote one of his treatises to the subject; I prefer to believe it disappeared, along with so many others. Nothing purges the City to such an extent from its "atrocigenous" pleonectic passions as mass sports. However we are envisaging yet another type of play: by play, we understand a form of art which has *effectively attained* what the avant-garde's "surpassings" aimed at: the suppression of the merely *spectator* attitude, an art in which everyone takes part.

Thus generalized play is the civic festival as dreamed aloud by Rousseau. Everyone *wants* to be the best; the point is to *give form* to this ineradicable propensity of the human animal to trans-appropriation. To formalize the pleonectic. We saw it with "democratic nihilism," and the man of compulsory irony: in parallel with the tremendous disasters of "egalitarian" societies, which said the last word of the illusion, which is death, in our societies we know that "the spirit of nihilisim" consists of a *perverted* game, a parodic egalitarianism of the following sort: "the nullest is the best; the best is the nullest." According to the complicated apagogical structure we examined above (see *Irony*), such a society, in actual fact, rewards the worse, and punishes the better. This society model is not livable in the long term; it is a society that survives the disillusions of the past, and does not count much on its future. Nonetheless, it goes without saying for everybody that such a society is, all in all, preferable to societies of *literalized* egalitarianism, that is to say, literally deadly societies: "democratic nihilism," at least, realizes its egalitarianism *aesthetically*, i.e. through the formal *catharsis* of a distorted *representation* of equality—but representation *nevertheless*. However, its illusion remains the same as the illusion of "actually existing communisms," and which is the most complicated path in which the SoN engages its brave readers: for our best ideals of the left to regain strength, we must radically *give up* the metaphysical illusion par excellence, which has overdetermined the History of the left for centuries, and which is precisely egalitarian *abstraction*. It is in this way that the so-called politics of emancipation made itself complicit with what it fought.

The society we seek must be a *catharsis* of the fundamental inequality introduced by the technomimetic animal on earth, of the "pleonexia" that is co-originary with our condition, which would *not* be, as in the case of American style democratic capitalism, a "sincere"[7] representation of this inegalitarianism and its injustice as the "law of Nature," in the ideologically assumed way. The American ideology is a self-assured assumption of inequality, accompanied by its representation *in the first degree*. We, Europeans, *represent* equality ideologically, but *in the second degree*. This is, ultimately, the "principle of irony" (see above). And this is why, in my work, irony is not a psychological but a political category; and absolutely full-fledged. It is an absolute historical singularity of the western *set-up*, after the Second World War, and definitive of democracies: it goes hand in hand, and increasingly blatantly for three decades, with an entirely novel *representation* of the political, and of course different from the old aristocracies, royalisms, tyrannies, that is to say, those which still exist in most majority of the globe. Subjective self-derision accompanies, as its implicit cost, the constant right of *ridiculing* the representatives of power: a genuine mediatic liturgy is organized around this new representational economy, which has not been analyzed to date, not even by Debord or Baudrillard.

Let us be ethically straightforward: if the United States has dominated, politically as well as culturally, the twentieth century, it is time for us to look— without affectation—at the reasons why it happened this way. To put it in very broad terms: the Stalinist ideal was the ideal of an equality without freedom; the capitalist ideal, a freedom without equality.[8] Are we going to carry on with the psychotic hypocrisy of the leftist, always ready to sacrifice freedom for equality? In reality, we do not even have the choice. Inegalitarian freedom has prevailed over carceral or genocidal egalitarianism, quite simply because freedom *is* essential to the technomimetic animal; it is an "ontological" trait that differentiates him unfathomably from the other species, whereas equality is a perfect transcendental illusion, produced precisely by those who incite inequality: technomimetic appropriation, scientific isomorphism.

Capitalism *represents* (see above) inequality while assuming it obscenely. Even so, this obscenity prevails over the *virtuous* obscenity of abstract egalitarianism (pleonasm) which, in the eyes of everyone except for a few willingly blind Platonists, has certainly recovered badly from the suntrap outside-the-cave, proved to be even more monstrous than what it fought, and we know this is quite something. What we need is a political *representation* of the pleonectic motor that is fundamental for us, which would *actually* be a *catharsis* of the following: a *preservation which is a suppression*, and not a suppression which is a shameful preservation.

In order to illustrate this point as concretely as possible, I will give an even more provocative example: poker. Here it is, a game-sport rapidly expanding today! What will the Pavlovian leftist simpleton dimwit say? That it is a game "in the image" of capitalism, born in the United States among the cowboy brutes (this is wrong, the origin of poker is … French), that it is a money game and therefore repugnant, etc. Not that he would be wrong! Yes, like all art and all games, poker is an *imitation*, of capitalism in this case, invented by the semi-outcasts of the said capitalism, where and when capitalism was in full expansion: at its *set-up*. We could put our Pavlovian leftist in his place, by making him see that the percentage of "leftists" in the French poker circles is by far higher than … probably all the other layers of the population! In the presidential elections, 20 percent have voted for Mélenchon, 35 percent for Hollande, only 25 percent for Sarkozy, and finally 10 percent for Marine Le Pen, which is the exact opposite of the other layers of the French population. In the United States, whose political criteria are obviously rather different from ours, a significant majority of the players voted Democrat. But we will leave it there with the in-itself insignificant statistics. We will add, however, a crucial consideration: *all* the great poker champions happen to come from modest or extremely modest social backgrounds. I mean all of them. I am not talking about the good or the very good, but about the indisputable geniuses of the game, the Mozarts of the discipline: Ungar, Brunson, Negreanu, Ivey, Chan ... Scotty Nguyen, of Vietnamese origin, one of the most splendid and unpredictable players, lived literally in poverty before he came to the United States. On the Internet you can watch games where he is telling the other players how he crossed the Pacific as a boat person,[9] dying of thirst, eating from a bowl. There is something poignant and wonderful about seeing him handle the chips that represent tens of thousands of dollars, talking about the hell he came from.

Of course the Pavlovian leftist simpleton is right. Poker *is* a parody of capitalism. But the reader now knows that, when you see the word "parody" in my text, you must look at it twice. The leftist will say, for instance, that he prefers chess, the more "rational" and, guess what, "Soviet" game. Yes indeed! But a great number of chess Grandmasters have taken up poker, while to my knowledge, top poker players have never become grandmasters. Why? The leftist Pavlovian simpleton will say it is no doubt for the money. Should we disagree? Yes and no. Almira Skripchenko, about whom everyone who met her says stands for the most splendid conjunction of the highest intelligence and physical beauty, encyclopedic erudition and "Slavic" nobility of soul, one could ever come across, sums up the stakes when she explains what led her to leave the "Soviet" paradise of chess for the "capitalist" purgatory of poker: "I'm originally a chess player, and in this game, you evolve in a perfect world: therein, everything is justifiable, you can entirely master every action. When I started to play poker, I said to myself, this is ridiculous: how can you set yourself up to be a potential victim of chance? It really is something I had trouble digesting and incorporating. At first, it made me crazy to lose because of a bad card, but then I got used to this imperfect world of poker. After all, it's like the one we live in every day."

Aristotle rather than Platon...

The truth is quite simply that poker has become a game as sophisticated as chess or bridge; and which requires skills, although different, still as complete as the other great games or great sports; like chess, poker is considered a sport. The cliché of a game exclusive to Texan outlaws bathing in whisky is a thing of the past. Its practice requires an impeccable hygiene of life, and an iron mental discipline. We often have the impression, even more than with chess, that in poker you have to do constant mental *bodybuilding*: the least strategic relaxation can prove fatal. It does not require fewer skills than chess, maybe even much more, because it is *impure*. In any case, the skills have to be much more diversified. Daney and Godard showed it: if cinema was the dominant art of the twentieth century, it is precisely because it was the impurest of all. Poker is to chess what cinema is to hermetic poetry or music:[10] a plebeian art, and yet as "superior" as the other elitist arts. I have a phenomenal admiration for Boulez, but after all, if the coming art has to be only "Boulezian" or "Mallarmean," the horizon is distressing and hopeless. The democratization of the world is irreversible and, whatever "nihilistic" collateral effects we have to endure, it is a good, and not a bad thing; and aristocratic postures have no chance of taking the wind out of its sails.

Poker requires more skills than chess, because the latter is, precisely, an aristocratic and self-contained game, requiring only two or three types of skills made exponential, which produces fewer *geniuses* than *gifted* players. Poker requires neither excellent logico-mathematical nor strategical-tactical skills, like chess; it requires a psychology worthy of Proust, the statistical memory of an elephant, a Don Juanesque sociability, an absolutely tremendous instinct (an affectual force), courage and many other qualities, all perfectly dispensable for a great chess player. It is not only in this regard that poker is much more "democratic," and therefore aesthetically egalitarian, than "egalitarian" chess. In chess, if you are not an international Grandmaster by the age of twelve (as Skripchenko was, among others), you will never have any chance of being classified among the world's top hundred. In poker, some of the greatest contemporary players started their career at the age of fifty!

Of course, Petrosian, Fischer, or Kasparov cannot be reduced to machines; they are not just gifted, they really are geniuses. But Stu Ungar, Johnny Chan, or Phil Ivey as well—and we must add that they are, on average, much more sociable than the great chess champions … The course of a Stu Ungar's career is similar to a Mozart's or a Rimbaud's; had he received the right education, he could have become a first-rank mathematician, or a great artist. The poker theories of Sklansky, Caro, or Negreanu are as lucid and complicated to read as a great philosophical or logico-mathematical theory. And the greatest of these theorists, Lee Nelson, precisely one of those players to have started their career in their forties, is as difficult to read, and as sophisticated to grasp as Brunschvig, Desanti, or Vuillemin.

A text which has always meant a lot to me, and which I never commented on in my books, is the digression that opens *The Murders in the Rue Morgue* by Edgar Allan Poe and also the addenda included in a short story that takes up the same characters, *The Purloined Letter*. This is the ideal place to talk about it, and quite at length. For a very long time, since my adolescence, I have so much considered this inceptive digression not only as a great text by one of my favorite poets, but also, as it were, an implicit component, written in invisible ink, of what the SoN's negative philosophy nevertheless positively lets loom on the horizon, that I can give myself the right to copy it almost at full length, for the necessity to give a comprehensive account of the present text. These sentences count among the very rare I would have liked to write myself, in my hours of madness or intoxication; and reading them again, I am thinking I *could* have written them myself. So much so that I will not specify the passages emphasized by Poe, and those I emphasized myself.

> The mental features as regarded the *analytical,* are, in themselves, but little susceptible of analysis. We appreciate them only in their effects. (…) The faculty of *re-solution* is possibly much invigorated by mathematical study, and especially by that highest branch of it which, unjustly, and merely on account of its retrograde operations, has been called, as if par excellence, analysis. *Yet to calculate is not in itself to analyze.* A chess-player, for example, does the one, *without effort at the other.* It follows that the game of chess, in its effects upon mental character, is greatly misunderstood. (…)
>
> I will, therefore, take occasion to assert that the higher powers of the reflective intellect are *more decidedly and more usefully tasked* by the unostentatious game of draughts than by all the *elaborate frivolity* of chess. In the latter, where the pieces have different and bizarre movements, *with various and variable values, what is only complex,* is mistaken (a not unusual error) for *what is profound.* The attention is here called powerfully into play. If it flags for an instant, an oversight is committed, resulting in injury or defeat. The possible moves being not only manifold, but *involute,*[11] the chances of such oversights are multiplied; and in nine cases out of ten, it is the more concentrative rather than the sharper player who conquers. In draughts, on the contrary, where the moves are unique and have but little variation, the probabilities of inadvertence are diminished, and the mere attention being left comparatively unemployed, advantages are obtained by either party are obtained by superior *acumen.*
>
> To be less abstract, let us imagine a game of draughts where the pieces are reduced to four *kings,* and where, of course, no oversight is to be expected. It is obvious that here the victory can be decided (the players all being equal) only by some *recherché* movement, the result of some strong exertion of the intellect. Deprived of ordinary resources, the analyst *throws himself into the spirit of his opponent,* identifies himself therewith, and not unfrequently sees thus, at a

glance, the sole methods (sometimes indeed absurdly simple ones) by which he may seduce into error or hurry into miscalculation.

Whist has long been known for its influence upon what is termed the calculating power; and men of the highest order of intellect have been known to take an apparently unaccountable delight in it, while eschewing chess as frivolous. Beyond doubt, there is nothing of a similar nature so greatly tasking the faculty of analysis. The best chess-player in Christendom *may be little more than the best player of chess*; but proficiency in whist implies *capacity for success* in all these more important undertakings where *mind struggles with mind*.

When I say proficiency, I mean that perfection in the game which includes a comprehension of *all* the sources whence legitimate advantage may be derived. These are not only manifold, but multiform, and lie frequently among recesses of thought altogether inaccessible to the ordinary understanding.

To observe attentively is to remember distinctly; and, so far, the concentrative chess-player will do very well at whist; while the rules of Hoyle (themselves based upon the mere mechanism of the game) are sufficiently and generally comprehensible.

Thus to have a retentive memory, and proceed by "the book" are points commonly regarded as the *sum total* of good playing. But *it is in matters beyond the limits of mere rule that the skill of the analyst is evinced*. He makes, in silence, a host of observations and inferences. So, perhaps, do his companions; and the difference in the extent of the information obtained, lies not so much in the validity of the inference as in the quality of the observation. The necessary knowledge is *that of what to observe*. Our player confines himself not at all; nor, because the game is the object, does he reject deductions from things external to the game. He examines the countenance of his partner, comparing it carefully with that of each of his opponents. He considers the mode of assorting the cards in each hand; often counting trump by trump, and *honor by honor*, through the glances bestowed by their holders upon each. He notes every variation of face as the play progresses, gathering a fund of thought from the differences in the expression of certainty, of surprise, of triumph, or chagrin. From the manner of gathering up a trick he judges whether the person taking it can make another in the suit. He recognizes what is played through feint, by the manner with which it is thrown upon the table. A casual or inadvertent word; the accidental dropping or turning of a card, with the accompanying anxiety or carelessness in regard to its concealment; the counting of the tricks, with the order of their arrangement; embarassment, hesitation, eagerness, or trepidation—all afford, to his apparently intuitive perception, indications of the true state of affairs. The first two or three rounds having been played, he is in full possession of the contents of each hand, and thenceforth puts down his cards with as absolute a precision of purpose as if the rest of the party had turned outward the faces of their own cards.

The analytical power should not be confounded with simple ingenuity; for while the analyst is necessarily ingenious, the ingenious man is often remarkably incapable of analysis. The constructive or combining power, by which ingenuity is usually manifested, and to which the phrenologists (I believe erroneously) have assigned a separate organ, supposing it a primitive faculty, has been so frequently seen in those whose intellect bordered otherwise upon idiocy, as to have attracted general observation among writers on morals. Between ingenuity and the analytic ability there exists a difference far greater, indeed, than that between the fancy and the imagination, but of a character very strictly analogous. It will be found, in fact, that the ingenious are always fanciful, and the *truly* imaginative never otherwise than analytic.[12]

In *The Purloined Letter*, Dupin will complement his friend's considerations by forcing a digression on a child's game that always serves as a propaedeutic paradigm for the great poker theory books:

I knew one about eight years of age, whose success at guessing in the game of "even and odd" attracted universal admiration. This game is simple, and is played with marbles. One player holds in his hand a number of these toys, and demands of another whether that number is even or odd. If the guess is right, the guesser wins one; if wrong, he loses one. The boy to whom I allude won all the marbles of the school. Of course he had some principle of guessing; and this lay in mere observation and admeasurement of the astuteness of his opponents. For example, an arrant simpleton is his opponent, and, holding up his closed hand, asks, "Are they even or odd?" Our school-boy replies, "Odd," and loses; but upon the second trial he wins, for he then says to himself: "The simpleton had them even upon the first trial, and his amount of cunning is just sufficient to make him have them odd upon the second; I will therefore guess odd";—he guesses odd, and wins.

Now, with a simpleton a degree above the first, he would have reasoned thus: "This fellow finds that in the first instance I guessed odd, and, in the second, he will propose to himself, upon the first impulse, a simple variation from even to odd, as did the first simpleton; but then a second thought will suggest that this is too simple a variation, and finally he will decide upon putting it even as before. I will therefore guess even";—he guesses even, and wins. Now, what in its last analysis is the mode of reasoning of the schoolboy deemed "lucky" by his fellows?

"It is merely," I said, "an identification of the reasoner's intellect with that of his opponent."

"It is," said Dupin; "and, upon inquiring of the boy by what means he effected the thorough identification in which his success consisted, I received an answer as follows: 'When I wish to find out how wise, or how stupid, or how good, or how wicked is any one, or what are his thoughts at the moment, I fashion the expression of my face, as accurately as possible, in accordance with the expression of his, and then wait to see what thoughts or sentiments arise in my mind or heart, as if to match or correspond with the expression.'

This response of the school-boy lies at the bottom of all the spurious profundity which has been attributed to Rochefoucault, to La Bougive, to Machiavelli, and to Campanella."

"And the identification," I said, "of the reasoner's intellect with that of his opponent, depends, if I understand you aright, upon the accuracy with which the opponent's intellect is admeasured."[13]

These few pages that open the two most amazing short stories of the whole history of crime fiction, are worth entire theses, and constitute an advantageous substitute for massive volumes of academic philosophy. For me, this would have been enough reason to cite them.

Let us simply say that it goes without saying, for those who know, that the description of the great whist player, given by the narrator as a prelude to the appearance of the criminal investigation genius called Dupin, is almost exactly the same as the description of the *very* great poker player. Type "Phil Ivey" into an Internet browser, observe for minutes on end his behavior at the table, and come back to this book. You will be astounded.

Poe is absolutely right. Three rounds are enough to learn whist. If you are a good player of the game, you will be so right from the start: the art of whist depends on the sole psychological faculty of putting yourself in the mind of your opponent. This is a "telepathic" faculty fundamental for poker and completely useless in chess, because of the "mathematical" transparency of the game. This is probably why great chess players, great mathematicians (or logicians), as well as great philosopher mathematicians, so often and so easily become paranoid. When *nothing* is hidden—and nothing *should* be—when this mode of thinking is transferred to politics, then one feels the need to *reinvent* the dimension of veiling, inchoative, for a Heideggerian, with respect to the originary ("natural") envoi of being, and "purged" by scientific transparency. Paranoia is the psychosis of the one who, having wanted to make *everything* transparent, quite logically, no longer sees anything but dissimulation everywhere: Cantor, Gödel, Fischer, the high-brow misanthropy of Plato or Badiou ... in these modes of thought, paranoid psychosis *shows* that the mania for complete transparency ends in the mania for generalized false semblance. Absolutized unveiling becomes equally absolutized veiling: the scientific transparency of the non-human makes the human fully opaque (see *Ontological Differend*; and *Science*).

Just as paranoia is common currency with the chess player (see Nabokov's amazing *The Luzhin Defense*, where this defensive paranoia, metaphorically absolutized in the strategic *style* of the chess genius, for wanting to fill in all the rear bases of existence itself, ends in suicide, which is revealed as the true meaning of the said "defense"), to the same extent, you can have a hard time finding just one paranoid poker player: I bet with my eyes closed that it will take you months to find one for me. A game which primarily metaphorizes the dimension of dissimulation and bluffing, is an insurance not only against the mania for complete transparency, but, for this very reason, against the equally delirious (and therefore symmetrical) presumption of a universal dissimulation.

In other words, games such as whist or poker obey the Heideggerian, i.e. aletheiological, principle of truth: the ceaseless economy of veiling-unveiling. They are somewhat far removed from the Badiouian doctrine of truth as "indiscernible," which is the (beautiful! I am not ungrateful either) concept of a kind of uniquely intelligible transparency of truth, which we can quite safely say is perfectly applicable to chess. For "my" own doctrine of truth, the Ontological Differend, I would say this Heideggerian concept of aletheiology, not to mention Badiou's, remains still too "nice," always ready to positivize any transcendental truths which, when you study their immanence, are almost always revealed to be abominable, and not only in the area of politics. All this not to spread my cultural jam, but to say something very specific: if "my" concept of truth (see *Ontological Differend*), in Schürmann's wake, aggravates the most worrying thing about Heidegger's concept of truth, while expelling its too "nice" dimension of veiling-unveiling, this *general* regime of truth, as tragic disruption of knowledge and truth, applied to the quasi-entirety of the anthropological closure, becomes inapplicable in the sole sphere of *play*, in the sense I understand it. Only in play does the tragic truth of Schürmann-MBK become (again?) a kind of "nice" Heideggerianism. *Aletheia* remains a luxury of the philosopher, who has the good fortune of being able to contemplate "from afar" the play of veiling-unveiling to which being surrenders, even in atrocity. Most human beings live their lives, mutilated alive by the ontological differend. The flaw of *aletheia* is precisely what makes it valuable for the academic trends of the time: it remains too "ontological" in being applied to the entirety of being, without particular consideration for the human, whereas the differend is the *singular* regime of truth introduced to the world by anthropological eventalness, in respect of all collateral damages of Science. As we have seen, play is, in a unique degree of intensity, the *catharsis* of truth, originarily tragic and blood-thirsty. Perhaps all my efforts are aimed at a complete change of paradigm for truth in philosophy: when the whole tradition follows the scientific paradigm, it is perhaps high time to change it. Let us hope that Schelling, Nietzsche, Heidegger, Bataille and a few others have not leveled the terrain into pure loss. In short: only in play does the ordinary mortal gain access to the aletheiological economy of truth in an "egalitarian" fashion, and takes pleasure in it, even when he loses. As to all the paradigms of scientist inspiration that fill up the history of philosophy, I never stop saying why the contemporary task of the concept is to demolish its facilities.

Let us reconsider, in this philosophical light, what Poe said about the gifted boy playing the guessing game with marbles: well, in poker, the very superior level consists precisely of this type of psychological speculation: "He thinks I think that I think he thinks that I think ..." And the winner has to be as gifted as the boy praised by Poe. Unlike what the ignorant (therefore) thinks, bluffing is not a primal dimension of poker; it is part of it, moreover only mastered by excellent players. And the level of supreme mastery is not so much "bluffing in the first degree," identified by the ordinary person in the very essence of poker, which makes the opponent believe, by making intimidating bets (in the game's jargon this is called "to tell a story"), that his hand is very strong even though he has nothing, for instance making an offsuit 7–2 pass off as a pair of aces. No! In fact, the supreme bluff consists in *a bluff of a bluff*. Meaning: when some genius player *deliberately* makes crazy, even wild bets, to make his opponent believe he is bluffing even though he has ... "the nuts." To pass the traces off as false, when they are actually the true, Lacan would say: this is the *archi-ludic* essence of man, i.e. the horrible technomimetic animal, all of a sudden *sublimated* by ludic *catharsis*. And a brilliant opponent will realize in time that the *degree* of the bluff does not lie where the "crazy reraiser" wants him to believe it does; that he actually plays the "maniac" even though his game is reasonably *relentless*. Nietzsche spoke of the "sage passing himself off as a fool"... Basically, the most sagacious will have anticipated it: poker is, *par excellence*, the game in which one should maximize the art of *pretending to pretend*. Which is perhaps art par excellence ...

Let us return to whist, in what it says about poker, to that very moment when poker saw the light of day in American working-class saloons, while whist was the game of high society. All nineteenth-century literary documents (I have in mind Poe of course, Balzac, Conan Doyle, Jules Verne …) attest that whist was the most popular game at that time. Hegel played it every day (and, in the last decade of his life, every evening, in the public house, in front of a good tankard of beer…). As for bridge, it is a game where you have to know hundreds of preliminary conventions just to become only a decent player. Bridge is a *Baroque* version of the classical whist, probably invented by those who got tired of whist's "democratic" simplicity, and therefore introduces all these Gongoresque conventions in order to "initiatorily" limit access to it. Whist is to bridge exactly what—Poe said—draughts is to chess. In these latter as well, and even much more than in bridge, you must learn an unbelievable number of conventions to perform even slightly well. And it is "paradoxically" for this very reason that whist, like draughts, reveals the player's IQ much more immediately and infallibly than bridge or chess.[14] It is forever more impossible for me to move away from Poe's demonstration: the most *complex* games, which are therefore the most revealing of profound truths, are always those with initially *simple* rules. The concern to bring complexity to the game must be left *to the players*. Contrary to *idée reçue*, the play *must not* be bigger than the player.

Poker sticks to the exact middle, and this is why it became the most popular card game, if not the most popular game in general, of our time. Its rules are very simple to learn. If you have talent, you will know it right away. If you do not, you will not want to know it, and you will go on playing. And poker has as much, if not more, need of bad players as of very good ones. A champion wins a tournament one out of three times. A good player, one out of ten times. A bad player can win one out of twenty times. And this is not the least of its beauties: *everybody wins in poker sooner or later, even the very bad ones*. This is not the least "democratic" aspect of the game. But poker demands *also* the learning of very sophisticated techniques, which are not exactly permanent conventions, as in chess or bridge, which makes these games more annoying than they should be: they refer back to this wound consisting of all those "second natures" we, as technomimetic animals, have self-inflicted. Poker certainly is an emulatory *catharsis* of the bloody "pleonexia" consubstantial with our conditions. In it, everybody has their place. Everybody has their chance, the best, as well as the worst. Justice is *equitably* rendered to everyone, to the artist of cards, as well as to the unsubtle simpleton.

Are they talking to us about "egalitarianism?" But which one? The one of the "scientific" complicity, depriving each and every one from whatever personal initiative they may have, imitating the frozen logico-mathematical isomorphism? Or is it an *aesthetic* formatting of the fundamental inequality between men, which leaves each and every one absolutely free in their acts, their successes as well as their mistakes, and which can make each and every one happy according to their capabilities, even when they are very bad?

Two of the best poker theorists, Sklansky and Schoonmaker (a prominent psychoanalyst as well!), who are also great players, recently wrote the following which eloquently says it all: "Poker provides an extremely 'level playing field.' In no other popular competition is everyone treated so equally. You can't play golf against Tiger Woods, but you can sit down at any poker table. You can play against anyone from a novice to a world class player, and you will all be treated as equals."[15]

The first passage I have *ever* read, where the word "equality"—which is redundant in fact—does not sound hollow! Why on earth does it come from poker theorists, and not from a left-wing academic? This is no doubt due to this game's so profoundly democratic dimension, which will most probably make the good mind of the Stalinist conclude that, since it is democratic, it can only be capitalist.

After all, poker is devilishly Lutheran, in that it is the only great "emulatory" discipline; in other words: the only *profession* where there is not the slightest hypocrisy concerning the reality of capitalism. Nobody or almost nobody inquires after the amount of money a Hollywood star makes, or a left-wing academic celebrity, a politician, etc. In poker, it goes without saying, it is "cards on the table": a player is classified exactly according to what he wins. Lacoue-Labarthe said, with his usual prowess, that we probably had to consider money as something as originary to our human condition as language. And perhaps, in this wake, we need to go even further, because the Neolithic documents make quite credible the hypothesis that money constitutes a language *even* more originary, remote, than what we understand by language: that money has, and by far, preceded language, and as such ensured it as its immanent-transcendental condition of possibility. Which staggeringly means that language, and therefore the derived "pure" sciences, are nothing but sublimations of the *techno-economical* age of proto-humanity—food for thought for the sensitive beautiful souls of all kinds of leftism. These *sublimations* alone made man enter the historical age itself, ours; and from then on this period is, perhaps, only the brackets on the way to an yet *other* language. In other words, science sublimates language, which sublimates money, which sublimates the archaic *technai* of the flint and hunting … none of these have really suppressed what they pretended to "surpass." Thus there must be a surpassing of science—and of the inveterate philosophical scientism clustered therein—which is a preservation, i.e. a preservation by *strata* of all the anthropological "ages of the world," archaic *technai* and money *included*. Where the *historical* age itself, that is to say, the properly *scientific* age—the age which discovered the *ages* preceding it—would in its turn be put into brackets ... but we are getting carried away, far beyond the limits of the present book. Let us get back to a more immanent matter ...

To put it by way of the oxymoron of a specific metaphor, the phantasm of chess has in common with mathematics—and their penetrating critiques by Poe—the fact of being concerned with truth only when the *chips are down*: when the truth is constituted for good, eternalized, and chance is entirely abolished. Whoever is interested only in the *post festum* victorious truth will constantly display a somewhat ridiculous triumphalism, which in return gives evidence, and universally, *against* this paradigmatic type of truth, which has cost humanity only too dearly. In poker, victory never ceases to be *constituent*; chance is never abolished. It is eternally recast, and this is why there is something in it for everyone, including chess players, who eventually become weary of their game's mechanical teleology, just as we have become weary of all those metaphysical teleologies, blank and regular as clockwork. And since it is victory that is constantly constituent—and you can lose in a second the rush[16] which made you win for hours on end if you happen to lower your guard— truth, itself, is *constantly constituted*. Each new hand unveils something new about the players, which was not revealed by the previous hand.

So I say it again: only play, *in general* (including chess, it must be well understood), is the *catharsis* of the archi-negative connotation underlined by "my" concept of truth. In this sense, can we not recast the timeless debate on Plato's "betrayal" of the Socratic attitude with the poker player/chess player paradigm? Plato considers as entirely constituted, sedimented, that which was, in all likelihood, constantly constituent in Socrates. Socrates, because he was the Prince of ironists, and therefore the Prince of philosophers, could he not have been as well the *first poker player*? Just as in poker, everything, at any moment, is put back into play. The highest of conquered knowledge is swept by the next dialogical patch: the movement of truth, well before Hegel, consisting in considering at each stage of dialectical progress the previously conquered knowledge as null and void (suppressed, in order to be "preserved" in an unrecognizable form). With Platonic transcription, the incessant, as it were pre-Franciscan, putting back into play the Socratic method, becomes a frozen, planning strategy, bureaucratic sorting and compilation of annoying conventions, favorably disposed to every Academy, where Philosophy becomes the essentially *capitalizing* recitation of acquired knowledge, and ceases to be the adventuorus navigation on sight, which meant somewhat "as far as the eye can see."

A skill less known by those who know poker only in its clichés is, precisely, the ability to know how to *lose*. There is in here the promise of a mental preventative for all metaphysical triumphalism, to say nothing of psychology. What is there to say? Not that the poker player is a high roller: this too is a cliché that has had its day. There are very few real high-rollers, only a majority of players who lose a little money and a minority who win a lot, by concentrating the losses in their own winnings. The great poker player is a *calculated* high roller. He mathematically and strategically takes his risks in the long term, never in the short or middle term, whereas the bad player generally does not see further than his present hand. All great players will tell you that the first thing to learn in order to go far in the game is to know how to *throw away your cards*, fold. No known discipline, no other game, sets up this *pedagogy of failure*, this long propaedeutic to the calculated assumption of partial tactical defeats called poker; no long-term *strategic* victory is achieved without this wisdom, this self-lucidity, of the countless hands—sometimes as tempting as sin—you have to sacrifice in order to win in the long run. We should not be afraid of the cliché: poker, as the paradigmatic ideal of generalized social play, is the best possible school of life.

We evoked *catharsis*. As we know, its function in the Greek City was eminently political: Tragedy, but the Olympics as well, formalized the community as *œuvre*, and *œuvre* as the way of binding the community together. It is pointless to insist on the function fulfilled by mass sports in our societies, which silently extend, here as everywhere else, the Greek creations. But let us see how all this takes place in poker.

It is enough, first of all, to observe the audience of the final tables in the grand tournaments in order to realize that poker equals, in fervor, the exaltation of the mass sports, perhaps even already surpasses them—no doubt owing to the much more egalitarian accessibility of this game, more than any other game or sport. Poker requires a discipline at least equal to any other professional sportive or ludic practice, but it is a discipline *accessible to everyone*. And this is still not the decisive point. The decisive point is that poker both unites and separates all its players: thus the "cathartic" effect *in the strict sense* rediscovers the lost secret of Greek Tragedy, which was "not yet Theatre," that is to say, demanded active participation on the part of an audience which had not yet waned into a flowerbed of passive spectators. According to a profound remark by Lacoue-Labarthe, if the function of tragic aesthetics was, as always, essentially political,

Aristotle lucidly isolated its two primordial affects, Terror and Pity, as the two affects of the supreme political *danger*, at the two extremes of the passions of the City. Pity is the disastrous affect of communitarian fusion; Terror is the no less disastrous affect of absolute separation. All politics, and all political destination of art, aims at finding the balance between the two. Now, we can say that poker achieves this superlatively: it is a game both extremely socializing, if not generator of *philia*, and at the same time, a notoriously "individualistic" game, maintaining in the reunion an essential principle of separation of the proto-citizens called the players. *Catharsis* in its pure state is always this "happy medium" between reunion, community as *oeuvre*, and separation, *right* to inviolable individuation: *dés-oeuvrement*, or un-working.

In all these respects, the year 2013 was preparing for one of the most significant events of this beginning of millennium: the biggest poker tournament ever to be organized in the huge London Wembley Stadium. On the pitch, thousands of professional players will have to pay a big amount to play at real tables, with real cards, real croupiers and physiognomically visible opponents. Yet, in the stands, for a much smaller amount, almost a hundred thousand players will be equipped with computers allowing them to take part in the tournament, like on the Internet. The best of them will be able to take their turn on the pitch; the winner will take almost seven million euros ... We should realize what profound historical novelty is emerging there: It is probably the very first time in History, since the Olympics and circus games, including the jamboree of contemporary mass sports or rock dinosaurs' concerts, that people gathered together in a stadium in order to *all take part* in the event. What the most demanding twentieth century aesthetic avant-garde will have failed to realize in the end, a *game* achieves. In my own "avant-gardist" adventure, with the collective that was called *evidenz*,[17] I had always dreamt of a "life-size game" in which everybody would take part. I must note that, at this time, it was an already existing game, the only one capable of realizing this aesthetico-political utopia of our time.

We then notice several delightul as well as promising facts. First of all, there are not any, or very few, milieus where you find as much solidarity between the top level players, and even between all the others. On the website Winamax, a big fraternity of average players have gathered together under the banner of "team Winarien." As we saw with parody, when it is pushed to its limit, even in the self-derisory mode, it allows playing at being oneself, and to benefit from it, even when one is bad. One is just happy to *join the club*. Mutual aid, accommodation, flat sharing, loaning, emulatory prop bets, etc., are absolutely commonplace in this milieu. But as soon as the two best friends in the world meet at the baize, they turn into ferocious beasts, and they give no quarter. When the game is over, even if one of them has stripped the other of a million dollars or euros, they go have a drink and eat together in the evening. Even a couple as glamorous as Phil Laak and Jennifer Tilly, Laak being a charismatic and drolly eccentric super champion, and Tilly, an excellent Hollywood actress as well as a player capable of playing at the top tables, will make no favors to each other when they are at the same table.[18] Finally a couple which *completely* puts into action the irrefutable principle according to which love is the continuation of war by other means. The rest is simply speculation. Just as there is so to speak no poker genius coming from a well off family, just as the meta-cannibalism that takes place at the baize, between people who are otherwise friends (poker is the yum-yum), the carnivorous ferocity, makes it so that the great players like to use the animal metaphor of the jackal (or hyena) in referring to themselves, well, likewise, we obtain an extremely surprising ethical outcome, which is doubtless the effect of the *catharsis* proper to this game: most of the greatest current players are militant vegetarians. Who would have expected that Elisabeth de Fontenay and Derrida would find their best followers in such a milieu?

In sum: *catharsis* in its as it were pure state, where play purges the community from its founding pleonectic impulses, and binds them *after the fact* by the famous "purging, purification of [its] passions." Because the mental violence of poker surpasses the violence of every other game listed today; because this violence is not the *passivity* of the post-Debordian spectator swamped with sadism, psychopaths and gore;[19] because anyone interested in poker *ipso facto* plays it, and so it is an *art* which knows no passive spectators; poker, even more than the other arts, other games and other sports, is, in respect of *catharsis* only, but in respect of *catharsis* entirely, the king of the arts.

And it is extremely striking that all enthusiasts of this game talk about the "poker community." We do not talk of a cinema community; neither do we talk of a plastic arts community, nor even of a theatre community. The philosophers' community—to paraphrase a nice metaphor by Baudrillard—is composed of nothing but thousands of venomous snakes, intertwined in connecting vessels. The literature community is even worse; the "literary community," considered so much in depth by Blanchot (and his admirers), designates but an extreme minority of writers and thinkers within the sinister society of literary men and women. The community of lovers, again considered by Blanchot following Duras, is never composed of more than two people, regardless of the efforts made by some of my friends in order to increase the telepathic number a little bit—resulting only in human disasters. So far, arts have all failed to achieve their highest original vocation; the "Wagner case" should always be held up as a counterexample, in order to understand how such a failure can be squared, and with what consequences, which are *always* political. Of all arts, only games have all in all succeeded, without really putting on airs, in binding a community by the *catharsis* of pleonectic tendencies, without which we would still be grazing on carrots. But even with games, there is never talk of a "chess community," a "football community," or a "canasta community." To tell the truth, the only domain where a homologous expression is used, is when we say "the scientific community." It should make us think on the philosophical paradigm of politics: scientific or artistic? And if the latter, is it passive-contemplative, or ludic-active?

Let us be clear on this: we obviously do not think that humanity will be joined back together again in the best of all possible worlds when this world is turned into a giant poker table. We are simply assessing, as phenomenologists, the universal traits of the promise of a society placed entirely under the aesthetico-*political* sign of play. Poker is obviously nothing compared to the "life-size" games that civilization—if it occurred to it to save its skin and ours—could develop here and now, conceiving it with all forms of art that exist so far, in order to make each member of the community take part in it, even if he or she should be the least talented or gifted of all, and even, in a sense, all the more so because of that. Ducasse had announced something similar when he said that poetry must henceforth be made by all, and not by one: the best of twentieth century avant-gardes, I am thinking particularly of the Situationists and Debord, would hear it. May '68 would be the revolutionary *game* of an art made by all. Even IRCAM should be made by all, and not by one.

Debord would say: the avant-gardes have had their day. They perished because of the fundamental contradiction within them: preparing a social age and area where art becomes the production of all, and on the other hand, not being able to renounce the status of individuated-artist-demiurge. What is left of Debord is neither the community of the other Situationists, nor an even more unlikely "community of May '68," but only Debord, fantastic Creator, but fallen and melancholic, inhumanly alone, in all this adventure.

The future games should preserve all that was great about ancient arts, from poetry to painting, from music to architecture. The only thing they must suppress is what the twentieth century avant-gardes wanted to suppress as well: the passive position of the *spectator*, which is ultimately nothing but its position as *consumer*. Here as elsewhere, it was the Situationists who realized the essence of all avant-gardes. I am using poker here just as a matrix skeleton for the functioning of the coming games, i.e. *arts*. We must, for instance, preserve everything of an art as great as opera; but we should create, so to speak, "life-size" operas, in which everyone takes part. We should make use of architecture, painting, design, environmental arts (Kant rightly considered gardening as a branch of fine arts) ... Without the slightest melancholia or passéism, we can preserve all that was great in the arts of the past; we only need to make them "interactive," suppress their figurative destination (in painting), representational destination (in narration), passively auditory destination (in music), etc. And not only every art, but basically every *profession*. Because the asymptotic appropriation of infinity by man results in an always more pathetic crushing of the singular finitude, which is ever revealed only in this way, it is probable that the division of labor will always exist. Rather than overbidding on the literally theological daydream of the *incarnation* of every competence in the total and polyvalent (over)man, does not *play* represent the form of social bond *par excellence*? Every *citizen*—just like in the Rousseauist conception—contributes to the constitution of play by his very own laborious competence; otherwise, he *plays his part*, just like everybody else, and with the same basic chances. Whatever his profession may be, no one, as such, would put any citizen above another. The great musician, only as the player that he is, would be treated on exactly equal terms as a mechanic. But we would call this process of concrete utopia not by the order-word "equality," but by a keyword of the poker vocabulary, and which is the one we need ethico-politically: *equity*.

In short: the leftist simpleton is quite right. Poker *is* a parody of capitalism. It has been so since its birth, because it has always been its *waste* as well: the game of the outcasts of the American dream, who hoped to reproduce at the table, to replay, the chance that fate had taken away from them.

We talked about the spirit of the now-defunct avant-garde, and their living fate for the dawning century. The leftist simpleton, theologically condemning poker as the obscene substitute of capitalism, would still need to explain by what unfortunate coincidence Debord, at the end of the day, made a very good living, at a given period of his life, by excelling in this game of ill-repute. That it parodies capitalism, illustrated eloquently by the fact that you sometimes play with tremendous amounts in the transferential form of plastic chips, means it is its *catharsis*. The great poker champions are never *afraid* of money; and this is why they are practically never sought and recruited among the very rich people, but on the contrary, among those of a poor, if not wretched, background. They all say their goal is a good game and victory; money comes as a bonus in the end, the cherry on top. The chips are an illustration of the great poker players' *childlike* relationship with money;[20] they are, all in all, relatively indifferent.

Scotty Nguyen became champion only to feed his wretched family in Vietnam, not to get rich personally. His brother died on the same day as Scotty became world champion; he called his brother on the phone to give him the news, so that he would go and tell it to the rest of the plethoric family, and on his way there, his brother was hit by a car. What should have been the best day of Scotty's life turned out to be the worst, he who had had more than his share of misfortune in life. All this to say that, as long as we are talking of *catharsis*, the *spectacle* of poker is not, as is commonly thought, the spectacle of a victory of the rich against the poor, but in fact, most often, of the poor against the rich. "Bang in the center!",[21] as Beckett said.

Let us talk about the even more unlikely virtues poker would require of the players, such as … discipline! But no! It does require discipline, and not only at the table, but existentially as well. Las Vegas, along with Amsterdam, is universally known as "sin city." There, a great player learns very quickly to beware of all sorts of temptation. He does not need the hollow prescriptions of the metaphysical functionary to do that. For him, what matters is to *have fun*; to take pleasure in his existence, which should be the case with every living being on earth. As the artist John Cale said: "Work is more fun than fun."[22] Whether some will like it or not, poker is a *profession* in its own right. And it is the only redeeming profession of this new global proletariat, more miserable than that of Marxism-Leninism, and which is the proletariat of the idle, the *désœuvrés*. This is not the least prophetic of its signs. I would not mention it in this book that is supposed to be a general summary, but I always supported the obvious: *désœuvrement* is the one and only unprognostic political problem that poses itself to a contemporary philosophy. All the analytical tools inherited from the common metaphysical archive are useless to it. It must create its own from scratch.

Which would mean, in general, and for the reasons we put forward, that only play has a chance of being the successful *catharsis* of politics, i.e. the great art, the total and communitarian art we all dream of, without it leading to fascism, neither on the left nor on the right: art democratized for good. A world where all of humanity will do nothing but play, where play and work become indiscernible, where perpetual emulation is not synonymous with crime, where the disastrous fiction of equality is every bit as short-circuited as expropriatory atrocity and injustice, will be a world which will have suppressed the political malediction which we owe to Science.

This is therefore an obviously Kantian reflection. The only artist who understood at his time what Kant meant in his third critique, linking it with what he said in his second, was Schiller: humanity is only fully humanity when it *plays*. It is for this reason that play, certainly even more than any other form of art, is *catharsis* par excellence. *As* in Kantian moral law, *or almost*, and it is in this "almost" that all this differs from a chasm, man stifles his sensible inclinations *as well* (his pleonectic ferocity): those which lead to the pure and simple annihilation of the other. This is what differentiates, just as well, play from the other arts, so that play is called to become their ultimate fulfillment, provided that art's *communitarian* function is always, in the last instance, *political*, for touching much more closely than other arts the negative essence of politics, which is the annihilation of the other. In play and in play only, *and already in a great number of singularly mammalian animals*, the annihilation of the other is just *feigned*: this is the good old *catharsis*. Only play is *fully* the *katharein* of the pleonectic: all other arts are deferred/differed, mediated *catharses*. Kantian moral law—meaning politics—demands a *painful* submission. Play is a just an unconditioned submission to the force of rule, only this time, *happy* and *consentient*. Politics is the mimetic perversion of Science; but play is the *positive* mimetic perversion of political negativity.

For me, then, poker is emblematic of what should be a *successful* surpassing of capitalism; that is to say, a surpassing that is no longer taken in by the illusion of a suppression *without remainder* of what is surpassed, which will then return inevitably in the form of monstrous waste. That is to say, not the "scientific," but the *aesthetical* surpassing of the originary political malediction, in the elite form of all arts, that is play. A society which will be, as in the Land of Toys in *Pinocchio*, a site of perpetual play, a democratic and *realistically egalitarian* formatting of emulation and the second pleonectic instinct of the technomimetic animal: its ultimate, ontological impulse.[23] A society where the best are rewarded according to their worth, *but where even the worst, the most stupid and the most wicked, have the right to win from time to time*; to *exist*, in their full singularity.

If "equality" truly means that the political sun must shine for everyone, anarchist realism will find the means to prevail over the "communist" idealism, of the republican breeding—whip at hand—of "mathematizable societies": it is through the extremely upwards re-estimation of the *aesthetical* eminence of play. Meaning: political. "Aesthethic," wrote Lacoue. Ludic emulation is the pleonectic that has politically become, no longer "equality," but *equity*.

Catharsis

CATHARSIS: Not more than *mimesis, catharsis* is not specifically concerned solely with the aesthetic sphere. Its alchemy concerns in fact the minutest details of our most everyday and endemic conditions. Aristotle, much more essentially than Plato: the philosophical creator of *catharsis* was also the conceptual champion in terms of the great repercussions of the notion of *techne*, against the calamitous primacy of the Idea in his Master. The only thing missing in Aristotle was quite simply the link between *catharsis* and *techne*. We would have to wait for a very long incubation period, the Hegelian moment, the re-reading of Rousseau by Lacoue-Labarthe, and finally my unfolding of the latter's ideas, in order for the primitive scene of philosophy, superbly illustrated by Raphael's painting, to be replayed in front of our eyes, and for Aristotle to win a second time against Plato. The eidetic transcendentalization of the being [*l'étant*] by way of mathematico-logical purification (see below) is *void*, literally and in every sense. The unconditioned surpassings promised by Platonism right hand over fist, and left hand on the heart, is the metaphysical fraud with the most atrocious consequences that philosophy will ever have had to fight *from within*.

On this point, I open another parenthesis. Our post-revolutionary times were intrinsically Platonic, for having fulfilled the wish of philosophy's Père Ubu, which had remained pious for a long time. *The Spirit of Nihilism*, especially in *Algèbre de la Tragédie* and *Inesthétique et mimêsis*, for the first time, takes the bull by the horns. But what bull? Well, a tremendous fact that nobody analyzed to this day: the post-revolutionary era, which, to a certain extent, is an era of *accomplishment* of Platonism (the Republic is realized: there is an undeniable Platonism in Rousseau, Robespierre, Saint-Just), also initiated the all too outrageously notorious era of "*poètes maudits*." Until that time, poets were almost always considered citizens in their own right, integrated in the City and its functions, as accepted Poets; starting with the French Revolution, and in perfect blindness, we witness a curious *testamentary accomplishment* of Plato's most famous prescription: the great Poet, the Homer of his time, is *systematically* banned from the City. The "*poète maudit*" becomes a cliché; but the fact of the matter is that Hölderlin, Rimbaud, Lautréamont, Baudelaire,

Poe, Nerval, Artaud, Celan and many others would suffer exile, just like Plato wanted to condemn their professional ancestors to exile, and in general without the laurels. There are profound reasons for this fact and the decisive implications concerning our destiny (or the lack thereof) that the SoN questions here for the first time (see *Algèbre de la Tragédie* and *Inesthétique et mimêsis*). One of the "intimate" reasons for the break with Badiou is the fact that he was the very model of the philosopher who never says what he does (and this is his major ethical *fault*), and never does what he says (fortunately for us). I close the parentheses here.

The complex of *mimesis-techne-catharsis-aufhebung* does not concern merely the "monumental" turnstiles of global History, as Hegelianism would have us believe. It touches first and foremost upon the most trivial aspect of our immediate material environment. The table on which I write is made of wood. A tree was eliminated in order to make it. The tree is suppressed as a tree, but is preserved as wood. Wood is surpassed, all the while being preserved, in the form of "table." Look at the *slightest* object surrounding you: for each one of them, you can apply the exact same processuality. *Catharsis* is not an operation that concerns us only in the case of art, which only essentiates its power. It is the smallest link on the basis of which absolutely everything that surrounds us is constructed.

You must of course have recognized here the teleological fourfold of the original great thinker of *techne*: the material cause, wood, is what the table is made of. The formal cause is what destines the tree technologically, and which is suppressed; the form of the table is that which is produced by the technological "surpassing" of wood. The moving cause, here, is nothing other than the technological impulse itself (however, in the motivity of *physis*, it will be of a whole other nature). The final cause, of course, is the productive aim of the whole process: the surplus value co-originary with the technological act as such. Last but not least:[1] we know that Aristotle's *teleological* definition of *techne* will be, precisely, that it is both the moving cause and the final cause of *physis*.

What had philosophical tradition forgotten until I adjusted this entire Aristotelo-Hegelian complex to my style? The waste. In the case of the wood, it is the wood chips, but implying in fact the destruction of natural harmony and the devastation of forests: the *lack* ensuing from the appropriation of the waste. The *nihilating* [*néantisante*] expropriation, in which "nihilating" is an adjective that must be understood in all its senses, but today, also and especially, literally.

Nothing touched by the operation of the complex of *mimesis-techne-catharsis-aufhebung* has remained intact on earth. This means that the price of degradation, execration, and excrementation, attains the fundamental *form* that is surpassed, as we know, by the event of technomimetic appropriation. Meaning: this first form of appropriation, of pleonectic archi-economy, that is *life*. Technomimesis is a *catharsis* of Nature, of primary biological appropriation. Meaning in turn that life is *preserved*, and not just surpassed, in the form of abominable *waste*. It is at this point that the terrifying Figure of Evil appears (see below).

Let us take the kind of phenomena which classical morality considers Evil: zoophilia. Transgression (see below). I often like to cite the following anecdote from an article that eloquently resumes the subject: "A sixty-year-old man who tried to have sexual intercourse with an elephant was sentenced to fifteen years of prison. Caught half-naked, perched on a wooden box behind the animal, Kim Lee Chong declared that the elephant was the reincarnation of his wife Wey. 'I immediately recognized her by the naughty glint in her eye',[2] he said in trial in Phuket, Thailand."[3] It must be said that this kind of sexuality, one of the most widely practised in the world, is also never talked about. This event, *formally*, has all that is required of a true event. Here we must turn to a distinction made by Meillassoux, between an event of a world, i.e. the Big Bang, accretion of the earth, appearance of life on earth, appearance of consciousness, then technology … and an "intraworldly" event, which is nothing other than Badiouian: the appearance of a new species in the biological closure, the appearance of a work of art or a scientific discovery within the anthropological closure. It is *there* that the torsion lies, which is a torsion between *physis* and *techne*, nature and culture, and which is precisely the type of event that is never questioned by philosophy: the archi-event of *techne* consisting not in a simple "surpassing" of *physis*, but, always and each *time*, in a *perversion* involving the torsion of the relation between *physis* and *techne*. That is to say, in a *transgressive parody* of the former by the latter: and this is what the somewhat bulky example of zoophilia allows us to illustrate (and hence to pervert as well Meillassoux's "simple" distinction between the "absolute" event of the advent of a world, and an intraworldly event; meaning, Badiouian). In fact, *if* an event such as the copulation between two different animal species (dogs and cats, cats and mice …) happened within the animal and biological closure *alone* (where things "bloom by themselves": *physis*), we would take it as an intraworldly event of the utmost importance. But it is precisely *through*, and not simply *in*, the technomimetic closure, which *perverts*, literally and in every sense, everything it touches, that an "evental" phenomenon such as zoophilia takes place. It will be considered therefore as a *parody* of event: this is what the classical metaphysico-dogmatic morality will do, and it is in these regions ("depravity," said Aristotle) that it will recognize Evil. Yet it is this absurdity itself that the SoN fights. Why? Because the archi-event, and therefore *every* real intra-anthropological (Badiouian) event, has *straightaway* a parodic structure: agriculture is a parody of food gathering, hunting is a parody of predation ... including even the maximizations where flares the metaphysical megalomania which literally acts as a *second nature* in us, and turns mathematics into a gigantic parody of being, and logic into a gigantic parody of appearing ... This is the problem of the classico-dogmatic metaphysician's systematic forgetting of the essential moment, which is *precisely* that of parody. For us, there is no other event than the event of *mimesis* (see below, and see also *Nihilism*). This event always *perverts* everything. Zoophilia is not *less* of an event than a "great" love story or mathematics: it even sheds a revealing light on these "positive" events of traditional metaphysics which, because of deeply ingrained professional reflex, is always turned towards the unmitigated Good. What zoophilia, or any other "malevolent" and "diabolical" event forecloses through classico-dogmatic metaphysics, Auschwitz or Fukushima, is that every event is a *catharsis* of identity, yielding a monstrous *singularization*. As the story of the Thai illustrates both drolly and terribly, often what appears, from the outside, to be a simulacrum of an event, is in fact genuinely an event for the person concerned. He is put into jail for having *monstrously singularized* himself, just like they burned sodomites in the Middle Ages. This time, in the wake of a certain Foucault, the SoN explores this always perverting torsion of the event such as it is incumbent upon *us*: the "good" event is always illuminated by those events that are secondarized, calumniated, foreclosed by metaphysical functionary work. To hierarchize these events in the direction of the "Good" is always to prepare, with new consequences, a whole accursed region of monstrous singularizations. It is *because* there is the event of appropriation of the Laws, called Science, that an avalanche of perfectly arbitrary Laws comes on top of the Laws of nature and being appropriated by men. Yet, an overwhelming majority of these Laws expropriate, exploit, ill treat, torture and kill the overwhelming majority of men. Justice is just a belated notion, intended to compensate for the insane exponentiation of injustices pouring down on the anthropological closure *due to* the collateral *action* of Science. This is what we call "progress," whose reality cannot be denied, neither the fact that our states of rights are heroic historical conquests over the expropriatory archi-evidence of the political facticity associated with human animality, in parallel to the benefits of *techne*. But even in these states, it is the transgressive margin as explored by Foucault that sheds light on civic legality itself, tells its truth, and not the opposite, as for the most part metaphysical thought. As the great poker player Fabrice Soulier writes:

> I don't want to hear about the tenacious image of poker's immorality … I think a banker, who suggests a lame investment idea to a worker who slaved away all his life and put all his savings into a house he will lose, is a criminal. A businessman who, in order to save costs, chooses to sail a supertanker as old as Methuselah which, when wrecked, decimates the entire fauna and flora of a coastal region, is a criminal. A white-collar worker who, in exchange for a bribe, decides to validate an ineffective and dangerous drug that is sold as a miraculous cure, is a criminal. An engineer who decides to stuff shower gels with carcinogenic preservatives, is a criminal. The list can go on and on …[4]

It is our poor Thai who has been put into prison and punished for his "Transgression," and not the overwhelming majority of "legal transgressors" exemplified by Soulier, to which we could actually add the list of communist tyrants who slaughter entire populations in the very name of Justice.

Bataille, Foucault, and Schürmann will have been the first to place emphasis on this paradoxical "positivity" of the transgressive over the legislative. The SoN takes the investigation further, even further than Schürmann, by *reversing* once and for all the order of precedence, by thinking no longer simply about the basis of transgressive margins but by showing that it is at the very heart of legislative appropriation, Science, that we need to look for the ontological core of Transgression, which is the counter-essentialist core of man, and explains why this core has always needed, and still needs, a whole infinity of normative *phantasms* in order to conceal the constantly transgressive monstrosity of its precarious "essence" (see *Transgression*).

Logic

LOGIC: Alas, it is Badiou's unquestionable merit to have established that pure logic is the "transcendental of appearing." I directly acknowledged (as I said, I am everything but an ingrate) the most prominent outcome of this real conceptual conquest in *Ontologique*: in appearing, there is neither absolute difference, nor absolute identity, only infinite asymptotic degrees of *differential identities*. But what Badiou did not notice, because he refuses even to recognize the existence of the techno-ecological problem, is that this means: the transcendental of *Nature*. In fact, in *physis* in the Greek sense, what blooms by itself, there is no absolute identity between two beings [*étants*], never. This identity is produced, much later, in and by technology, and *technology alone*.

The error of mathematics (see below), which is the cost of archaic techno-mimetic appropriation itself, probably consists in *maximizing* the infinite and asymptotic *identitarian* approximations of Logic. In logic, identity remains *what it is*: a utilitarian *fiction*, which is never absolutized. This absolutization only takes place with the imperceptible mathematical transfer. As this great philosopher called Dupin said (but through which Poe, who knew everything, and always more than we think, perhaps copied *The Phenomenology*'s Hegel, who says more or less the same thing):

> I dispute the availability, and thus the value, of that reason which is cultivated in any especial form other than the abstractly logical. I dispute, in particular, the reason educed by mathematical study. Mathematics is the science of form and quantity; mathematical reasoning is merely logic applied to observation upon form and quantity. The great error lies in supposing that even the truths of what is called *pure* algebra are abstract or general truths. And this error is so egregious that I am counfounded at the universality with which it has been received. Mathematical axioms are not axioms of general truth. What is true of relation—of form and quantity—is often grossly false in regard to morals, for example. In this latter science it is very usually untrue that the aggregated parts are equal to the whole. In chemistry also the axiom fails. In the consideration of motive it fails; for two motives, each of a given value, have not, necessarily, a value when united, equal to the sum of their values apart. There are numerous

other mathematical truths which are only truths within the limits of *relation*. But the mathematician argues from his *finite truths*, through habit, as if they were of an absolutely general applicability—as the world indeed imagines them to be.[1]

The root itself of the mathematical transcendental illusion is first and foremost *the very sign of equality*. We can say that originary transcendentalization, which is written x=x, never comes up in Nature. In the originary envoi of being as *physis*, the fact is that there is absolutely no ontological identity anywhere. No man is ontologically "equal" to another man, no pear to another pear, etc., up to the tiniest constituents of Nature. As I wrote at the time of the *Esthétique du chaos*,[2] the twentieth century added to the Kantian transcendentals of space and time (save for the absolute transcendental that is being itself) the transcendental of difference. It then seemed that we would never have to get back to it, and that the philosophy of our century could henceforth never change track again. But then Badiou entered the scene, giving the stunning impression of bailing out all the most hackneyed prerogatives of metaphysics ... and this, with the brilliance of laying all purloined letters on the table, that is, by recasting metaphysics *on its rear bases themselves*: the logico-mathematical.

What about the fate of the transcendental of difference, of Heidegger's as well as Derrida's, Wittgenstein's as well as Deleuze's? This transcendental meant that even two "identical" letters or glasses are different because of their respective locations in space and time. Here the Badiouian square mind would tell me: "But no! You are bringing in these inexistent transcendentals where they have nothing to do. That two beings [*étants*] are *ontologically* identical does not change the fact, as the Master has shown in *Logics of Worlds*, that they are 'different' in the simple sense of being localized in a world; it is a difference of topological localization, where time and space have nothing to do with it. You yourself, Mehdi, do you not pay tribute to the point that in appearing, there is neither identity nor absolute difference? It is at the level of *being* (mathematical intelligibility, whose essential "syntactic" component is the sign =) that we can talk, if need be, of absolute identity. Take the example of two glasses made in the same factory. They are absolutely identical in their ontological composition. But it is their simple *localization* that differentiates them; what you weakly call 'transcendentalization by space and time' is just a difference of topological marking. Ontologically, in their respective elementary compositions, it is self-evident: they are perfectly identical."

What is the illusion of the Platonic fiduciarism and sophism here that hides behind the always peremptory challenge of the Badiouian square mind?

Here as everywhere else, since Rousseau our only access to the *concept* of Nature is negatively mediated, and precisely by what supplements it: technics itself which, having been sublimated, becomes "pure Logic" only belatedly, and mathematics, even more belatedly.

What is *techne* since Aristotle? It is that which is produced by the hand of man, and not that which blooms by itself. This is exactly why no one—except for the artificial, i.e. the technologically produced, paradise of mathematics—will *ever* be able to find the slightest example of absolute ontological identity—only "localized" differentially in the topological distribution of appearing—anywhere else than in what is technically, therefore *anthropologically*, produced. This is why Logic wins over mathematics in ontological dignity: it keeps closest to the essence of scientific appropriation, which is *mimesis-techne*. Here as elsewhere, the bad image philosophy has made of *mimesis* must be overturned: Logic is a discourse which continues to keep, mimetically, as close as possible to the being [*l'étant*] such as it gives itself "naturally," in the absolute absence of identity between two literally "given" beings; whereas mathematics goes astray, for hypostasizing the acquisitions of transcendental-logical appropriation as identi-tarian isomorphism, extended so as to include all that *is*, i.e. exists.

Logic is a *mimesis* that is faithful to what it transcendentalizes *by the void*; mathematics is a deceptive *mimesis* of the being's [*l'étant*] "egalitarian" putting in equivalence. The eidetic conception of the being begins with mathematics; a conception which would be Plato's and would be renewed with the Kantian doctrine of the in-itself—a *doubling* of the being which is the more or less the darling original sin of philosophers. This empty "essentiation" of things, merely *enabled* by logic, is "consecrated" by mathematics.

In Plato, the hatred of *mimesis* conceals the profound truth of a mimetic essence of thought that is much more perverted, *precisely because it is mathematized*. Because nothing spiritually rhymes better with *mimesis* than *mathesis*—and it is above all not artistic *catharsis* that can rival it in this respect, not more than any other. *Only mathematics suppresses what it subsumes without preserving anything of it*. Hence the calamitous ethical consequences, as Dupin would say, drawn therefrom by the metaphysician who places his paid work under this paradigm.

The critique of metaphysics which we owe so much to Heidegger does not indemnify him from having carried on the philosophical absurdity par excel-lence, which is the hatred of *mimesis*. Kant inaugurates the philosophizing by the critique of metaphysics; he would fail to cross out definitively the essence of the latter, which is the secretly pleonectic propensity to "double from the bottom" [*dédoubler par le fond*] the being [*l'étant*] with his doctrine of the in-itself and the noumenal, which Badiou takes up again as it is, all the while inveighing against Kant. The SoN "puts things back on their feet": it shows that the operation of doubling is indeed fundamental, and fundamentally metaphysical: but this doubling in fact never leaves the *surface* of things. In this respect, like in Deleuze, there is something profoundly "Stoic" in the aggressively anti-Platonic strategy of the SoN; and it is the anti-metaphysicist envoi advocated by Nietzsche, rather than Kant, that continues here, in fidelity as well (long-time critical, but fidelity nevertheless), the tremendous French moment of the "philosophies of difference," which was almost made null and void by Badiou's impact on contemporary philosophy.

Against these proclamations, to mark firmly the primacy of Logic over mathematics is also to reaffirm the archi-ethical primacy of difference over Identity. But the SoN's move is even more radical: if Logic is the transcendental of things that remains "at the surface," without doubling them into a truncated identitarian "in-itself" (pleonasm, because pleonectic), as in the case of mathematical drifting, it is still necessary, in the Derridean mode, to inquire into the conditions of this transcendentalization: the technomimetic. The *techne-mimesis-catharsis-aufhebung* complex is a philosophically more fundamental Logic than the entire formal Logic dissected by analytic philosophers or Badiou. Its archaeological "empiricity," in the Derridean mode then, is the transcendental of the logical transcendental (of the empirical, modeled on infinite asymptotic approximations of differential identities, and *never* on the absolute identity of mathematics, not more than on its aberrant doctrine of indiscernibles [maintained by Leibniz as well as Badiou], or the theorem of the point of excess [see *Mathematics*], etc.).

And it is precisely because it creates teleologically (including Descartes and Galileo: "man as master and possessor," etc.) the transcendental illusion of the identical that the technomimetic animal can then industrially *manufacture* the identical: two glasses, two clones ... In nature, even the two most conjoined of twins can never be "ontologically" identical. The Leibnizian principle of indiscernibles is mathematically valid; philosophically, since Kant's critical envoi, it is no longer worth anything. The following has been the mainspring of my theoretical thinking since its first autodidactic steps:[3] I showed how the transcendentalization of difference by the best philosophy of the twentieth century proceeded from the celebration—in the history of philosophy—of the transcendental as such by Kant, in the instances of space and time. It took hardly a century for the—empty—universal transcendence of time and space to vouch for what metaphysics had disastrously ignored for twenty-three thousand years: it is difference itself, by the always singular conjunction of the time and space of a being [*un étant*], that constitues the third transcendental accompanying the former two, until Badiou arrived, and took advantage of the adjective "transcendental" in order to neutralize this apparently irrefutable triumvirate: For the Pol Potist, only just recovered from his erring, there was no longer any space, any time, and no longer any difference. I am not forcing here the trait of a philosophy I studied more than any other. This philosophy truly constitutes the "final solution" of difference, and as such, the most Titanesque contemporary attempt to make the metaphysical Phoenix rise again from its ashes.

This speaks volumes on the hypnotic trust we are supposed to put, without further examination, in the "ontological dignity of mathematics" in general. And, in the face of the essential international philosophical audience, it is this very principle that Badiou would celebrate with his literalized, i.e. "Wolffly" mathematized neo-Platonism.

In his (admirable) commentary on Hegel in *Being and Event*, Badiou says Hegel is incapable of thinking the simple difference between two letters. It is true, but with new consequences, of Badiou himself: two letters are "ontologically" identical, he will tell us; it is their topological localization, their being-there, their appearing that produces their simple, ontic difference of place. Ontologically, they are perfectly identical. But the two letters are *still* and always technological, anthropological examples; it is by the transcendental and illusory appropriation of identity (therefore: of mathematical equality =) that man *produces*, and only *afterwards*, the identical being [*l'étant identique*]. Once again, the metaphysical fraud, reactualized by Badiou with great pomp, consists in reversing the order of things, literally and in every sense, by putting the mimetically *appropriated*, pleonetically *produced* Principle "in the origin," as it were, "in the posts of command": the principle of identity, condoned by the very precarious event of technomimetic appropriation, from then on claims to "condone things," to be *at their origin*.

Thus when you come up with an immense "phenomenology of appearing," on the basis of Logic, in order to infer therefrom that, in the ontic being-there, there is never identity or absolute difference, you are *not* really talking of appearing, but of *physis*. Technology, which territorializes identity "ontologically" appropriated by man, *makes appear* absolute identity, differentiated only in the topological localization of two identical artifacts: two letters, two glasses, two clones ... *Then* can we say that the doctrine of indiscernibles is applicable. But *only* then. Meaning, only in the *technological appearing*. The ontological in-itself of mathematics, and, for instance, of the scheme of indiscernibles, is nothing but a phantasm; here my refutation of Badiou is, after all, exactly the same as Kant's which shattered the age of metaphysics, in its Leibniz-Wolffian embodiments, in his famous "Appendix on the Amphiboly of the Concepts of Reflection." Only its *phenomenalization* takes place, first in mathematical writing, and then as technological production. Everything is at the surface; the in-itself has never existed.

Then Aristotle is right, and Plato is wrong: mathematical pleasure, before being epistemic, is first of all aesthetic; it is a matter of the childish happiness felt by the "natural metaphysician in us" for simplifying/dominating the influx of the diverse, through the purely noetic emulsion of an equivalence that is not really there. It is only in a second instance that this appropriation becomes "epistemic," i.e. political: instrumental. The old Platonic wish to recover the erroneous general "ontological" equivalence plated on the diverse, and by the very means of this fictitious noetic equivalence, failed the first time and hence has no chance of better succeeding the "second" time. The political destination of the mathematical is not "communism," which in its turn is purely noetico-programmatic, but capitalism, which realizes it in general equivalence.

In the kingdom of the "natural" being [*l'étant*], there is not *one* example of absolute ontological identity or equality. A rose is never absolutely identical to another rose, nor is any being which "blooms by itself" identical to another. The generalized relativism of identities and differences in the appearing is a rule of the pre-anthropological *physis*, and not of "the appearing" in general. Within this *physis*, there is *one* and one only region of being=event that transgresses this "Law of general relativity" of always differential identities, and always *approximatively* identical differences: it is the technomimetic region, belonging to Aristotelian *production*. The *instrumental* illusion introduced by anthropological noesis in the presumed "ontological" noumenon—"nature written in mathematical language"—that is based on the principle of identity and therefore equalization of the being, is precisely nothing but an instrumental-transcendental illusion. There is no in-itself and noumenon except as specifically *produced*; the essence of mathematics, even more than Logic, is technological. In Kantian terms, mathematics is the *schwärmerei* of Logic, and Logic the *schwärmerei* of *techne*, etc., etc.

Mathematics as the "in-itself" of things, as we have seen with the ontological differend, has historically proved to be nothing more than a fiction that is turning against us today, with the devastating violence we know too well. The mathematical fiction of equality and identity allows the production of *afterwards*, through technics, two in every respect identical artifacts, such as two glasses coming from the same factory. In *2001: A Space Odyssey*, if the regular appearance of the monolith is frightening, it is because we *know* that nature, unlike what Galileo held, is *not* written in mathematical language. There are no "perfect" circles or squares in nature: geometrical forms and mathematical idealities constitute a *simplification* of natural forms, "just like" life was a simplification of matter.[4] For instance, the planets are formally *simplified* by our geometrical spheres, which are not "at the bottom" [*au fond*] of things, their ontological in-itself being forbidden by Kant, and delivered turnkey by the equation ontology=mathematics; only technics *makes appear*, for instance in the regular angles of the buildings in which we almost universally live, the square and the rectangle in the heart of Nature, like hair on soup. The monolith's appearance in *2001* is terrifying—and would be so, if it should happen in some extra-human reality—because we confusedly, but very profoundly, *know* that we are the *only* depositaries of the technological event; we also know with which terrifying prerogatives this fortune has corrupted/spoiled us in the heart of all being [*l'étant*]. And so we are scared that suddenly another being could, even virtually, attain the means to do to us what we have done to others: we are terrorized by the monolith in the same way we would be terrorized by monkeys if they started rubbing flints together, or producing sophisticated tools. This is why, once again following the metaphysical critique launched by Kant, and aggravated by Nietzsche-Heidegger, the distinction "being-appearing" has become absolutely worthless. Mathematics, more severely than Logic, remains at the *surface* of things. Its claim to ontological "depth" is the very heart of the ancestral metaphysical calamity. Logic is *explicitly* the art of the *link* between things, of the always asymptotic degrees of similarity and dissimilarity, of always relative identities and also always relative differences. This is why it is precisely more "profound" than mathematics, in the very sense that Nietzsche said the Greeks "were superficial … out of profundity." Hegel calls his great ontological work, "The Science of Logic." We cannot even *imagine* that he would call it "The Science of Mathematics"… When Spinoza, for instance, lays down *more geometrico* as philosophical Ideal, the fact still remains that he produces a general Logic of the Relation. As we saw, mathematics can constitute an absolutely admissible paradigm of philosophizing … provided that pure mathematics itself is not taken too seriously. The mathematics of the affect (see above), or the mathematics of play (see above), must be completely different from pure mathematics.

Evil

EVIL: The properly anthropological and *gratuitous* [*gratuite*] ability of humanity to make natural (i.e. animal) sufferings exponential, virtually infinite.

Although of questionable taste, the play on words "cacathartic" unfortunately says more on the subject than a "serious" account. The event of animal appropriation does not yet produce Evil: animal sufferings are *necessary* evils; a necessity that is contingent in its envoi, as all this type of necessities are, but ultimately necessary. It is because the price of the difference between life and matter, the price of the conquest of movement, consciousness, and sensation is the precariousness of the animal appropriative being-there, and therefore suffering and death, that subsequently, in the second degree event of appropriation called the technological event, there is Evil. However, contrary to appearances to the contrary, this one is in no way necessary, and the entire ethics of philosophy is grounded therein. Very speculatively speaking, this means we can consider that suffering and death are in no respect necessary *transcendentally*, as phenomena sanctioning vital appropriation.[1] It happens to be the case, however, and a universal *Law* of the biological being, that he should suffer and die in the exact proportion to the ability to live and experience jouissance: to (self-)appropriate. Life always already [*d'ores et déjà*] exponentializes an absolute Law of the matter: every being is sooner or later called to disappear; nothing is eternal. We can thus uphold that the event, every event, converting a miraculous contingency into repetitive necessity, makes sure that even if it is transcendentally "contingent" that vital appropriation results in suffering and death, this contingency well and truly *becomes* a universal necessity which, it seems, only Promethean technics considers itself capable of challenging.[2] Therefore we may feel justified in asserting that the huge amplification produced by technics on vital matter at the same time *necessarily* amplifies the negative phenomena that have appeared with the pleonectic stage, that was technics itself; and so, that Evil itself has something ineluctable, necessary about it.

For once, I cannot bring myself to make Billancourt despair. Man is usually called the animal capable of reason, and reason makes us see that nothing *obliges* us to amplify the sufferings disproportionately, and to infinitely refine the prolongations of the ways of dying, on the pretext that technological overbidding has taken over the entire vital matter that preceded it. And yet this is what we do, what we have always done. Where suffering and death turned out to be *intrinsically* necessary to the vital stage of appropriation, it must be recognized that the amplification of these phenomena by technology is but *parodically* necessary. We could confine ourselves to the purely animal sufferings and cold hard death; we could even—and it is for instance the contemporary ethical debate on euthanasia—do all we can in order to alleviate the sufferings and make death itself perfectly painless. It was Adorno's ethical point of view—the categorical imperative, "after Auschwitz," to inscribe the question of suffering, not on the periphery nor directly outside, but at the very core of a philosophy—and, in this respect, I adopt it without reservation. The one thing Adorno did not have, and his relentless lucidity as to man's ability to transform the earthly world into hell, even whilst "considering the stage of productive forces, the earth could here and now be paradise," was a *genealogical* theory of Evil. In other words: by what twist was the perfectly *gratuitous* character of the amplification of sufferings, and death, converted precisely into "second nature"—into itself *gratuitous* automatism, as "luxurious" in its mode as all the obvious supernumerary luxuries with which technological appropriation overspoils us. The necessities of technological, i.e. metaphysical, life, what we also call "civilization," are *all parodies* of necessity. And Evil is nothing other than a gigantic and tortuous compilation of parodies of animal sufferings.

In fact, the proto-form of technological *catharsis*, or second degree appropriation, is quite obviously ingestion, or nutrition. Animals, in ingesting immediately the food they need, suppress the latter and preserve it as the energy which daily renews their existence. But there is a "price" to this proto-*catharsis*, which is the unthought of all philosophy, from Aristotle to Hegel's *aufhebung*: this price is the waste, the excrement. For the excremental necessity of the animal kingdom does not produce *by itself* any supplementary evil: it is precisely reabsorbed in the cycle of Nature. It even happens that one animal's excrement is another one's food, for instance our household garbage is food for the maggots, or bovine feces is food for the flies. "Philosophy in the bousoir"[3]... *But*, just as there is no autophagy in any animal species, which would sanction their immediate extinction (which proves that in Nature, the scheme of impossible self-belonging as event is already at work), in the same way, there is no phenomenon of *auto*-coprophagia, which we come across, however, in certain human specimens considered more or less rightly as "perverse." "More or less rightly," because one of the major casuistic difficulties I am confronted with in my philosophical move is the impossibility of finding the slightest conclusive criterion to determine *who*, in the anthropological closure, is *not* intrinsically perverse, i.e. perverted by the technomimetic: by the parodic. This may sound quite offensive to delicate ears, but "normal" marriage and family are no more nor less perversions of the natural envoi than zoophilia or coprophagia—phenomena we come across, as it happens, only among us humans. We do not have the slightest normative measure in order to be able to say which one of these respective practices is the "more or less" perverse. "Normality" itself, as the SoN demonstrates without the shadow of a doubt, is the *first* of the perversions instituted by post-appropriative expropriation.

Event in the second degree, technology, is mimetically modeled on this natural functioning. Technology is the *catharsis* of nature, and food gathering is exponentialized, through mimetic appropriation, as agriculture. But it particularly produces a certain waste, this time *non-recyclable*, as they say very rightly today. We recognize here the historical problem of ecology: the luxurious gigantism of western technology dumps megatons of waste in poor countries, increasingly "considered" the dumping ground of the civilized world. This process obviously begins with the treatment of the literal excrement itself, with the installation of our toilets in order to divert our feces and urine from the places we live in, and their dispatch in immense varying circuits.

Now this is, ontologically, what Evil is: it is more generally the "modulation" of the affect of suffering in increasingly sinuous and sophisticated circuits, which increases them inordinately. This is what Lacoue-Labarthe, with his usual genius of historial ellipsis, summarized for us: "Auschwitz is the waste of western art." Meaning: the waste produced by the complex of *mimesis-techne-catharsis-aufhebung* does not only lead to the "non-recyclable waste," the one fought by political ecology precisely. It produces, above all, *the living itself as waste*. The living skeletons of Auschwitz or Ethiopia, with their deformed or fused bodies of Hiroshima or Chernobyl, mutilations caused by torture or scientific experimentation, war or industrial diseases, Evil is what *techne* does to the living *without knowing it*. *Techne* parodies *life*, i.e. what the Greeks called *ananke*, natural automatism. "Evil is born when I do *in the face* of the Law that which I automatically do *prior to* it."[4]

It is the same with so-called mental sufferings. They consist of affectual depressurization produced by the "great détournement" of technoscience upon the soul of the human animal—the body ("without organs") of his affect (see above). Badiou, like Leibniz before him, is delighted by the fact that man is "the being [*l'étant*] that dwells within the most worlds." The dreadful sufferings of the schizophrenic are the other side of the pleonectic ubiquity of science. It is a question of a kind of technically describable oxymoron: the appropriative deterritorialization of Science, which *deports* human consciousness and affect well beyond their simple given ontic being-there, is reterritorialized as thinking and affectual tormenting expropriation. The overwhelming majority of human bodies, and animals caught up in the apparatus set up by the latter, quite simply do *not* endure what Science makes them undergo. They succumb to it *alive*, incorporate death by parodying it, and see their animal sufferings increase at an incredible rate before the technological stage of appropriation.

Birds or cats go and hide before they die. It often happens that man does not even have that chance, and forbids other animals, often immediately after their birth (in "Schürmannian" terms: technology does not only expropriate the living from their mortality, but very often from their natality itself), the minimal being-there of animal death. Death is already the trait of expropriation that stigmatizes the living stage of "pleonexia" inchoative with respect to the event. The living almost always have at their disposal a minimal being-there where it can "shelter" its death. The only mode, which is the premonition of Evil, in which we witness an *expropriated death* in the animal kingdom, is obviously when one animal is devoured by another. This expropriation lasts for an extremely short while. Technological expropriation, Evil itself, *eternalizes* these furtive temporalities that sanction the living appropriation of singular expropriations. Evil is the waste of Science, that is to say, animal sufferings and death *endlessly* parodied through technology.

In this respect, only two philosophies "anticipate" the region explored by the SoN, and those are Schelling's and Schürmann's. The former proposes a very "spiritualist" interpretation of Evil. The latter proposes a very "ontological" interpretation of Evil. I take the opportunity to make a most elementary self-presentation: coming from a non-academic background has certainly enabled me to discover very quickly what constituted the favorite *poses* of a given philosophical period, and especially to take liberties with them, overcoming possible intimidations. The least of these is indeed not the pose of "anti-humanism." That humanism, for reasons the SoN underlines at least as well as other negative philosophies, has become untenable for us, is one thing; however, what is designated above everything else by the pet name "anti-humanism" is the claim—with implicit and often dubious intentions—to think in a manner completely outside the anthropological closure. We might as well say that this contemporary pose of the philosopher is perfect, self-refuting nonsense. The SoN, within the most classical tradition that exists (Spinoza, Hegel ...), considers itself entirely as philosophical anthropology. Only the human can access the non-human [*Il n'y a d'accès au non-humain que pour l'humain*].[5]

That only the human can access the non-human is a simple truism, which gives no licence to spare—without serious ethical consequences—the anthropological trait that marks the maximally appropriative animal's every path of access to everything that is not he. However, that most of these paths of access, such as Science namely, are *never* communicated to any other species than ours (music has more chances than an algorithm of being communicated to an animal—and of course, play!), now that is not insignificant; and hence the genealogical inquiry, exclusive to philosophy, reveals of what "monstrous setting" we are the epochal heirs.

Mathematics

MATHEMATICS: For a modern, the transcendental is confused with ontology itself, i.e. as Kant would translate from its Latin definition, the "science of the most universal properties of all things." It is with what François Regnault called his "stroke of genius", i.e. the equation mathematics=ontology, that Badiou (and a few others, constituting what is typically called a "philosophical generation") hit me for such a long time on the head. We had to admit in fact that this simple but devastating equation constituted the mightiest answer of the history of metaphysics to the ontological question. In fact, since science is the art of appropriation of the "eternal" Laws of Nature, i.e. of the being-necessary of everything, what discipline of thought could lay claim to the rank of ontology more than mathematics? All in all, Badiou's "discovery" is so powerful that it appears, after a (long, very long…) digesting period, somewhat trivial. We ask ourselves why metaphysics did not think of it before, and for such a long time sought "ontology" in other places than where it was obviously to be found. Mathematics is the science of "the most universal properties of all things" in such an obvious manner that everything should have been said on that point. And yet, it would seem that Badiou alone discovered it.

However, even this point is not so self-assured, if we decide to take a more serious look at it. I will give the irrefutable proofs in one of my two as yet unpublished, "posthumous" books, but even the equation mathematics=ontology eventually seemed to me not only suspect, but finally null and void—which is by no means a simple "anti-Badiou" polemic, but a real conclusion which, on the pretext of the latter, constitutes a perspective turning point embracing the entire history of metaphysics and its false paths. I explained above why, at the end of the day, and in agreement with the rest of the tradition on this point alone, I confirmed the superiority of the logical paradigm over the mathematical (see *Logic*). Here I will argue, with more specific examples, why I think the equation of mathematics with ontology is nothing more than deceptive: like the previous chapter's conclusion, this too will show how the heavily interested position of "anti-humanism" openly falls into its own trap. The demonstration will illustrate, *en abîme*, the concept of irony (see above), by laying bare the semblance of semblance of the naked king, which is the match without remainder (see *Ontological Differend*) between being and mathematical thought, just as the police prefect had to wait for Dupin to steal the stolen letter of the Minister. Even more *en abîme*, it is pure analytical logic, again in the sense theorized by Dupin, that dismantles the metaphysical postulate of an "inhumanist" equivalence of ontology and mathematics.

And if Logic *alone* is a legitimate transcendental, i.e. the *empty* ontology of all possible link between the beings [*étants*], without taking account of any singular properties, but mathematics is delegitimized with respect to the claim to say its contents, *Ontological differend* (see above) *oblige*, then the necessary outcome sanctions, collaterally, what the philosophical twentieth century sought for the most part, that is to say, the institution of a thought of being which no longer lays claim to any "ontology." It is therefore rather in the original fruit of metaphysics that the deadly worm must be sought.

The sciences—every science—divide things up into their components that are inaccessible to animal perception. Etymologically, "to divide" means: to introduce the void. From the moment we remain on the level of the pure practice of pure sciences; it cannot do any harm to say, with dear Badiou, that these sciences are "innocent." But as Hegel said with his solid Lutheran sense, only the stone is innocent. For the void is *literalized*. It is all the forms of Evil. It is the perversion of predatory cruelty into tormenting jouissance. It is the most literal decomposition of the very matter of things by mathematized physics. The latter in turn literalizes the fact that "ontology," by claiming to apply to "the in-itself" of things, the in-itself itself created as it were from scratch, had always lied. In short: the equivalence mathematics=ontology "triumphantly" completes metaphysics. It says the *very* last word, as a truism. Yes, mathematics *is* ontology, and that is the *whole* problem.

I think mathematics refines the metaphysical lie par excellence: the equality formula, x=x. This should be enough to call into question the whole of what I call "Platonic fiduciarism," that is, the blind confidence in the epistemological, i.e. absolutory-ontological status of mathematics. Only in the light of this formula so fundamental to itself does mathematics as a whole appear as what it is at its origin: the ultimate sublimation of the mimetic impulse through which the human animal (self-)appropriated things, in instrumentalizing them. The formula of equality is in a way "the absolute weapon" which made man "Master and possessor of Nature," as Descartes, Platonic fiduciarism's second great historial kick-off, thought. And nothing is less innocent than a sublimation that lays claim, precisely, to the most immaculate innocence. We know well that in love, the domain reserved for the inspection of the operation of sublimation, there is just one step between the fact of saying that Helen is divine and the fact of realizing that she is nothing but a bag of guts and excrement. The amorous countersublimation should enlighten us about all the other types of sublimation, which are always pleonastically metaphysical, and therefore never more innocent than the lover interested in his sublimation who, when disappointed, becomes the worst slanderer of what he had only just deified.

Yet this is not the only argument against the equation mathematics=ontology. Once again, it is the unpublished book on Meillassoux that will get to the bottom of things. But I will make do with just one striking example here. It is about the famous "point of excess" discovered by the greatest paranoid of the twentieth century, Kurt Gödel (whose rivals were not few in that), and which Badiou, as you might expect, makes into a primordial "ontological" category, since all that is mathematical is *ipso facto* ontological.

All that is material is structured by what mathematics calls "membership" or "belonging," the relation denoted by $\in$. (Incidentally, perhaps this choice of the word "belonging" alone, to designate the essential structure on which modern mathematics is based, already betrays the pleonectic *prejudice* the human mind can never help applying to things.) Crudely put, my body "belongs to"/"is a member of" this room, which "belongs" to this house, which "belongs" to this village, which "belongs" to this country, which "belongs" to this planet, which "belongs" to this solar system ... and so on to infinity, without any end point. No end point "bottom-up"; but no end point "top-down" either: everything is indefinitely subdividable, decomposable into always smaller atoms. Even with quarks, physics will someday discover smaller subdivisions, and this is why mathematics *transcends* the other sciences, literally and in every sense.[1] The question is, as usual, what transcendentalization will *cost* sooner or later, in the face of the compulsory euphoria of professional metaphysicians.

On top of this comes the relation of inclusion, denoted by $\subset$. It indicates the *doubling* of the relation of belonging into *representation* of a "belonging of belonging." It is *materially* that my arm belongs to my body, but it is immediately a matter of representation (what twentieth-century philosophy, for a long time, determined transcendentally as "language") when we *say*: "my arm." Thus I separate (I divide ...) *artificially* the universal intrication of material "belongings" into *parts* represented as "separate." By what do I do this? By the pure void of this representation itself: my arm is only ideally [*idéallement*] separate from my body. Naturally, a virtuoso of the chainsaw, an instrument we owe to the appropriation of the void called science, can come to literalize this separation and cut my arm off, or other less avowable parts of me. Yet it changes nothing in the structure of things, which is universally governed by "belonging." I put the word in quotation marks in order to refer to the parenthesis that inter- venes in the preceding paragraph. It is very likely that the sole *fact* of calling this structure "belonging" is *already* a more than interested representation, betraying the inveterate pleonectic "second nature" of the technomimetic animal. Then it is perhaps a poor choice of words, but we must obviously agree that "belonging," in fact, coincides universally with the structure of things—as logic spells out the universal structure of their relations.

Is this the case with inclusion? What Gödel's theorem—certainly one of the most admirable logico-mathematical discoveries of the twentieth century—tells us, is that the set of the parts of a given being always *exceeds* the structural set of its members. The *representation* of a being, which divides the being into infinite—infinite because arbitrary—parts (I can, in an intelligible manner, cut my body up into as many odd parts as I will, for instance), is always *superior* to the simple structural *presentation* of the being in question. Very well.

Because of Badiolism, that is, accomplished metaphysics, mathematics is ontological, then inclusive, and the ensuing representational excess, is "ontological."

Must it be conceded? Obviously not. No being [*étant*], in its compact materiality, overflows its own representation. The parts of a planet do not spend their time exceeding the elements that compose them, the inclusions that are supposed to ontologically haunt my coffee maker do not seem to be in a hurry to overflow in every direction. The representation of a tree does not pounce on my face with all the might of its excess, and even a rabid dog, if he jumps at my throat, does not do so because of a point of excess, but rather because of its singular material structure, which is after all still too nicely pleonectic compared to any human being, even communist. Conclusion: it really seems that the "ontological" scope of the famous point of excess, which Badiou applies to the political situation for instance, is caught in the anthropologizing "correlationism," where human thinking *plates* [*plaque*], on the very inside of things, a process that shows merely his own power to (self-)appropriate them. It is us who divide the being into "excessive" parts (it is even a particularly eloquent example of the techno-appropriative operation), and not things that subdivide *themselves* into partitive representation that exceeds their universally elementary structure.

Therefore the equation mathematics=ontology is worthless, but not because ontology would have to be sought in a safer place. It is because ontological propensity itself, the scientific universalism that sublimates the ferocity of technomimetically appropriative animal, is the oldest of metaphysical illusions—practically the definition of the latter all by itself.

Thus we see by this single example that mathematics is *not* ontology. It is rather "the ontology"... of the noetic-noematic *link* that unites the technomimetic animal with the being [*l'être*] it appropriates. The keyword here is the one that is indiscernible from every "ontological problem" since Kant: transcendental. And with *Logics of Worlds*, it must be admitted that Badiou got quite closer to what he wanted to reach with the first version of *Being and Event*; but as if despite himself, and as if on the flip side of what he says. If logic is the transcendental of appearing, then logic alone is *properly* ontological.

But it is so, precisely, transcendentally: it says nothing of the *singulars* (see below) it subsumes, in reducing them to their "most general properties."[2] Whereas mathematics claims to apply to those singularities *themselves*, and this is the disastrous error where Plato, Descartes, and Badiou join each other. Such is the price to pay for it to be what it is: the "purest," i.e. the most *purifying* of sciences. We know to what sweet engagements some were led by the "passion of purification" ... But such is especially the—mostly disastrous—price that will have to be paid by the beings to which these purifications *will be applied*, by mistaking representational excess, principle of identity, indiscernibles, or relation of biunivocity for material structure, pleonectic-evental exception, or alimentary or reproductive instincts.

We can henceforth formulate this disastrous error in several oxymoronic ways:

- Mathematics "is" ontology ... *but there is no ontology*. The critique of metaphysics launched by Kant and Heidegger must be dramatized "after Badiou," and after the many effects of neo-dogmatism it gives rise to at the contemporary philosophical university (what we call "Speculative Realism").
- Logic is ontology, but provided that it never says anything on the singular contents, of which it merely enacts the transcendental laws of relation.
- Logic prevails over mathematics in conceptual dignity, precisely because, according to Badiou, it describes "appearing" [*l'apparaître*] and not "being" [*l'être*]. But there is quite simply no being outside appearing: this naive Platonism, or positivized Kantianism (which holds that the in-itself of things can be appropriated, in Kantian terms, being God[3]), does not take account of the exacerbation of the contemporary critique of metaphysics

by Nietzsche: "with the true world, we also abolished the world of appearances." For transcendentalizing the appearing into *empty* eternal and universal rules, Logic is in fact "ontology," because in (self-)appropriating these empty rules, it does not pretend to create an inaccessible world "in-itself": these are strictly correlational rules.

We saw earlier how mathematics, in its turn, perpetrated the metaphysical overturning par excellence: by applying a *typically anthropological* operation to the being [*l'étant*], whether it be the principle of equality, identity, or excess of parts over members, it takes this instrumental operation for the in-itself and claims to have discovered the "ground" [*fonds*] of things. From then on the terrain is leveled for all forms of religion, which a Badiou will replace "advantageously" with all forms of "laicisized" egalitarian fanaticism. In appearing, which is being [*l'être*] itself, there is nothing but the elementary: neither parts in excess—except in the anthropological closure that *creates* this excess (and this is … "ontological" capitalism)—not representation (see below).

From this point of view, yes, mathematics is much more "evental" than Logic, for the fact that it *adds* to being [*l'être*] things *that are not there*. Only Logic is really faithful to the things outside humanity; whereas mathematics *contaminates* these things with the anthropological ability to represent, that is, technologically (self-)appropriate them. *The excess of representation lies nowhere else than in ourselves.* This contamination, it should go without saying at the point we are now, becomes, in the middle of the twentieth century, more literal than it has ever been, with the nuclear fission we claim to see "in" things. The problem is that things dreadfully show that they themselves do not recognize themselves therein.

Then the history of mathematics is by no means "the history of eternity" as Badiou sees it.[4] It is a "bank" of phenomenal appropriations, and the greatest scientific "conquests" of the human animal are based, in fact, on the mathematized sciences. Whereas Logic is much less generous in terms of appropriative "gifts," but this means that it is much more "respectful" of the being outside-humanity [*l'être hors-humanité*] than is mathematics. Which comes down to rethinking the one and the other on completely different bases than those laid out a first time by Plato, a second time by Descartes, and a third time (this poisonous credit should be granted to him) by Badiou.

So how do "we pass" from the infinite approximations of logic (see above), appearing, and the "identical in the nth degree," to *absolute* (=God) identity[5] that founds mathematics? Because it is this principle that is essentially false, and it is from this falsity that the set of "eternal ontological truths" of mathematics are deduced, which lead to nuclear fission for instance. The mimetic decomposition of *physis* through the most archaic *technai*, sublimated by the "pure sciences" of logic and mathematics, is accomplished, after the second Galileo-Cartesian break with nature, in a *literal* decomposition of the latter. The Neolithic and Paleolithic technique, despite its violence, merely "diverted" nature into new outlets, like efflorescence into agriculture; it is by way of this first violence which is then sublimated by pure sciences that we entered history itself, and it is this beginning that would then be recapped by Platonism, i.e. second degree sublimation of appropriative violence. In the second, Galileo-Cartesian beginning, sublimation, having reached an *apocalyptic* stage that could not have occurred in any way even to Galileo and Descartes, does not take more than two or three centuries to display the *new* mode of its destructive violence. In any event, what is confirmed is the anthropological illusion par excellence, through which we will have sublimated and made "disinterested" our selfish interest and our literally unlimited pleonectic voracity: the identitarian illusion, i.e. the *mimetic* astuteness which made us, for a couple of thousands of years, "stronger" than our planetary rivals. On this point, Hölderlin is very much ahead not only of Fichte and his colleagues from the Stift, but still today of Badiou: the question of *being* must be radically distinguished from the principle of identity. Heidegger or Derrida will understand something of this. Others, still today, turn a deaf ear to it.

If being thinks itself [*se pense*] effectively as event, then all "ontology" is done for. Forever. Schürmann is the guiding thinker of the coming century. Badiou is not only useless and uncertain, but potentially disastrous, if we take him at his hyper-thetical word. It is moreover because of this that Badiou's theory of event, particularly concerning arts and politics, but also at bottom the mathematical formula he gives of the event, as well as his falsely bland theory of love, is, for those who can read, perfectly lame and false. What is false is what I call the "masculine" side (see *Appendix*) of the philosophical process: the tightness of the "truth procedures" between themselves. It is basically absurd to think that the truths of science, politics, love, and art follow a course independent from the other procedures: as such economically giving themselves the means to maximize the segregation, by putting the "Good" itself in a bureaucratic isolation room.

The minutest detail of the SoN shows that it is strictly impossible to think such tightness, and that, on the contrary, the procedures do not stop interacting with each other. A name for this perpetual interaction, "perpetual movement" as they say, when it is foreclosed, is the one Deleuze and Guattari turn into a philosophical category: schizophrenia. It is the assumption of this *objective* schizophrenia of the technomimetic animal that opens the path for a properly *modern* Wisdom. Conversely, the rococo philosophical promotion of all the rational *nec plus ultra* of all domains, from Cantor to Pol Pot, is the safest path of thetic raving with a funnel for a headpiece. The more metaphysics hardens its pretension to founding rationality on supposedly irrefutable bases, the more it predisposes humanity to all forms of irrationalism and superstition; prompted by always *singular* (therefore pleonectic) motives, the more it claims to sincerely *believe* in the existence of principles, archetypes, eidetic and subsuming conceptions of the being [*l'étant*] modeled on scientific and ultimately mathematical purification, the more it encourages "the entire humanity" to chase after phantoms.

Then let us be clear on this: the polemic against mathematics is essentially aimed less at mathematics, and its admirable discoveries, than at the paradigmatic appropriation philosophy makes of it right in its Platonic envoi, commiting us to two and a half thousand years of horrors. I share with the majority of philosophical judgement (Kant, for instance) the idea that mathematics probably consitutes the *nec plus ultra* of what a human mind is capable of thinking *technically*. The great mathematical inventions are to the intellect what athletic or acrobatic exploits are to the body. In fact, many mathematical propositions well and truly have an ontological scope (such as the fundamental question of the zero). Yet, in this respect, there are obviously things to take or leave—especially to leave when you take a closer look, and especially when you look at the effects. The task is henceforth that of an infinite weight of being which will use mathematics, among others and always critically (the actual ontological scope, for instance, of real numbers). As to the history of ontologies, it is behind us for good: we should give our thanks to Badiou for unintentionally having us get rid of it.

In terms of scholastic protocol, this translates as follows: the thesis of "the univocity of being," which is merely the narcissistic projection of the philosopher-king as old as Plato himself, must be abandoned. Being is impure, muddy, plurivocal: even the Deleuzian virtual reabsorbs somewhat too much the differential influx of the being [*l'étant*] in the univocity of Bergsonian duration. Heidegger, Schürmann, a part of Derrida are safer invocations: no point of Sirius to the treatment of the question of being, which is said in more than one way, and is distributed in regions as impure as they are non-communicating, dissymmetrical. I am simply urging to *think differently* the situation of mathematics, and perhaps in the respect I just mentioned, in the heart of human thought, and thus to place it in an entirely different manner within philosophical strategies.

As long as this change of paradigm does not gain the upper hand, we will have to go on launching attacks against what I have also called "Platonic fiduciarism," of which Badiou will have given the ultimate historical expression with his equation ontology=mathematics. Because ontology will not recover from it. And this is not as bad of news as it sounds.

Mimesis

MIMESIS: *Mimesis*, as we saw with the question of irony-parody (see above), is not—against the prejudice conveyed by philosophy—semblance. We implicitly gave its proof, with the absolutely anthropological property called irony, showing that semblance *cannot* be doubled. A semblance of semblance always "resolves" itself, in the para-Hegelian mode, in the monstrative display of that on which it "took off": a black person who pretends to pretend is still black, a woman, a nonentity, etc. Whereas *mimesis* is infinitely doubled, and turns upside down everything it touches. The clever ones will then blame *The Spirit of Nihilism* for being just a deceitful copy of this Hegelianism without reserve; they will have missed the essential point, which is the fact that this philosophy develops, right up to their ultimate consequences, all the foundations laid out in outline by this great man called Philippe Lacoue-Labarthe. I hope to be, in my own right, the Adorno of that Benjamin.

Why? Ironic "resolution" does not indicate the least "progress," as it happens in Hegelian double negation. Henceforth the reader must know well what I think of the notion of progress in order to avoid such a misinterpretation, which is one of the points which separates me most radically from the one I otherwise consider the greatest philosopher of all time. There are many other differends that my already published work, and also my few as yet unpublished, "posthumous" books elaborate in depth.

This is what I owe to Lacoue-Labarthe: *mimesis* is also *catharsis*; it never leaves intact that which it grabs hold of. The appropriation of repetition is the most violent "alchemical" weapon ever seen on earth. It is the very name of the archi-event by which we are what we are. It does not produce the slightest "progress," except for illusory, always as the fig leaf of the pleonectic *second nature* through which alone we became *everything* we are, without an atom of exception.

Semblance is certainly a direct consequence of *mimesis*. Man lives in simulation and dissimulation for being the mimetic animal. But simulation and dissimulation never change anything to what they simulate or dissimulate. And this is what decisively *proves* the ironic faculty: by showing that semblance can never be doubled, without at the same time *exposing* as purloined letter that which it is the semblance of. *Mimesis* divides itself (is doubled) infinitely. Agricultural *mimesis* changes *nothing* to the laws of botany it takes hold of, and yet it changes *everything*. Art changes *nothing* to the archi-political horrors it lays bare, and yet it changes *everything*, for the fact that it "simply" exposes them. Alas, only pure, i.e. mathematized sciences *concretely* alter that which they take hold of, and this is what I call "ontological differend" (see above). From nuclear cataclysms to eugenic disasters past and future, from ecological exhaustion to the enormous anguish of cosmic solitude provoked by Galileo's telescope and spatial conquests, from human and animal slavery to indus-trial exterminations, the mathematization of sciences, at the same time that it quenched the "Promethean" impulse inchoative to the human being-there, and provided it with all these "Goods" in which it delights still, and beyond shame, philosophy "itself," provoked all the abominable evils (see *Evil*).

Mimesis, needless to say, thrusts its proto-pleonectic roots deep into the vital stage of appropriation. The emergence of a phenomenon such as sight is evidently the latent prototype of what technics will later reduplicate with the techniques: at the very level of vital, physical emergence, appropriation and *mimesis* seem to be the two metaphysical "principles," in other words, the two ultimate phenomenological traits, of the event. In this sense only, and in this sense entirely, the animal perceptual region of being [*l'être*] is always already a *parody* of matter.

The event *as* repetition is what is the most difficult to think, but also the most urgent. For an upwards revising of this concept, so calumniated by metaphysics, we can have recourse to *mimesis*. We also need to go all the way: what differ-entiates the anthropological life from all the other known cosmic events is that event, for us, *is* well and truly repetition understood as *mimesis*. Hegel, with the *aufhebung*, is *already* a philosopher of the event, and *The Phenomenology of Spirit* is the vastest philosophico-historial inquiry ever made for "taking stock of" the crucial events-repetitions secularized blindly in our being-there.

Techne-mimesis is the archi-event from which we proceed. Philosophical modernity, from Kierkegaard to Deleuze, had already discovered that repetition produces difference. But we must go further, and show that the most decisive, the most evental and intensive difference *is* repetition itself, understood as *mimesis*.

It is the glory of the French philosophical moment of the seventies to have radicalized what Heidegger and Wittgenstein had sensed: being is difference. Once and for all. In this respect only, but in this respect entirely, Kant was a more profound philosopher than Hegel, for having anticipated that the destruction of the dogmatic age of philosophy could only lead to a transitory phase of *pathetic endurance* of being as difference, as Schürmann brilliantly analyzes in *Broken Hegemonies*. He still remained anchored in the contested metaphysics, treating this transcendental difference as a kind of parasitical incongruity of sensibility. Schürmann will say: if singularity *appears* incongruous to understanding, it is by the deep-rooted virtue of the "natural metaphysician in us," and the subsuming power which Kant himself continued to trust.

The French sixties complete the critical project by letting being [*l'être*] be as absolute difference. Hegel and Schelling's "drama" was the will to save, for a last time, the originary project of metaphysics: the accounting for being [*le rendre-raison de l'être*] as identity. Only Hölderlin, by precisely laying out the foundations of what I call "archi-transgression" (see *Transgression*), anticipated that the thesis of being as One and as Identity was the oldest error of thought. Because of it he succumbed before his time. Only Badiou, in the twentieth century, ventured the gigantic anachronism of resurrecting philosophy as architectonics of identity, that is, of the mimetic impulse that takes its subsuming power for the "ground" of being. Ubu, philosopher king.

Being accomplishes itself maximally as event. Event is the maximal entelechy of being. In other words: at each macro-event, Big Bang, molecular life, animality, consciousness, technics, the event *intensifies*, and as if explosively, "the identity" of being as difference. Being is each time *concentrated* into event as if into the eye of a needle and *exposes* itself therein as difference. Event is the exponent [*l'exposant*] of being as difference.

Technomimetic event, this purely anthropological *astuteness,* this brilliant subsuming artifice that appeared on earth as miraculously as nature itself, for almost two and a half thousand years, took itself for what it took hold of. With this metaphysical illusion finally cleared away, the French philosophical moment of the sixties wanted to affirm straight out the full positivity of difference. But it was too early to pop the champagne. Evil, literally and in every sense, had been done already a very long time ago. *The Spirit of Nihilism* extensively argues the reasons for Deleuze and Derrida's failures: the former wants to make an ontology of difference which is an untenable oxymoron. Ontology is the science of the most general and particular; to liberate difference while claiming to make it into an ontology was to fail in advance, by definition.[1] As for Derrida, who purely and simply transcendentalizes *metaphysics*, and its whole archive, *by way of* difference, he fell into what Schürmann calls the "Sirius" trap: Derridean deconstruction requires that one "decide to change terrain, in a discontinuous and irruptive fashion, by brutally placing oneself outside and by affirming an absolute break and difference."[2] Derridean deconstruction, thus by affirming at every turn the architranscendental difference, also called "différance," or "trace," as more "profound" than all differences *fixed* by metaphysics, eventually gives the strange sensation of *undifferentiating everything*. For instance, in a testamentary interview for a French magazine, Derrida explained that the difference between manual labor and intellectual labor is worthless And the same goes for the difference between *physis/techne*, man/woman, empirical/transcendental, being/nothingness, etc., etc. The SoN is, to a great extent, a relentless "deconstruction of Derridean deconstruction."[3] I cannot get into detail here, since this book is just a vast "insert" to the SoN; but let us simply say that, after Schürmann—who saw clearly that transcendental difference *cannot*, ever, *not* be identified by the "natural metaphysician in us"—the task is not to affirm, quasi-mystically, the deconstructive difference at every turn, because the trap closes back on the Derridean, while "Différance" *in language* [*dans le langage*] eventually undifferentiates everything. Language subsumes; it does violence to the different by restoring it to a case of the Universal (including in Derrida! Because all the differences "fixed" by metaphysics are merely *cases* of the architranscendental of difference); singularity is precisely this difference *assaulted*—even if hard to admit—by idiomatic subsumption. All we can do is thwart this violence. This is what Schürmann, much more effectively than Derrida, does in his own way. This is what I do too, in my own way, but such as enabled by Schürmann as its condition of possibility.

Of all the famous "philosophies of difference," only Foucault would sense that difference, "liberated" in thought alone, could not start to suddenly caper about in nature, being ecstatic over itself: metaphysical sedimentation was far too old. Difference could only affirm itself by an always painful, if not deadly, *transgressive negativity*: that which responds to the subsuming, un-differentiating negativity by which metaphysical idiom affected it: by caesuring it, crossing it out. Empirically: by exploiting, torturing, killing it before its time. Schürmann.

But this is why *The Spirit of Nihilism*, at first glance faithful to this uncompromising ontological negativisim, does not stop there. Considering identity, for the first time, no longer as being but as event, the event of technomimetics, it demonstrates that this exorbitant power of man never ceases to be phenomenally in *continuity* with the entire immemorial and cosmic "logic" of being as event. In other words, metaphysical astuteness will not have *only* oppressed difference under subsuming identity. It will have *also*, but in the most perfect obliviousness up until Kant-Heidegger, *produced* difference.

Singularity is not *only* difference as caesured by scientific isomorphism. It is, precisely, *production* of unprecedented differences. For twenty centuries, this production was surreptitious for the longest time: and overall, a constant ordeal, precipitating humanity into the arms of all the forms of religious consolation. Humanity found solace therein from its own oppressed, singularized difference. Singularization, lived as a disgrace, a defect, a mutilation, a deformity. Still today, despite certain "democratic" appearances. Schürmann more or less says that it is in the name of Nature, the hegemonic phanstasm of an entire age, that sodomites were burned in the Middle Ages—and still today in many parts of the world. But we would be quite naive to think that, in our western democracies, the violence done to the different as deadly, outlawed singularization, is not regenerated under strategies obviously much more sophisticated than those of the good old witch hunt.

This *Evil* that identity did to the different here-below, that is, producing difference in the very movement by which it negated it, well, perhaps in the up-above, this identity would finally do what it said: make everything equal; even though when in applying this programme explicitly here below, the implicit thing everyone saw was that identity produced only, always and still, more inequality and dissymmetry: non-assumed difference which, as such, is always perceived as *monstrous*. Schürmann more than brilliantly showed how, for the entire metaphysical tradition without exception, singularity had always been recognized as Evil. Hegel would liminally recapitulate the Whole of the most fundamental metaphysical prejudice: singularity is absolute negativity.

Being [*l'être*] is, always and everywhere, *as if* [*comme*] ceaseless differential production. But "being is accomplished as event" [*l'être s'accomplit en événement*] means: therein production is intensified maximally. Event is being as intension [*l'être en intension*]. There is infinitely more difference after the Big Bang than before. And, after the appearance of Life, there has been more concentrated *qualitative* differences on the small planet earth alone than everywhere else in the incommensurability of the cosmos to date. Finally, more differences appeared in historicity in which the long period of technomimetic prehistory is accomplished; in a word, more differences in the few thousand years of Civilization alone than in all the preceding tremendous biological cycles. Event *is not* "outside being," as Badiou irrationally asserts. Event is *concentration of being*, and thus its exponent. And the illusion from which we are just barely beginning to come out is that identity was nothing but an astuteness—of which we were just the transfixed smugglers—of the immemorial history of being accomplishing itself *maximally* in the event.

We then get the actual purpose of the manner in which *The Spirit of Nihilism* seeks and renews the modern philosophical intuition of a repetition creative of differences. To say it in the form of an oxymoronic provocation: *The Spirit of Nihilism* is a Hegelianism of difference. Revisiting, with Lacoue-Labarthe, the concept of *Aufhebung* (see above) in the light of the *mimesis-catharsis-techne* complex; assuming the discovery of the metaphysical modernity of being's horizon as non-Whole, non-One,[4] and non-identical; we discover what Hegel could only ignore: the "surpassings" of each *aufhebung*-event will never be reabsorbed in the destinal, eschatological horizon of a Whole. Each operation of suppression-preservation-surpassing produces a divergent difference, and the speculative "totality" is no longer anything but the ever-growing dissemination of the *remaining singularities* of each operation of subsumption.

And all this for an astoundingly simple reason, which effectively destines Hegelian syntax to a diffracting revisitation: identity was not the primary principle of the One-Whole in charge of making the absolute of events come back to the identitarian house, at the end of the life span that suffered from absolute knowledge; identity was *in* the *aufhebung* itself, and not in the final horizon of being. Identity is nothing but an extremely circumscribed accident of being, which at the same time maximally concentrates the latter, as maximal producer of difference. Every event is a maximal accident, a monstrous anomaly.

Hegel did not see what Lacoue-Labarthe saw *via* Rousseau: *aufhebung* is nothing other than *mimesis*. Food gathering imitates grazing and suppresses it while preserving it at the same time. Not only does the negation of negation not amount to the simple initial affirmation; but it does not destine itself, this explaining that, to any decisive identitarian reconciliation, any reabsorption. The cycle of negations, and negations of negations (thus of surpassings, and surpassings of surpassings) that consitute the *aufhebung,* produce only diffraction of singularizing, differentializing events. Identity, as *singular*—and singularly human—event of "the history" of being, lies nowhere else than in the mimetic *operation* which identifies what it suppresses, preserves, and thereby surpasses, each time singularly. It in no way resides in the *fact* of an ontological identity, a principal identity of being hallucinated by classical metaphysics, including even Hegel and Schelling (and Badiou ...). Identity is an event that is very bluntly and empirically confused with that of the technomimetic itself. The proof is that in *physis*, there is only infinitely asymptotic similarity, never identity (see *Logic*). Only technology in the trivial sense comes to *produce* two beings "indiscernible" in every respect, like two glasses, or two hundred thousands, coming from the same factory. But Kantian space and time transcendentalize this solely ideal [*idéalle*] "identity," and assign *again* to each of these artifacts its own place and time, keeping it different. Only technology phenomenalizes metaphysically maximized identity, for instance in mathematics.

Yet this phenomenalization *never* ceases to be *still* difference. The dialectic of identity obliterated from itself the fact that its fundamental operational link was the mimetic impulse. Identity is not ontological, but operative: a very late coming event in the cosmos. Such is the illusion of a little less than twenty-three centuries of metaphysical functionary work. The dialectic of *mimesis* alone thwarts the traps of identity.

Nihilism

NIHILISM: Contrary to what the title of the undertaking seems to indicate, and therefore to what we hastened to think we understand, the SoN is not a "philosophy of nihilism," which, after so many others, would come to diagnose our age as the age of "accomplished nihilism." The SoN is not only a deconstruction, but a *destruction* of the concept of nihilism. Indeed, as a great philosopher[1] said in an unpublished lecture, the *Algèbre de la Tragédie* comes *first of all* as a "Homeric" crossing of contemporary "nihilism": not only the being-for-parody [*l'être-à-la-parodie*] which we so thoroughly talked about, and which constitutes, *de facto*, the sophisticated spirituality of what I provisionally called "democratic nihilism"; but, *on the very inside of democracies,* not to even mention the horrors still perpetrated in 80 percent of the planet, how this spirituality of compulsory sarcasm and derision results in *new* sufferings—shorthanded well enough by the words "depression" and "suicide"— in ever-increasing factual inflation in our affluent western democracies. But at the *end* of the crossing, nihilism appears to have been nothing but the pet name of a much deeper and older concept which classico-dogmatic metaphysics never wanted to know anything about: the concept of Evil. Let us go over the essential outlines of this deconstruction-destruction.

Philosophy, already in its Platonic envoi, is haunted by a specter: the specter of Evil. More precisely still, it *defines* itself, literally and in every sense, by the making a specter of Evil: the phantomizing, irrealizing of it. This is the famous myth of the cave which would rule over almost twenty-three centuries of philosophical *a priori*: Evil is no longer considered as a form of the "less good" [*le moins bien*], an anthropological illusion that bars our access—by the degrees of the better [*le mieux*]—to sovereign Good. Evil is no longer anything but the hierarchical terracing of simulacra in the direction of the Best [*le Meilleur*]: it is considered solely with respect to Good, all Evil being nothing but a degree of the "less good" in the direction of the decisive qualitative difference of the final Good. It is in *The Republic* that the chips were down, and now for almost twenty-three centuries, from which we are only barely coming out.

In the exact same movement, that is, in the primitive scene of *the Republic*, philosophy is defined purely and simply as *that which must come to replace Religion*. The exclusion of the Poet and Tragedy from the ideal City has ultimately no other meaning than that. Art (see above) is attacked on the account of the civic Religion it conveys (sanguinolent paganism). Philosophy is not there just to be simply the parallel rival of Religion. It is not a question of putting philosophy and religion, glaring at each other, cordially hostile but democratically compatible (hence, also, the foreclosure of Democracy), each in their proper place. No: philosophy actually is that which must come to *replace* Religion. What Plato solemnly declares, in Hegelian terms *avant la lettre*, is a death duel. One of them must win without remainder; and the other must disappear. This is the originary project of Philosophy. This is what philosophers almost always forget, even while we live in an age where, more than ever, the question asserts itself with the final violence. The "return of the religious," in the form of monstrous global *parodies* (see *Irony*): Islam in Islamism, Christianism in Evangelism, Judaism in Zionism.

Plato historically failed. Philosophy did not suppress Religion in its deadly struggle with it. It is Religion that "Hegelianized" the struggle: It is Philosophy that lost in the conflict. Religion, as the Hegelian Master, consented not to suppress Philosophy without preserving anything of it: it consented to spare Philosophy's life, provided that it becomes its ancillary, just like in the Hegelian struggle through which humanity begets itself as such. The slave becomes the Worker, therefore that which shapes Humanity (St. Paul: "we are all God's workers"—beginning with philosophy); the slave, instead of dying really and disappearing, becomes a symbolic death, a valet, a living *instrument*. The technomimetic animal is also he who transforms the other animals, and most of his kind, into technological means, and that is one of the figures of Evil.

Ciceronian, and then especially Augustinian-Christian Romanity, will take on the task of putting the bit between the teeth of the philosophical scapegoat for the benefit of the Master of Religion: what Plato wanted to do to Religion (artists merely standing in place of it), Roman paganism and then Christianism did to philosophy; but as in Hegel, in the mode of parody. The slave is the one who *pretends* to die, who shows to the one who defeated and can destroy him that he accepts his death provided that his life is spared: from then on he will work for the one who humiliated him in battle. For almost eighteen centuries, Philosophy, which would have had itself as the historical succession of Religion, has been nothing but its docile, hypocritical, and spineless soubrette.

My hypothesis is that the two moments are in profound solidarity with each other, and that this point has gone unnoticed until now. What is the difference of—first Tragic, then Judaic—Religion from philosophy? Religion was not *less* of a thought than philosophy. Today philosophy must have the minimal-unionist humility to recognize that it has historically lost to religion. Recognize, but what? That Religion *did think* the question of Evil, without trying to irrealize it. It is the genius of Aeschylus and Sophocles among the Greeks, the genius of Judaism with the doctrine of original sin. In the first (Greek) philosophical archive, it is impossible to find a single *concept* of Evil: one must turn to the Bible and Tragedy, and then, at the moment of birth of the philosophical, which is defined purely and simply by the foreclosure of the concept therefrom, to the "philosophers" who subordinate their practice to Religion, Paul, or Augustine.

What does this latter, but also the tragedians, tell us? The exact opposite of what Plato says. Let us come back to the myth of the cave: Plato tells that art, as vehicle of the religious, is wrong to present Evil everywhere (these are the "shadows" of the cave), and that in order to get rid of these hallucinations, one must draw inspiration from Science: epistemological positivity and transparency proper, in particular, to mathematics. With this done, philosophy will secure a wholly rational Politics for the City, where everybody is happily assigned to their appropriate place, a Politics that Religion plainly failed to organize. Therein Evil is therefore conceived as a simple accidental hierarchical "delay" over Good: as simply "less good"; and therefore, ultimately, in light of the sovereign Good, the supreme principal mensuration, as *nothing*. Thus the concept of "nihilism," right at the outset, is a concept *prepared* by philosophy: that is why Nietzsche, in putting the surpassing of the division between Good and Bad forward as the supreme *surpassing*, cannot help repeating despite himself the most originary metaphysical gesture. Philosophy, having nihilated Evil, eventually attributes to the latter, under the pet name "nihilism," *its own* responsibility of nihilating the donation, the positive, the affirmation (that is to say: the natural metaphysical drive in us all). Not a Hegelian, but a para-Hegelian move: it is by nihilating (transcendentalizing) the purely given difference (*physis*) that metaphysics, unwittingly, will have *created* an infinity of not only "positive" (the Good, the Immortal, the Eternal, etc.), but also long *accursed* differences, insisting as a malediction in all the figures of deadly singularizations and transgressive incongruities that have haunted History like the nightmare it did not want to awake from (to paraphrase Joyce).

Now Religion said something completely different, which made it prevail historically, and whose diagnosis remains more than ever overwhelmingly

legitimate (this having explained, and explaining with completely new consequences, that): Science is not *only* the source of positivity, technical and
cognitive appropriation, overwhelming supremacy of man over the other beings
(the philosopher never ceasing to be ecstatic over it), from Plato to Descartes'
"man as Master and Possessor of Nature." Science, i.e. technics, along with all
the Goods it provides us with, also brings about a trail of abominations and
sufferings unknown even to the realm of animal cruelty and predation. No
slavery or torture without chains and swords, without iron; no Auschwitz or
Hiroshima without railroads, gas, and nuclear power. Evil is the Creation of
abominable sufferings, *non-necessitated by Nature alone.* An animal cannot give
up predation without disappearing. A tyrant could give up war and oppression
and an executioner could give up torture, without jeopardizing their biological
survival.

Learnedly, philosophy did not stop playing deaf. Starting with the seventeenth century, especially with Spinoza, philosophy does, once again, want to
subtract itself from Religion. However it still wants to come clean, and does
not yet call into question the Theory of God. Most of all, it perpetuates the
great blindness that is co-originary with it. In Spinoza, Evil is nothing but a
deprivation of Good, an imagination, an imperfection of human understanding,
absolutely impervious to the divine understanding to which leads the Sage's
reconstruction of this understanding. The same also goes for Descartes, then
for Leibniz, and his famous "the best of all possible worlds," so readily taunted
by Voltaire. To say it dryly: there is an originary *inanity* of philosophy, the
inanity of its blind confidence in Science, in its contract with the latter, renewed
indefinitely in full fiduciary blindness. *More geometrico*, and eventually it will all
turn out for the best. In an unpublished seminar, Pierre-Henri Castel makes a
good summary of the move. He evokes a famous letter in which Spinoza makes
exemplary use of his negation of the question of Evil, and

> has this hard-hitting formula: for Nero to put a dagger in his mother's chest
> is never just an act determined entirely by the order of causes; it is all the
> natural power of Nero's arm that expresses itself, and it so happens that it is
> in the breast of his mother Agrippina that it thrusts the blade. We see how an
> act—precisely for someone like Spinoza—can be presented as something that
> only poses a problem for *those who believe in the free subject.* However, in the
> order of Nature, the Sage has absolutely no reason to feel concerned about what
> our imagination comes to *cut out* [*découper*] there, such as someone hurting
> someone else. These are things that fall under the imagination, come from an
> imperfect knowledge of causes.[2]

What would the Sage have to say to us about Auschwitz? Answer: there is no need to resurrect Spinoza himself, when technology will allow us to do it one day. Today it is enough to read the Resurrection of the Classico-Dogmatic Sage that is Badiou in order to find the same age-old rationale, which has very fortunately become perfectly untenable for us, as has all metaphysical necessitarianism (pleonasm). Jean-Claude Milner, speaking with all the facts, was able to say that modern Platonism could only be accomplished in Sadism.[3] As to Pierre-Henri Castel, he shows that Sade would not say anything else than what Spinoza says:

> By definition, the only act is crime, because it is the void which will succeed in making emerge these two points of intensity which are the two sides of the same jouissance, in other words, extreme pain/extreme pleasure, and because crime, moreover, never manages to be criminal enough to be as criminal as it should be, and be equally creative of acts; and where, at the same time, one affirms that anyhow it is in Nature, and since everything is in Nature, there is no crime.[4]

The simulacra and the shadows of the cave—Evil—are not, as Plato thought, the stigmata of a *defect* of Science. To take the example of a very "cavernous" animal, the mole lacks absolutely nothing, and certainly not scientific "light." Animals are unaware of Evil because they are unaware of science. They are unaware of its "goods" of course; but they are unaware of its atrocities as well, which only technics, from ancient slavery to Auschwitz, enables to perpetuate. (They eventually get to "know" something of it, passively, in our industrial batteries and slaughterhouses.[5])

In this respect only, but in this respect entirely, Luther, for instance, is, and always a length ahead, a conceptual creator as important as Descartes, Spinoza, or Leibniz. This is because he, in an extraordinary manner, sets out to *rethink* original sin and demonstrate how humanity is marked by it as if by a stigma. He *philosophizes* Evil, although still in a religious manner, and changes the world more decisively than the hopeless eudaemonism of philosophers. It is in a Protestant country that Spinoza, a renegade from Judaism, would find refuge. Renegade, in this context, means renegation of any intelligibility of original sin. Evil is still not falling under philosophy; when, with the arrival of Leibniz, philosophy claims to make a "concept" of it, it is as astonishingly flat and grossly inane as all the philosophical concepts of Good and Truth are thoroughly elaborate. No matter how Badiou continuously wants to distance himself from Leibniz, there are few metaphysics of the past that are as close to his as the Monadology; that is to say, the perpetuation of the Platonic error, which explains all the rest. The original, the empirical being [*l'étant empirique*], is passed off as a confused parody of mimetico-mathematical *purification*; while this latter, the child-king of metaphysical *mimesis*, is passed off as the Original of which the real being [*l'étant réel*] is no longer anything more than the declining degradation (*monstrously* incongruous singularity). Henceforth, all the forms of Evil, in their turn, become merely confused representations, duplications of the intelligible divine, exempt from those regrettable confusions that disturb the professional metaphysician's peaceful tranquility.

With modernity, that is, the French Revolution, things begin to creak. Kant, the guiding philosopher of democratic laicism to date, for the first time ever, assigns to philosophy *and* religion their respective and tight limits. However, the move is not radical enough, because Kant's historical teleology, as project of universal moral noumenon and "project of perpetual peace," continues to think Evil as a transitional patch of the Good. As Pierre-Henri Castel says: "what we see here is the emergence of a theme destined to a terrifying posterity, is it not, after Kant: it is that every thought of History implies the elimination of pathos. To think history, is always fundamentally to cease looking at the atrocious misfortunes, the crushed bodies, the massacres, etc., thinking it would be unbearable."[6] For the first time, with Hegel, Evil and Death are thought in philosophy *in their immanence*—because Evil is a living Death, as Auschwitz would provide the overwhelming proof. The words Nietzsche would later popularize, but which are a paraphrase of Luther, "God is dead," teaches Hegel, and us all, that henceforth we must think Death *otherwise*: as an *incorporation* in the living, which defines man as such. Historical man is a constantly deferred/differed death; it is this infinite differentiation that is described in *The Phenomenology of Spirit*. But it is made, yet and again, so that the question is resolved at the end in the eschatology of Absolute Knowledge, that is, with the perpective opened up by the French Revolution, of a City of Universal Law [*Cité du Droit universel*] where the dialectical synthesis of Master and Slave gives the Citizen that is free and equal, in rights as well as duties, to every other. In short: in the usual philosophical happy ending[7] of a sovereign Good, here below. Marx would only pad it out. They were the secular equivalents of Augustine's Heavenly Jerusalem.

It is with Hegel's two friends of youth, Hölderlin and Schelling, that things would *finally* fissure for good. Hölderlin, with his brilliant reflection on the Tragic,[8] which would lead him to madness, discovers that the entire History is a catastrophe, that the French Revolution risks not living up to any of its promises, that the irrealization of Evil, always reabsorbed within the One and the Identical of philosophers, is the oldest of their illusions. Even more radically, Schelling, with his *Philosophical Investigations into the Essence of Human Freedom*, for the very first time in the history of philosophy, finally puts forward a *concept* of Evil. Heidegger would consider this text as the major accomplishment of German speculative idealism, and an anticipated refutation of Hegel. We must give the full extent of this estimation, which is nonetheless the greatest moment of world philosophy since the Greeks. Man is free because he is capable of Good *and* Evil. If man was not *capable* of Evil, he would quite simply not be what he is; he would still be an animal [*ani-mal*] among countless others. A philosopher pays a price for attaining the acumen of the most ambitious speculation since the Greeks, by coming to this unpleasant conclusion. For this very reason, after this book was published, Schelling would cease all attemps at editorial manifestation, without ceasing to keep writing. He would let his friend Hegel, who owed him so much, conquer all Europe (his simplifier Marx would conquer only in the next century): today, as yesterday, the philosopher is the one who must not "make Billancourt despair." Schelling caught a glimpse of an *abîme*; his philosophy, unlike Hegel's, could no longer promise a worldly paradise of any kind.

Before all those glorious Germans, inspired by the grandiose caesura of the French Revolution, there was a cursed precursor: Rousseau. And he happened to be Swiss: a Protestant, although he tried hard to be unaware of it. By localizing all Evil in the caesura between Nature and Culture that is man, it is Rousseau who *laicizes* original sin for the first time. By the same gesture, he revisits the Aristotelian caesura between *physis* and *techne*. A thought that is greatly distorted still today; yet a thought that would yield all the most radical revolutions of our age, politically of course, but also philosophically (Kant and Hegel would not have emerged without Luther; but they would not have been able to come up with their founding concepts without Rousseau, Marx, and Darwin as well), literarily, and artistically (modern lyricism, Romanticism). It is also with Rousseau that, for the very first time, philosophy learns to *beware* of Science. Thus, anti-Rousseauists such as Nietzsche and Heidegger, who would also become relentless critics of the philosophical Ideal of Science (a pleonasm since Plato), owe to Rousseau infinitely more than they think.

After Kant, Hegel, and Marx, it is the end of at least one thing: the historical teleology in philosophy, the positive eschatology that tied it to the religious. No more Heavenly Jerusalem, no more rosy futures. Schopenhauer introduces philosophical pessimism; Nietzsche promises us a beyond Good and Evil, an assumption of the world in its injustice and cruelty; Freud locates an implacable source for human Evil in the unconscious; Heidegger destroys the very possibility, for a modern, of founding a positive practical philosophy.[9] Benjamin, after Hölderlin, will think History as an endless martyrology; Bataille will talk only of Evil; Adorno, Derrida, Foucault, Blanchot, Lacoue-Labarthe, Lyotard, and many others will no longer turn a blind eye to the Platonic counter-blindness, that of the phenomenal hegemony of Evil. Except for Badiou …

However, none of these philosophers would propose, like Schelling, a *concept* of Evil as sophisticated as what the Classics built, in terms of conceptual cathedrals, in praise of the unadulterated Good. When Arendt evokes the "banality of Evil," the one thing she fails to do is, yet again, provide us beforehand with the concept. Such is, still today, philosophy's *schizophrenia*: either we read and write philosophy "classically," meaning, always trying to find a eudaemonism in it, which can almost always be found, without looking at the each time specific conditions endorsing it, which is an always methodical and obsessional foreclosure of Evil. Or we recognize the blinding obviousness of Evil, but then philosophy is blinded in the second degree, in considering itself free from the obligation to propose its concept. At best, it is fought or limited; never really explained (this is true even for Adorno, who merely finds sociologico-political explanations for Evil).

The last philosophical eschatologies, the Kantian, the Hegelian, and the Marxist, would nevertheless give the illusion, for almost two centuries, that philosophy would *finally* succeed at that which Plato failed: suppressing, supplanting the religious once and for all. This was particularly obvious with Marxism. And it is, without the slightest coincidence, since the patent collapse of the latter that Religion prevails once again in the world, over a philosophy beaten hollow, indeed practically fallen into the state of being just another cultural and consumption practice, more marginal and folkloric than all the others.

The last and monumentally anachronistic attempt at erecting an entirely "positive" philosophical cathedral, laically devoted to the maximal Good, to unadulterated eternal truths, to fully lived Life, to triumphant Immortality and Eternity, is Alain Badiou's. For this reason, he has to repeat the oldest error, while amplifying it, in other words, making it monumentally gross and inadmissible for us: Evil is nothing but a category of theology, or of morality, which is a degraded theology; death does not exist; the Chinese Cultural Revolution is a creation of eternal truths; Pol Pot is Robespierre; Auschwitz is not a subject for philosophy (and furthermore, it is "anecdotal," like everything that comes from Evil), etc. The undertaking is crowned by success and he becomes the most read and translated author in the world, and, despite the abyss separating their respective conceptual geniuses, this triumph is essentially not very different from the success of a Michel Onfray[10] within the limits of the French scene. Philosophy is yet and again what comforts us, guides us, turns us towards the better, through the sophisticated irrealization of Evil. Philosophy is, yet and again, a eudaemonism whose sad fate is to serve as a "shrill" cultural leisure, whether it be the case of Žižek or Badiou.

One of the very rare authors to display a conceptual genius almost equal to Badiou's, although of a quite superior *philosophical* lucidity, is Reiner Schürmann. As opposed to the Frenchman, Schürmann aggravates the problems, removes the casts, destroys our most self-assured beliefs, brings us—dumbfounded—face to face, perhaps without recourse, with the disaster that is ours, on the edge of the twenty-first century. Never had philosophy been so dark, so implacably lucid about our conditions, so cleverly lacking in the illusions that professional metaphysicians of all ages had strived to build. For this very reason, he is still very little read, very little known, even if, twenty years after his death, the rumours are starting to spread about his greatness: the greatest philosopher of Evil since Schelling; *Broken Hegemonies*, whose scope is comparable to that of *The Phenomenology of Spirit* or *Being and Time* in their day. Must we wait long in order to understand why we are reproducing, here and now, and in a weaker version, the occultation of Schelling by Hegel?

Someone formulated the problem to me in the following way: since Nietzsche, we had been thinking that the question of Evil was "settled," belonging to a somewhat outdated past. After Auschwitz, the question returns with a traumatic force. Problem: in Nietzsche himself, the foreclosure of the question of Evil, its atheistic elimination (the anti-Darwinian "Darwinism" that says the big fish is "right" in eating [*a "raison" de manger*] the small; the overman, in crushing the last of men; the Master and Genius, in using and abusing the slave, "the weak and the failures shall perish," etc.), returns as all foreclosures do. Nietzsche's "nihilism" is the specter under which the death of the question of Evil, seemingly buried by its perpetrator, returns to haunt, like the bodies buried alive in the short stories of Edgar Poe. From then on, it will haunt all modernity, to such an extent that among the majority of philosophers the question of nihilism will take up even more space than the question of Evil. Nietzsche recognized in the Jewish and Platonic double envoi the Origin of nihilism; antisemitism in general is nothing other than the attempt at exorcizing the people through which the *thought* of Evil historically constituted us, westerners, in the conception of original sin. Auschwitz, in the last instance, will have *meant* nothing else: the huge "pagan" technological sacrifice to get rid of original sin, by immolating its historical representatives.

As to "nihilism"s Platonic envoi (according to Nietzsche), today we see a striking effect: the self-proclaimed and legitimate resurrection of Platonism called Alain Badiou, the most sophisticated and grandiose attempt at rebuilding a total prescriptive metaphysics of the Good and the positive True[11] [*le Vrai positif*], through a just as sophisticated irrealization of the question of Evil, thus does not cease to *recognize* nihilism *absolutely everywhere*. Contemporary poetry and art are nihilist. Democracy and capitalism are nihilist.[12] Most of the other philosophers are nihilists. The overwhelming majority of western citizens are nihilists. You and I will always be presumed nihilists even before we open our mouths, not to mention after ... with the exception of his own philosophy, Wagner, and Mao Zedong, the inflation of the nihilistic vision of the world is even greater in Badiou than in Nietzsche or Heidegger themselves! Which is obviously no small thing; and shows that this was what remained problematic of Platonism in Nietzsche himself.

I take this opportunity to make a genuine call for tenders to the Anglo-Saxon public. In France, the challenge was "taken up" only by the courage of a unanimous Law of silence, and indeed first of all on the part of the person concerned. We saw above (see Mathematics) what I think about the "ontological" scope of the theorem of the point of excess. Here, the call for tenders will unfold certain consequences, and will give, in a funky[13] manner, a panoramic view of my differend with Badiolism, and hence of my hostility towards the pompous *revival* of Platonism, that is, together with the prejudices of *every* classico-dogmatic metaphysics that have become untenable.

I would like to know first of all, of course, whether representation's excess on the presented is well and truly an ontological law that applies always and every-where, eternally, to every being [*étant*], or whether it is *only* a matter of a typical law of anthropological "transcendental schematism" alone, to talk like Kant, as was conceded to me by all those mathematicians I talked about. In other words, of a faculty, as infinite power of division, that is perhaps actually confused with technological power as such: the power of inspecting the being, literally and in every sense, and opportunely, *re-presenting* it in a "pleonectically" convenient manner, allowing us to instrumentalize it.[14] In short, I would like to hear once and for all whether this famous excess is an effectively intrinsic law of the being [*l'étant*] or a *purely instrumental* (and therefore anything but "innocent," as Badiou says) anthropological projection onto the being: I am at the disposal of anyone who would like to discuss this.

Then, since the excess of representation is an ontological law for Badiou, and one of the other names he gives to this representational excess is the State, I would like to know how, say I, Badiou can only claim—with his stereotyped Marxism[15]—that the State can be abolished in the political order, since it is an ontological Law that thus applies eternally to every being, the sun as well as the earth, a black hole as well as a kitchen sink, and that hence there is not the slightest hope for abolishing the State anywhere. This is the case, by definition Badiouian, *except* (a miracle!), he says, *in the anthropologico-political closure!* Once again, I am at the disposal of any brave volunteer who would like to discuss and explain this to me. Because, evidently, the result is the complete negative of Badiolism's wobbly "construction": Nowhere is the State an ontological Law of any being [*étant*] whatsoever, not even animal; it turns up *only* in the anthropological closure. It is the monstrous maximization, across the communitarian organization, of its *singular* aptitude to re-present things by abstract divisions[16]... Henceforth the abolition of the State could only mean: to uproot the representational drive in us, extirpate the pleonectico-techno-mimetic root within. We might as well talk about birds without wings, or aphonic sopranos.

Finally, and because, on the one hand, the State is ontological, hence eternal, except, it seems, in the anthropologico-political exception that Badiolism ("inhumanism") precisely does not consider to be an exception, even if we all know—including up to the most well-informed—that, on the contary, the State is the crushing and omnipresent reality of our *mere* human being-there. I would like to hear someone say, knowing all this, what these could actually mean, these incessant considerations of Badiou's on the fact that there be an inextricable link between State, Representation, and corruption, what I call Evil; and this, even while Badiou, always in line with the metaphysico-dogmatic traditionalism, considers that Evil has neither being [*être*] nor existence, while at the same time thinking that almost everything is reprehensible, corrupt and, last but not least,[17] "nihilist." I beg the Anglo-Saxon reader's pardon for the convolutedness of this latter sentence, but it is the subject matter itself that is so, and not a regrettable writing defect on the part of its author (hoping the rest of the book proves to be the exact opposite for the reader). In other words, we see clearly that in Badiou corruption is eternal and universal, which is much worse than the Evil and Sin of Religions—which circumscribe moral corruption where it should be, in the human adventure—because, in Badiolism, it is an inextricable predicate of Representation, the eternal essence of the being of every being [*de l'être de tout étant*], even if, on the other hand, it does not exist. On the one hand, everything is corrupted, and on the other, everything is innocent; on the one hand, the State is an inexorable ontological fatality, on the other, we can abolish it tomorrow, in the sole anthropological closure.

In sum: I would like to know whether this compossibility of all these contradictory and self-refuting considerations are not the indication of pure and simple schizophrenia, and can drive the reader crazy as well, under the pretext of the most unassailable rationality which, according to its author, ever existed. In this case, perhaps the author in question should ordain "purifying" charity, starting with himself. Once more, placing myself most faithfully at the disposal of anyone who would like to sharpen the arguments to settle the debate, the question I ask is indeed the following: how can a philosophy that claims to be so *puritan*, namely fanatical on the question of purity and purification, can ultimately, fully in line with the most inquisitorial religious puritanism, end up seeing Evil, ugliness, and mediocrity absolutely everywhere, even while denying their existence on the other hand.

And it is on this point, under the sole pretext of the gigantic symptom that is Badiou—like Wagner in his time—that I could conclude the call for tenders, returning to what is formulated by the present chapter: the still "nice" hypothesis which says that classico-dogmatic metaphysics had been incapable of thinking Evil, hence its humiliating defeat against Religion, thus makes way for a "wicked" hypothesis. Classico-dogmatic metaphysics would in reality be much more *directly responsible* for Evil than supposed by the "nice" hypothesis of a semi-involuntary omission, conditioned by the professional atavism inherited from Plato: Badiou, with his fanatical will to stick to this classicism, furnishing the proof through *reductio ad absurdum* and schizophrenia: the omission of Evil would be both voluntary *and* innocent. Following the untenable speculative antiphrases we just reviewed, we come to a crude casuistic oxymoron: dogmatic classicism in philosophy, of which Badiou is the "giant" and colorful caricature, considers all in all that Evil is nothing but a *phase* [*passe*] on the way towards the Good (this is self-evident with the Hegelian dialectical machine). On this, I am in fact *very close* to agreeing with him.[18] But I cannot, because what I criticize, in the last instance, in the philosopher's originary gesture, is well and truly the *effacing of the traces* of the crime (something even Hegel no longer did exactly, not to mention Schelling and Hölderlin). Nietzsche said of Wagner that his deadly weapon was the "magnifying glass": "(...) one looks through it, one does not trust one's own eyes—*everything looks big, even Wagner*—What a clever rattlesnake! It has filled our whole life with its rattling about "devotion," about "loyalty," about "purity"; and with its praise of chastity it withdrew from the *corrupted* world.—And we believed it in all these things."[19] Each word here coincides disturbingly with what I experienced in my "Great Alliance" with the philosophical Redeemer of the German musician. Our contemporary speculative Wagner uses a similar magnifying glass, and blows the dogmatico-classical process of the effacing of traces to absurd dimensions never reached before. A speculative exponentiation, at the moment when it is *no longer possible* to obliterate the overwhelming proofs.

The crime, the Evil, resides not so much in the *fact* that it had been necessary to overbid on the crime which was not yet a crime (i.e. predation), but *well and truly* in the operation of obliteration. Thus dogmatico-classic metaphysics from then on will have to *answer* for its *direct* responsibility in the perpetuation of Evil: by the fanatical, let us dare say psychotic,[20] denial of the latter. This is what (with Badiou taken as the "magnifying glass" of the classico-dogmatic tradition of metaphysics) we thought had been expired since Kant and Heidegger. Plato could still obliterate "innocently" the fact that, in order to build the Acropolis, thousands of slaves had to be martyrized. Spinoza, who brought the principle of metaphysics, that of real necessity, to its peak, perpetuated the tradition in attributing all evils to an imperfect comprehension of the chain of causes, which disturbs the too nearsighted view of imperfect understandings upon the necessitarian perfection of God. This is in fact why Sade and Spinoza say strictly the same thing: everything is rational, hence necessary; Evil is not a concept of Nature. And this is also why, contrary to the clichés, it is not Sade but Rousseau who is a *philosopher* of Evil. In this respect, he is still the "Newton of moral philosophy," as Kant recognized in him. Sade sticks to a last referent, a principle, that the Middle Ages had already made extinct: Nature. It is this ultimate referent that Rousseau precisely caesures: what I call archi-transgression.

Schelling fissures the edifice even more decisively: if Evil is one of the proofs of freedom qua *human*, it is because it does not come from any real necessity. And it is on this point that the most recent, "Platonic" attempt at obliterating Evil turns out to be not only desperate and anachronistic, but, by a curious twist, in complicity with the capitalist ideology it claims to fight: on the one hand, obliteration of Evil by the Laws of "ontological" necessity, namely of the logico-mathematical,[21] which for the latter make death, torture, horror into simple cases derived from the universality of the concept, and hence non-beings [*non-êtres*] just as well; on the other, the Leo-Straussian ideology of the White House, Reagan, or Bush, which coolly explains to us that the injustices, inequalities, and finally abominations of expropriatory facticity are nothing but a consequence of the Laws of Natural Necessity. In our terms: it is said that *techne* is hardly more than an extension of *physis*, which ultimately changes nothing to it. As in Spinoza or Sade, facticity comes under necessity. The expropriatory injustice which arises from the technomimetic closure remains "Darwinian"; the strongest crushes the weakest; "the big fish eats the small," said Mao, saying the last word on his Idea of communism.

The fact will *always* remain that it is wrong. Man is the one who can *know* that the avalanche of expropriatory injustices and atrocities that poured down on earth because of his "fault" had in fact nothing irreparably *necessary* about them. That is why Schellingian freedom, which is *properly* born in its ability to do Evil, discovers *afterwards* that it is capable of Good.[22] An animal can by no means "surpass" predatory cruelty without self-suppressing himself. We could renounce exploitation, expropriation, torture, the atrocities without self-suppressing ourselves. *Evil is a non-metaphysical philosophical question, because it does not fall under any real necessity: it is tied to the contingency of the event of technomimetic appropriation.*

And under the invocation of the great negative philosophies born in the twentieth century, Benjamin and Bataille, Adorno and Blanchot, half of Heidegger and half of Derrida, Foucault and Lyotard, Schürmann and Lacoue-Labarthe, the only ethical question of coming philosophy should be the following: why does man, who *could* rationally pull himself out of suffering, in other words, who *already* can do it, not *want* to do it? Why does he waste his energy with trivialities, some theological, others metaphysical or biogenetic, for wanting to be more eternal, immortal, and infinite, and thus perpetuate the abominable sufferings, by turning away from them over and over again? The *ethical* superiority of negative philosophies over the most sophisticated positivisms and eudaemonisms lies therein: it asks *the right question*, recapitulated by Adorno: "Given the level of productive forces, the earth could here and now be paradise." *Here and now.* Then it really is these negative philosophies that hold the only stone of non-despair worth something on the edge of our century: because, unlike classico-dogmatic metaphysics whose "great" revival today is Badiou, they *know* that Evil is *by no means* an insurmountable fatality. But because, in the latter, the hallucinogenic deluge of "nihilism" comes to compensate this classico-dogmatic foreclosure of the question of Evil—including even in its "truth procedures" where the atrocious sufferings of Cantor, Gödel, or Grothendieck, of Schönberg or Beckett, of the originary erotic situation called "archaic rape," and of the fact that 90 percent of the "loves" in the world are but simulacra conditioned by social convention, and therefore sufferings that are in most cases gratuitous, and finally of course the monumental sufferings Mao and Pol Pot inflicted on their peoples in the name of their Good, appear to be nothing more than the negligible prices humanity has to pay in order for the comfortably bureaucratic Good of the philosopher to arrive—then the *spectacle* of the metaphysician, the tobacconist of the Good, who now has only to put his feet up on the *tabula rasa* and count the "eternal truths" like stamps, by nihilating the insane stock of sufferings and the *eternalized, non-necessary death* they cost, this spectacle appears finally as it is: as comical as little Wagner in his fuchsia silk dressing gown. Only for a little while did the magnifying glass manage to pass a mouse off as an elephant.

"Beyond Good and Evil" was not a triumphant conquest of Nietzsche's, but his final drama: because in lieu of this "surpassing" comes the insurmountable "nihilism." Which recapitulates well enough the SoN's undertaking: not to propose another surpassing, after two centuries of surpassings of all kinds involuted into "nihilism," "postmodernism," "spectacle," "simulacrum," parody, but: to think surpassing *otherwise*, to *live* it otherwise. Philippe Descola's great book of anthropology, *Beyond Nature and Culture*,[23] gets caught up in a similar impasse: he thinks to "prove," with the description of primitive cultures, unaware of the "western" caesura of Nature and Culture, that this caesura can be "surpassed." But the question is not even broached in this book; that is to say, Rousseau's thought, in terms of modernity, and, historically very prior to the latter, the Greek, and especially Aristotelian caesura of *physis* and *techne*. Every attempt at "surpassing" this "old" cleavage is doomed to failure, but why? Because *our* concept of surpassing thrusts its roots nowhere else but into this caesura. The caesura of *physis/techne* (hence: Good/Evil) cannot be surpassed, because *our* historial concept of surpassing *is this caesura itself*.

What the SoN shows, owing to the brilliant discoveries of Lacoue-Labarthe, is that the "modern" concept of "surpassing," carried by Hegel to its speculative perfection (see *Aufhebung*), was nothing other than Aristotle's *catharsis*, in other words, the mimetic operation that separates *physis* from *techne*. So when one claims to surpass this disjunction, it is always by means of this disjunction itself: and the squaring of the vicious circle always closes on its perpetrator, Nietzsche or Descola. The latter's design is praiseworthy: in a way, "ecological." He proposes, somewhat more than in-between the lines, to inspire us with all these primitive wisdoms in order to change our relationship to Nature. But in the end he only *irrealizes* the latter in a brilliant relativism ... *cultures who live on that side of the Nature/Culture caesura* think an essential continuity (for instance: animist, or hylozoic) between the two. He reproduces Nietzsche's impasse, who, with the concept of "nihilism," rediscovers, exactly as in the metaphysics that was supposed to be surpassed, a hopeless inflation of non-being in lieu of the appropriative "Good," which in Nietzsche functions as a kind of voucher of innocence, delivered with brand new consequences, to man's pleonectic rage. Where dinosaurs were, it seems, the "champions" of purely animal pleonexia, man is the dinosaur of spiritual pleonexia, meaning: of Spinozist *conatus* perverted by the technomimetic. Like Spinoza, Nietzsche wants to prove the innocence of *conatus* that is supposed to be universal, without wanting to know anything about the pleonectic perversion produced by the birth of man as such: technomimetic astuteness, the unthought root of the process of irrealization that classical metaphysics labels as negligible "Evil." When, according to Nietzsche, Geniuses and Tyrants should always and everywhere triumph without remainder, on the contrary, it is that which keeps the human pleonectic from resulting in a happy ending that triumphs: the *victims* of pleonexia and their strategies, the slaves (and the Jewish thought remunerates it according to Nietzsche), the losers, the weak: "nihilism." In other words, the same inflation of non-being that classico-dogmatic metaphysics dismisses as unreal "Evil," yet latent everywhere, in the dreadful becoming-nihilist of the world.

Thus, as proved a last time by the Badiou symptom and its overbidding on "nihilism" in lieu of irrealized Evil, "nihilism" actually was the very last, and the most sophisticated, of the ways in which philosophy irrealized Evil all throughout its history. Following Nietzsche and Heidegger, several generations of philosophers and writers would rack their brains in order to find the Holy Grail of the "surpassing of nihilism," and each time come back empty-handed. The solution was very simple: it was necessary to stop considering "nihilism" as a facticity, and dismantle piece by piece the mechanism whereby Nietzsche reconstructed the very question of Evil there where he thought he had eliminated it.

The views of Hölderlin and Benjamin, their embryonic, spectral philosophies of history, sent to us like bottles to the sea, allow us to do without the historial *thesis* of nihilism by Nietzsche and Heiddeger. There is no golden age, neither before, nor after, neither Roman, nor Renaissance, nor Belle Epoque. There is no Heavenly Jerusalem, no rosy futures, and neither is there a non-contradictory God. All ages have been wretched, all successes and "Civilization" have been constructed on the obnoxious ground of ultra-majoritarian existential failures and martyrdoms, and "barbarity" that is always denounced as the opposite of the civilized world, without being amazed at the fact that it arises *only in this world*, that is, in the anthropological closure. Then only disconsolation remains, Schürmann's, Lacoue-Labarthe's, or mine. Yet, even so, the energy that animates these philosophies, which *know* that theirs is henceforth the most urgent task of turning the concept against that which it is usually made to serve, the artificial paradise of the maximal Good, so that Evil is not perpetuated with too much impunity, holds the only true glimmer of hope. Despite appearances, only those philosophers are *not* desperate, for envisaging the situation in its epochal gravity, and for being the only ones to become aware of the means of escaping it at least partially. To limit the damage would be already a much more significant and ethically upright victory than to assign humanity yet one more time to the Promethean tasks of universal work for the Good, which will result in nothing but another case of collectivized enslavement.

This is why *The Spirit of Nihilism* is the only attempt at rising to the outrageous challenge issued by Schelling and Schürmann: philosophy must radically change its basis and priorities; if it wants to have the slightest chance of finally prevailing over Religion, it must take over that which the latter made into its *thinking* [*pensante*] area of specialty, Evil; it must do as did all the great metaphysics of normative foreclosure, from Plato to Badiou, including Thomas Aquinas or Spinoza, and put the positive universal at the bottom of the ladder, and singularity (for classico-dogmatic metaphysics, the trivial root of all "Evil"), at the top. It must propose as rigorous a phenomenology of Evil as the Platonic phenomenology of Good, or the Hegelian phenomenology of the spirit. To that end, it must deconstruct the concept whereby we obliterate the question of Evil: precisely the "nihilism" whereby we diagnose our age. I showed that when we go *all the way*, up to the utmost limit of the diagnostic resources of the concept of "nihilism," the concept falls apart: the essence of nihilism has nothing nihilistic about it. Contemporary "democratic nihilism" is nothing but the ultimate form—and hardly the most violent—of a much more immemorial question, which is the question of Evil.

We must say in conclusion: philosophers, make one last effort if you want to bring down both Religion and the "nihilism" of contemporary laicism at the same time (the two being dialectically complicit, as we see every day). Be truly brave, even sacrificial, in a word, heroic. Stop lazing around in the prescriptive, in eudaemonism, in more or less tempered utopia; following Rousseau, Schelling, or Schürmann, tackle the root of contemporary "nihilism," a question even older than the question of the "Good" of philosophy that arose from an error in diagnosis: the question of Evil. Thereby we would stop both selling false promises—the only point whereby we will have been the immemorial and ever submissive accomplices of the religions—and comforting ourselves. But we would, perhaps, contribute to avoid what these false promises, and especially the diagnostic errors that made them, resulted in: a definitive catastrophe, absolute and irremediable, which, for the first time in all History, has become an actual possibility, already happening before our very eyes.

Parody

PARODY: Parody, at its origin, is a *religious* musical genre. We might as well say, it is very possible that the contemporary triumph, not of the simulacrum, but of irony, is the sign of a *purification* of religion: of cult. Sexual compulsion itself has the structure of a *celebration* of the sole trait of *immanent* immortality that marks our body: biological reproduction. For this entirely rational and lucid reason, the sexual affect is the heart of all the anthropoid affects. The rest is metaphysical small talk, in other words, rash maximization of the pleonectic drive whose libidinal manipulation is, for man, the essence, and especially for a philosopher, even and especially communist. As we saw in the section on Desire (see above), for us sexual jouissance is a paradigm of "our" own pleonexia, and more essentially than alimentary necessity. This is because, unlike most other mammals, we can pervert this jouissance by all the convolutions of possible technological repetitions. When the professional metaphysician tells that his functionary work has nothing to do with jouissance, he admits that in reality he only ever deals with jouissance: his own, his singular pleonectic delirium raised to "the universal," without seeking the opinion of the future concerned ("entire humanity" he considers from his desk).

In the SoN, the word "aesthetic," for instance, should not be understood in the weak sense of a philosophical examination of art. It must be understood in the strong sense: a theory of affect. I am going to say something completely outrageous for which most of the metaphysical functionaries are not going to forgive me: orgy, debauchery, depravity, pornography are not bad but rather good things. They are a lesser evil, and there is good reason to prescribe making love, instead of war. Why? Because, originarily, *all* our sexuality has a parodic, in other words, commemorative, in other words, ritualistic and religious, structure. Religions themselves, if humanity does not self-destroy itself before that, will eventually understand and fade away by themselves: the "religions" called "nihilist" like sports, games, and technicized lechery, are *in their essence* more religious than religion. Religion will sooner or later have to confess the void that inhabits it since the very beginning: and the last priest's head will fall, when it admits that the *empty* parodies that humanity gives itself hold better than the "full" parodies of religion, in all its variations. Parody, in its "democratic-nihilistic" form itself, is a *participative* form of ritual. The Baudelaire of this "nihilism," Jean-Jacques Schuhl, illustrates this fact in his description of a Pink Floyd concert: "English bands are, first and foremost, bands. They are musicians only secondarily. Music serves as a pretext to do things *together*, and to say things *together*."[1]

The *mimesis* of the Inexistent is play. Play is essentially religious, whereas religion is not essentially ludic. This is why the one will eventually disappear, in favor of the globalization of the other.

Aesthetics is the regime whereby the technomimetic animal organizes its affects *collectively*. We saw that *play* (see above) was the inevitable form of a humanity getting rid of all supersensible recourses. Because man is originarily parodic being [*l'être*], he has yet to put behind him the metaphysical binarities which expropriate him from this parodic jouissance, maximizing the binarities produced by the event of appropriation (sensible/intelligible, immanence/ transcendence, fallen world/higher world, finite/infinite, etc.). The becoming-play of humanity is a reappropriative becoming, in a very precise sense defined in the passage devoted to the question (see above).

Our whole *being* [*tout notre être*], for better or for worse, is marked by the seal of parody. And all our affects are, through and through, parodic: this is what the thought of *catharsis* became aware of, early in the philosophical "rise." Because we are the originarily parodic beings [*êtres*], our own avatars, we are yet to reappropriate our own doubles, which are our sole originals, expropriated by the metaphysical spirit of seriousness. Because we will give ourselves the possibility of this reappropriation, we know already that there never was an age of the "spectacle," the "simulacrum," the "postmodern," nor even and especially not of "nihilism." Never did we cease to be the imitators of Nothing. To play is to know this.

Yes, art has long been alienated, because it was subjected to great metaphysical, i.e. representational binarities. Only play is the non-representational art dreamed by all the twentieth-century avant-gardes, who finally ended up running into the most originary of all art forms themselves, coinciding with the profoundest mimetic impulse to ever inhabit the human animal: the ludic impulse. Because play is art that is finally accomplished and destined to every human being without exception, and even—who knows?—to animals, it is the only livable political world that humanity can make, if there remains for him any chance of survival.

Provided that we add the following: play is also the art that is *as least representational as possible*. It is not at all non-representational. Every epistemological, political or aesthetic claim to abolish Representation (see below) leads only to disaster—and technological, political, and artistic disasters always communicate, at some point, around a common claim to having *abolished* all representation. Play will be the *minimally* representational art, for being the paradoxical *assumption* of the indelible anthropological fact that is *mimesis*, in other words, representation.

Politics

POLITICS: As we saw, the other, singularly animal beings [*étants*] cannot *will* [*vouloir*] and therefore are not *capable of* [*pouvoir*] their own repetition. The event that singularizes us humans is the event of the transappropriation of our own repetition: a repetition of repetition, technological *mimesis*, which hence produces the alchemy of a whole catalogue of upheavals of what is "imitated," in actual fact *transfigured* by this imitation. *Mimesis* is nothing other than *properly* anthropological, that is, techno-scientific repetition. The event "man" does not consist of a particularity of such and such characteristic organic features: it coincides, absolutely, with the mimetic impulse, the ability, unique in the entire known cosmic realm, to repeat repetition. To *fictionalize identity* [*fictionner l'identité*].

We might as well say that every appropriation is *transgression* (see below). The emergence of life is, always already [*d'ores et déjà*], a transgression of the "laws" of matter. In doubling the Laws of Nature by *mimesis*, we appropriate them. And such is our difference from our ontological congeners, the other appropriative beings [*étants*], animal or even vegetable. The latter, for lack of (self-)appropriating the laws of their own repetition, repeat *themselves* over very long periods of time, interrupted only by a change that is itself outside of their grip (a climatic upheaval, a genetic mutation, itself always taking very long to incubate). What happens when technomimetic appropriation, that is to say, the event of Science, the only event of which we are the decisive Subjects, occurs? We transgress these laws, in two senses of the word: in (self-)appropriating them, we dominate them; and we can "override." This transgression of the Laws of Nature is not necessarily an abolition of the latter:[1] the exponentiation of sexuality, which is a compulsive over-repetition of the instinct of … repetition, obviously does not abolish any biological law of procreation (even artificial implantation, contraception or biogenetic and clonic production by no means *abolish* the pre-given Laws of Nature): it "suppresses" them (parodically!) and preserves them all the same. More importantly: it *surpasses* them. In other words, it *creates* brand new Laws which, quite far from abolishing the old, *perverts* them and pushes them to the background. In the meantime, the operation always produces a *waste*, and such is Evil.

This emergence of *new* Laws is the birth of politics: that which *doubled* the act of the technomimetic appropriation of the necessary Laws of Nature and being, as soon as a primate discovered *repeating* the rubbing together of two flints. This means that this appropriation-transgression of the Laws of Nature is doubled, just as well and just as soon, by a new regime *not only* of Laws, but also of new *transgressions*. It is moreover these *latter* transgressions that everyday language means when it says "transgression": crime, blasphemy, madness, etc. In my conceptual vocabulary, the first understanding of the word "Transgression" more or less overlaps with its ordinary sense. It even sheds brand new light on the concept of what we have always commonly understood by "Transgression."

The "Laws" of politics are all supernumerary: having surpassed those of Nature, they become established in their lieu and stead, in order to organize (in one way or another) the human communities. The Laws of Nature, having been surpassed, that is, pushed to the background, all become agents of what is commonly known as Evil, the harmful, the diabolical, etc. Evil is born when I do in the face of the Law that which I automatically do prior to it. Natural laws, bloated by the appearance of the conventional "Laws" that overhang and dominate them, challenge the latter and become their literally *automatic* transgressions. The *thwarted* Laws of Nature take revenge for the sublation that scientific appropriation made them undergo. Besides, the cruelty and suffering that reign supreme in the animal kingdom are very probably, already, a "revenge" of the immutable Laws of matter on their biological sublation. Disappearance being the inevitable lot of every being [*étant*], whoever *accelerates* their being-there through transgressive appropriation, here the animal and already the vegetable, pays this appropriating acceleration by an acceleration of their disappearance: such is etiolation, drying up, extinction; such then is suffering, predatory cruelty, and death.

Politics is a parody of science, which delivers the negative truth of the latter, to which it has always turned a blind eye, with the complacent endorsement of philosophy. It wants to act "as" [*comme*] the shrewd discoverer, who equalizes the beings under the isomorphic regime of the Law he has (self-)appropriated. "As" the archi-scientist, which is already the one who rubbed the flints together or the first gardener, this Law *throws* the *singularity* (see below) that is appropriated, exploited by Law, outside the field of the exploitable. This is what gives the figure of the Tyrant, already found in embryonic form in the Scientist, at an earlier stage. But this is also what gives the singular Victim (pleonasm), at a later stage, the one being complementary of the other, as confirmed by the entire section of my work that constitutes a commentary on Agamben's admirable notion of *homo sacer*. This notion is discussed at length in the first part of *Ontologique de l'Histoire*; in that book I show how this notion communicates with the first Heideggerian, then Badiouian, notion of "evental site": the new event always comes from the discarded, the remainder that is singularized by an anterior event. This is the SoN's version of the Nietzschean eternal return: every event of appropriation produces a waste, a singularity not captured by the positive universal; it is always this waste that is the site of the next event; when the latter takes place, a new singularization takes place as well, which in turn will give the following event, etc., etc. This is the vicious circle of History, since it would actually seem that the *more* we go towards the appropriative event, the *more* we produce "accursed" singularizations, that is, waste. This is, by all appearances, what detains every historico-political teleology since Marx: we can no longer see an end to this process, an ultimate event which would redeem all of a sudden the set of the singularities "damned" by the archi-event of appropriation, the technomimetic, or the original sin of Religion, which promises that redemption. *Modern*, i.e. German philosophy, because it is a laicized theology, still promised, with Kant, Hegel, and its Marxist vulgarization, such a final Reconciliation; today, Badiou is trying to piece together a prescriptive philosophy of infinite and unachievable truths, a kind of teleology without teleology, and Meillassoux lays cards on the table: only a non-contradictory God can still save us. The SoN rejects these solutions, and proposes to look into the *roots* of the Evil that the species has self-inflicted on itself since it raised itself, parodically, above the other species. The stakes should be extremely simple: even though we could rationally abolish all sufferings, why and how do we still and again do nothing but find pretexts, metaphysically fantasized by our inveterate "pleonexia," to perpetuate them and make them worse?

Let it be said in conclusion: this one discovery of *The Spirit of Nihilism* alone leaves behind one of the most immemorial prejudices of philosophers, from Plato to Badiou, including Condorcet, Marx, or Althusser: for the "good" politics, the day it exists, Science cannot be of *any* use. Summoning any kind of scientific discourse in order to correct the "bad" politics by the supposedly "good" is the worst absurdity ever committed by philosophy. Science is the set of the appropriated laws of *Nature*. It is their *mimesis*. Politics is the set of the Laws *resulting* from this appropriation, *none of which* tallies by any means with scientific laws. Politics is, very possibly, the *parody* of the event of science and its "laws," but this fact precisely aggravates even more the fault of philosophers, for condoning this belief of all tyrants in a "scientificity" of their being-there: philosophers themselves also *parody* science *unconsciously*, in administering the rules of "good" politics *as if* it were a matter of science, and like tyrants very mistakenly believe.

As to art (see above), it is the *mimesis* of politics, otherwise more faithful than science could ever be, no matter how little: every collusion of the scientific and the political—and philosophy for a long time has been nothing else—*intrinsically* leads to nothing but disaster. Art's repetition of politics gives something else—which is precisely art. As anticipated by the most lucid part of twentieth-century philosophy, which is also the most "negative," Benjamin, Adorno, or Lacoue-Labarthe, it is in the questioning of the link between the "laws" of politics and the "laws" of art, as their reciprocal regimes of "transgressions," that resides the one and only chance of politics itself. The more you "harden" the *truncated* collusion of science and politics, pretending that the recourse to the first is the only panacea for the second, the more you play the pipe of Hamelin to humanity, pretending to want its Good. It is to the appearance of the scientific "Good" that we owe all political "Evil"—a pleonasm for the Son, needless to add any more. Yet this is what philosophy has almost always done. It is perhaps not too late put an end to the consequences.

Art has secretly always been the immense collection of preparations for the "*grande politique.*" Taking play as that which it has always been, the essence of art and its childhood, this politics could in fact finally emerge before us at the dawn of this century.

Now is the time for the discussion with a Master of mine, before Schürmann and Lacoue-Labarthe: Adorno, who, with his *Aesthetic Theory*, produced the twentieth century's most powerful philosophical reflection on art, much in advance of Heidegger for instance. This thought is still too little known not to become what it is: untimely topical. "Art that seeks to redeem itself from semblance through play becomes sport,"[2] he writes for instance. Adorno is the only one to have anticipated that art was unique in hinting at the utopia that politics could not fulfill; and that at the same time its modern self-destructive negativity was its ethical faithfulness. As long as the earth is not what it should be, paradise here and now, art must show both "the star of redemption" and its immanent abortion.

Representation

REPRESENTATION: Is it not high time we stopped telling fables? There is no representation except in the anthropological closure. Never does a tree come to represent another tree, a dog another dog. Everything in nature, and especially in the animal kingdom, considers itself, although "blindly," as completely *singular*. But because it is in full *possession* of its own singularity, the being [*l'étant*] outside science never becomes aware of it. Only science makes singularity aware of itself, in the mode of the pathetic: precisely because it is what science leaves as remainder (see *Science, Singularity*); expropriates, literally and in every sense.

The *Platonic* error of the twentieth-century avant-gardes was the compulsive desire "to have done with representation." This is why these avant-gardes ended up falling into postmodern parody, that is, the most deflationary form of the supreme form of the parodic called "play." The politically "revolutionary" will to abolish representation, which so often went hand in hand with avant-garde art, has hatched nothing but monsters. In a filmed discussion, Lacoue-Labarthe defines totalitarianisms as regimes which claim that their gigantic representational installations are not representational, that they coincide with what they represent. Moreover, no political regime is entirely exempt from this professional vice. And this is not the least aspect in which politics is a *parody* of Science: "like" science, but with very different means and outcomes, it claims that the (mathematical, logical, neurocognitive) representative [*le représentant*] coincides with the represented [*le représenté*]. Both ignore the *ontological differend* that fractures them immediately already in their technomimetic envoi.

"Art," says Lacoue in the same interview, "in other words, the *critical* distance with representation."[1] We will not surpass the death of the avant-garde and its artificial postmodern survival except through an *active* assumption of representation, our originarily-parodic-being. In other words, through play, in which the representational distance is both continuously maintained and continuously tempered by the fact that *everybody* takes part in it. Yes, Ducasse was absolutely right: poetry must be made by all, and not just one. The more representation is monopolized by one, such as the Savant, the Tyrant, or the Philosopher, who lays exclusive claim to the latter's legitimacy, and hence hypertrophies it in what was only recently still called "alienation," the more representation becomes the opposite of what it claims to be. The more it claims to stick to things and living beings, the more it moves away from them in reality, devastating them in almost always exact proportion to the distance that opens up as it is hushed up. On the contrary, the more representation remains *close* to that and those it represents, the more it will be conscious of the distance *in principle* that separates it from what it represents. It is this requisite that is fulfilled by the political utopia of play, already present among us, in an immanent manner, in all the actual games. Because each and every one fully takes part in play, only play is the aesthetical, hence destinally political form that is an assumption of the ontological differend (see below): a happy medium between representational accuracy [*justesse*] and distance with respect to representational being [*l'être représentatif*].

The Platonic Idea itsef, as Heidegger demostrated, is nothing other than the re-presentation of the being [*l'étant*]. It is this re-duplication, this schematic *mimesis* of the being (Kant will say: transcendental schematism) that is the pale copy of the always singular original, as such irrealized through the alleged universal archetype, and that, historically, ends up appearing *pathetico-parodic*. The SoN, by the deconstruction of "nihilism," urges us to make one last effort to pull out of Platonism: it is a philosophy of *mimesis*.

Singularity

Singularity: See *Science, Ontological Differend.*

Science

SCIENCE: The ontological differend, the absolute and universal principle of *inadequacy* of Science and what it appropriates, universalizes also the Hölderlino-Heideggerian style figure of "the further away it is, the closer it is." Translation: the more a science is said to be *pure*, the more its effects are impure; the more a science is impure, the more its effects are "pure." In order to clarify this point, I will cite an excerpt from an open letter I wrote to the young philosopher Tristan Garcia:[1]

At this point, I tell myself perhaps there is a rather extraordinary theory of knowledge that would have to be produced on the basis of a dialectics which would cross your two very strong theories of the compact [*le compact*] and the comprehending [*le comprendre*]. Besides, this is why I do not consider Badiou a dialectician. In this regard, for me the guiding, brilliant, recapitulating words come from Adorno: "Dialectical thought is an attempt to break through the coercion of logic by its own means."[2] And we are fully there. I really find it very powerful, the manner in which you basically "shift" the prohibition of self-belonging into a *radical impossibility of self-comprehension* [*l'auto-compréhension*]. That which would comprehend itself maximally (there is no self-comprehension except as tendentious [*tendancielle*], never absolute), such as the stone, the compact, would be *precisely* that which would appropriate the least possible something else, and would be the furthest from all "knowledge" [*savoir*]. The thing that almost absolutely comprehends itself, the compact, would precisely be that which would be practically incapable of comprehending anything else. *Then the thing capable of comprehending the maximum of other things would be the most incapable of comprehending itself, despite its claims* notably, the human thing. Here "Platonic fiduciarism" receives the deadly blow: Mathematical "certainty" is precisely never as certain as when it applies to that which is *furthest* from itself. This is moreover why the more a science gets "closer" to ourselves as object, as in the case of biology, or surgical science, the more it is hesitant, uncertain, groping, blurred, perhaps hardly-a-science. The prehensile (vegetable, animal), and then appropriative (cognitive, epistemological) being [*l'étant*] loses in self-comprehension as it gains in comprehension of something other than itself. Thus it would seem that you have laid out the basis of a spectacular reversal of the evental dialectics inherited from Badiou, on the basis of self-belonging. And besides this is the key of my own quietus: the "mystery" of self-belonging, of the event as "miracle," is entirely literalizable as a dialectics of appropriation. The Platonist, *for want of comprehending things*, takes refuge in the forms; he comprehends things only as forms; and first and foremost because he does not comprehend *himself as thing*. Yet this is the *banal* condition of the human thing, and precisely his singularity. The Platonist, through his tendency, is simply the one who does *not* want to know that man is—because he appropriates formally the maximum of things and hence comprehends them—the thing that pays the price, the price of being less and less capable of comprehending *itself*, of being compact. Yet again, I had felt that you attained something like a quasi-ontological theory of the uncon-scious. You told me you did not read psychoanalysis. What a shame! You should study Lacan's counter-*cogito*, which your theory (your *ethics*) of comprehension terribly reminds me of: "I think where I am not, therefore I am where I do not think." If you wish, I will find the seminar where he develops this most in depth, it would most certainly appeal to you.

Science is nothing other than the maximization of the pleonectic. Indeed, even the word "philosophy," for a long time translated somewhat syrupily as "love of wisdom," seems to have meant much more literally: "appropriation of knowledge." In other words, once again, this quasi-pleonasm is also the pure and simple synonym of the pleonectic.

It will then be said that the SoN, for being anti-pleonectic, is to be put away on the shelf of "anti-philosophical" accessories. But one would be wrong: the (evental-technological) archi- and hyper-appropriative essence of the human animal is not something to be "fought," otherwise we might just as well become one of those "anarcho-primitivist" philosophers who think that even the Neolithic Era was the beginnings of a long decadence, and that in short we must go to the Paleolithic, in other words, destroy every trace of technological civilization itself: return to its fossil. This somewhat manic Rousseauism is not ours. The SoN is not an "anti-philosophy" either, but the suggestion of a radical revolution of the *narcissism* whereby philosophy draws its ethical postulates. According to the SoN, the pleonectic as such is ineradi-cable from the being [*l'être*] of man (metaphysical Lutheranism). It attacks the philosopher's narcissistic foreclosure, whose very title indicates that he is, in a way, the "champion of the pleonectic." The tragicomic manner in which he gives big lessons on the best means of destroying every appropriative trace of the anthropological closure can therefore, historically, no longer be seriously defended: the meta-fairground spectacle that is the network of academic discourse contradicts every word pronounced therein. The SoN promotes the *assumption* of the pleonectic, a surpassing of capitalism, which does not picture itself as the final *suppression* (yet another "final solution") of the universal play of appropriation-expropriation that constitutes historical humanity as such. It fights the performative contradiction that philosophy has been to date. It wants to cure philosophy of its casuistic infantilism that has remained deep-rooted, until now.

Science produces a vertiginous alienation [*extranéation*] of the being [*l'étant*] which (self-)appropriates that which was not itself. There is an asymptotic logic, a yet coherent paradoxy of appropriation as logic of the impossible self-appropriation [*auto-appropriation*]. As I point out to Garcia, in terms of tendency, the stone is much more in (self-)possession of itself [*se possède elle-même*] than an animal wasting his being-there hither and thither, flapping his tongue around. But the logic lies exactly there: because the stone is maximally in *self*-possession of itself, what Garcia calls the "compact," it *self*-appropriates nothing that would be external to it, and therefore in the end does not (self-)appropriate itself either. The maximum of self-possession, "compactness," in the being-there, coincides with the minimal degree of pleonectic propensity. It is in this sense that Hegel's famous Lutheran saying, "only the stone is innocent," must be conveyed. Conversely, the being [*l'étant*] that comes out of itself, and thus (self-)appropriates that which is not itself, vegetable and then animal, paradoxically *ceases* to be entirely in "self"-possession of itself, in perfect blindness to this uniquely tendentious, never absolute "self-belonging" (a full self-appropriation would be the living contradiction of a God that would have nothing external to itself). Appropriation is all about expropriation. With specifically scientific appropriation, we may say that man appears to have come closer to the maximum a being is capable of, and, for this very reason, for the fact of (self-)appropriating what all the other beings are unconscious of, for the double infinity of space and time, he self-inflicts a dispossession that the other beings cannot know either. His purely material being-there is *crushed* by the insane mental alienation [*extranéation*] that is scientific knowledge, and he henceforth becomes the exact opposite of the stone: the maximally *expropriated* being, and he becomes so in the pathetic *knowledge* of this expropriation that costs him the positive knowledge itself of science, from the consciousness of cosmic infinities to universal Laws of Logic, from the consciousness of evolution and History to the quasi-butcher's-knowledge of his organic interiority as psychic: and there are no literal butchers among cats.

The material being-there vertiginously *relativized* by the exaltation of learned, i.e. expropriated appropriation is what the SoN calls Singularity (see below). Singularity is the being [*l'étant*] seized by science, which science makes into the particular of a universal. Hence, everything that is *not* included in the subsumption of the abstract universal is *as if it were not* [*comme s'il n'était pas*]. The metaphysical tradition for a very long time incorporated with blind confidence—fiduciarism—this processuality of Science. For instance, the third part of *Ontologique de l'Histoire* includes my "great" discussion with Hegel on this point. For him, singularity is literally *nothing* but the force of pure negativity destined to be reabsorbed in the play of the terminally positive Universal. There is a very strong intuition in this schema, but which is exactly like the other side of what I am trying to systematize. In my work, the singular is rather the "negative" that *falls* from scientific isomorphism which reduces the beings whose laws it draws to interchangeable particularities, as indifferent instances of these Laws. Concrete difference, scored out therein by the "positive" universal of science, hence transmutes into what the SoN determines as singularity: *negated*, and as such *negativized* difference. To say it in as demagogical a manner as possible: the Singular is the Difference that is purely and simply *victimized* by Science. The unbearable paradox, whose ceaseless defense is the cause of the whole tragico-horrific condition of the technological living being, is that without this victimization singularity would have never *appeared* as such. Art exposes it in all its purity; yet, without the primitive crime of Science, never would have art had at its disposal its somewhat primary matter, which is, as we saw, for this very reason quite often the Evil of a same movement.

Thus "negativity" should be understood in two senses here: not in the sense of a "dialectical motor" that implicitly considers every singular to be precisely nothing more than a particularity destined to be reabsorbed in the positive Universal according to a scientific model, but in the simplest sense of the manner in which the being *suffers* from expropriation. Hence "negativity" in this sense overturns Hegel's: it points to the above-mentioned "as if it were not," in the following sense: the appropriation of the isomorphic laws condemns the singularity subsumed by these laws to *non-being*. The singular is that which, of the different, inexists to scientific isomorphism, or isotropism. The being-singular [*l'être-singulier*] becomes a simulacrum, a semblance, the shadow of its "true" being said [*son « vrai » être dit*] by the "positive" universal of science. The pathos of this traumatized singularity is, of course, often the "motor" of events, but events always play for very high stakes by (self-)appropriating something new: always costing new expropriations. Therefore always new sickly modes of singularizations; such is the anti-Hegelian dialectic of the SoN, and such is also its version of the eternal return. History is the squaring of this vicious circle, whose dialectic is unfolded entirely in the *Algèbre de la Tragédie*. The SoN asks whether we are capable of pulling ourselves out of this historical vicious circle (awakening from this nightmare, Joyce said): appropriation of the universal=reduction of the beings to subsumption which makes them into the particulars of a universal=production of singularity as waste, expropriatory negativity of the immemorial anthropological process of ferocious appropriation.

Be that as it may, the original epistemological consequence necessarily follows: the more a science is appropriatory, such as logico-mathematics, the more it is expropriatory; the less it is appropriatory, such as medicine or biology, the less it expropriates. In other words, the more a science is pure, the more it is impure; and the more it is impure (empirical, approximative, etc.), the more it is pure. The more it applies itself to the near (medicine and biology again), the more the near proves distant; the more it applies itself to the distant, such as mathematics or mathematized physics, the more it *deceptively* makes near the distant. The universal self-evidence of appropriated laws is blind to the singularity martyrized in the meantime. It is this illusory eidetic transparency, obtained by the most violent appropriative *mimesis*, that great metaphysical maximizations feed on, often with delight, and with the most obscene impudence.

The SoN is not opposed to science, even if it reminds that with Rousseau, Nietzsche, and Heidegger[3] a new relationship is established between the latter and philosophy. The philosopher no longer genuflects, through atavistic reflex, before the eidetic transparencies of science, whose fundamental opacity is revealed by the nightmare of history. But to simply and purely fight science, as the "anarcho-primitivists" do, is to redouble what one is fighting, inviting the species to immediately commit suicide, precisely what science has historically prepared it for. To uproot man from his fundamental epistemic, i.e. technomimetic impulse, is still to dream of clearing him of all pleonectic "malignancy." It would be to reproduce the oldest casuistic illusion of the metaphysical functionaries. The SoN simply invites philosophy to think its relation to Science *otherwise* than in simple paradigmatic admiration. It insists, here as elsewhere, on the necessity of a healthy *critical* distance.

Techne

TECHNE: Once again Kubrick's movie is our modern Odysseus, as its title promises. An ape grabs hold of a bone and makes it into an instrument: it is the dawn of humanity. As Jean-Clet Martin[1] writes, the animal

> gets directly in touch with an environment and introjects its givens as if in order to negate them by devouring and contest the distance that separates them. The dog eats the meat almost without chewing it, destroys immediately whatever gives him appetite without either delay or deferring the satisfaction. There is no stepping back for the animal; a grain is the invitation for swallowing it up. No bird could wait to see it sprout. (…) The cow (…) is entirely determined by the green of the grass, it lives only for that and, as a result, its passive existence remains purely thingly: a natural life, aimed with all its might at a natural object, the grass. This hunger could never be satisfied in that always yet another clump of grass will arouse it again on the endless path of an inexhaustable infinity. The animal dies without having touched itself, having brought forth a new herbivore that chases after the same grass according to a cycle impossible to close.[2]

Which is why life is actually the *first* stage of appropriation; but because the latter is solely *ontic*, it does not get out of the circle of immediacy and hence does not know the expropriatory gigantism that characterizes the anthropological, i.e. techno-scientific stage of appropriation. In other terms, there is no politics, that is, no exponentiation of the play of appropriation/expropriation by representation. Save for the "possession" of territory, which always depends on the physical *presence* of the "possessor" or "possessors," animals do not double this *play* of appropriation/expropriation through the representational cut. I can possess a land while being perfectly absent, and this faculty alone deserves to be called "representation" (see above). For this very reason, the animal world expands neither in historicity (in time) nor in geoplanetary and cosmic consciousness (in space).

The animal directly devours the grass; whereas man breaks this cycle by (self-)appropriating *the being* [*l'être*] of the grass. "Instead of devouring the seed, he plants it; he suspends his instinct of self-preservation and does not throw himself on the earth's produce,"[3] like the animal or the Master who, with the slave's produce, acts like an insatiable animal. It is only later that the archaic *techne* of the simian tool or of representational repetition that makes food gathering into agriculture becomes "pure" science.

Let us make it clear: *techne* dialectically constitutes the moment of the *materialization* of *mimesis*. The latter is an empty repetition. We would have to wait for an incubation period of only a few thousand years, with the appearance of logico-mathematical sublimation, for this emptiness *in its turn* to become literal and material, closing the loop. This is why Aristotle is more crucial than Plato, that is to say, he is both more lucid and more useful. If *mimesis* were not *materialized* into *techne*, it would remain an act of consciousness among so many others, meaning: among those countless others that, beyond all doubt, fill the heads of other animals. If in these pages you see the "high road" of an infinite debt of Hegel to Aristotle, it is because only Hegel, in near modernity, truly overturned Platonism by instituting ceaselessly the proceedings of the Idea to the court of its effectiveness, *or non-effectiveness*. Platonism's henceforth *conscious*, and for this reason unforgivable, trickery is that it knows that all its prescriptions, just like in the original version, are destined to remain *dead letter*; or else can really mortify, on the the pretext of "true life," "eternal truth" and "immaculate immortality." If the SoN, to a large extent, consists of an encyclopedic revisitation of the Hegelian concept of *aufhebung*, its archaeology digs up the remains of the concept never mentioned by Hegel, and which Heidegger will mention for him: *techne*. It is the name of Hegelian effectiveness, but such as empirically accessible to everybody. If, as the SoN pleads following Lacoue's discoveries, *aufhebung* truly is a meta-Aristotelianism that is unaware of itself as such, in other words, a combination of concepts which Hegel does not mention much by name, i.e. *mimesis*, *catharsis*, and *techne*, in a stunning anachronism we will see Hegel clarify Aristotle in return: Hegelian effectiveness translates *techne*; the rightly famous and universal mediation (or representation, see above), *mimesis*; and finally the famous surpassing, *relève*, or sublation translates *catharsis*.

The Differend with the absolute Master of modern philosophy[4] becomes clear exactly on this point. The Hegelian *aufhebung* is what "lifts up" [*relève*] difference in order to lead it to identity. The *aufhebung* as reworked by the SoN demonstrates that it is a fictitious operation of identification, a technomimetic appropriation, which produces difference (see *Mimesis*).

Transgression

TRANSGRESSION: Ours is the age which shows that the whole of anthropological experience is under the sign of transgression, and not of legislation. Philosophy, with the exception of Bataille, Foucault, Schürmann, and myself, is lagging much behind this obvious fact. And again as religion suspected, this originary transgression which I also call "archi-transgression" is nothing other than scientific appropriation that doubles things in order to take anthropological appropriation to both trans-historical (consciousness of the Big Bang, the accretion of the earth, its possible dissapearance, etc.) and cosmic-geoplanetary dimensions (complete "trustization" of the planet, including sea depths, spatial conquest, etc.).

Now, we should be aware of a literally crucial detail where the SoN's whole contribution is perhaps concentrated: it is that "*transgress*" has the same etymological root as "*transcend*" that is so dear to philosophers since Kant. Having said that, I almost have the impression of having said it all, and that I could pick up the SoN's whole undertaking in a Heraclitian fragment, or in a haiku which says "only" this, which says absolutely all. This sole consideration drastically clarifies the *tragic* overdetermination which makes the "natural metaphysician in us," and which a great majority of professional metaphysicians want to know nothing about. It is because the human animal is that which transcends the given by science that the appropriation of the laws of nature has an essentially transgressive structure, that transgression *then* becomes the essential reality of the world's anthropological age (after the age of "pure" matter, and the age of non-technological life, not appropriated by science).

For instance, and as it has become commonplace to observe, in sexuality, fundamentalists of all kinds are absolutely *right*, and not wrong, to observe in horror that the sexual life of the human animal is essentially a "transgression of the Law of Nature." Their only mistake, which nobody ever says anything against, is that they are not *less* in this Transgression than the adulterous, the sodomites, or all the "deviants" they want to cast out. And this is one of the crucial points that my philosophy turns upside-down: it shows that the supernumerary laws governing anthropological coexistence are nothing but the "masks"—the *semblance*—of Transgression. Hence the whole overturning, which seems to do more than just emerge in my undertaking, to which I subject the treatment of the question of semblance and parody. *It is first of all Law that parodies Transgression and not the other way around.* The appropriation of the laws of nature by science unleashes such a potential of violence—and this is the political *fact* as such—that man feels the necessity to transgress these laws *in the second degree* by "doubling" them with "laws" not inscribed therein. This is why the transgression *of* these laws by the rebellious, the rascal, the sexual deviant, the artist, etc., has been historically recognized as a fundamental reality of the anthropological situation—as disturbing as it is ineradicable. Art, starting with Sade, makes these rejects of humanity into heroes, and philosophy will have to wait for Bataille, Foucault, and Schürmann in order to probe what this unprognostic heroization was all about.

Indeed, this was one of the SoN's "eureka" moments which, in the same way as the diagnostic of the ironic era, merely drew an obvious fact that did not weigh lightly on the mental landscape of a whole generation—at the very roots of every "nihilist," "postmodern," etc., sentiment. It is that, since Sade, art has overwhelmingly been the art of a heroism of Transgression, unprecedented until then. A teenager who grows up reading Sade, Baudelaire, Lautréamont, Rimbaud, Bataille, Artaud, Genet, Burroughs and many others, enters the world of literature—and art in general—taking for granted this categorical imperative of "transgressive heroism," born almost a century and a half ago with aesthetic modernity. But he very quickly realizes that the era of transgressive heroism had indeed entered the *parodic* mode decades ago. There are still a few creatures who seem to believe in the discrepant virtues of Transgression in the first degree, but they are in general somewhat pitiful. The age of heroic transgression certainly died with the assassination of Pier Paolo Pasolini, the last "holy transgressor." The part of the *Ontologique de l'Histoire* called "La forclusion, le vide et le Mal" analyzes this historiality in depth; *Algèbre de la Tragédie* coins the adjective "pathetico-parodic" in order to characterize the "postmodern" age of the deflation of transgressive heroism in art; and finally *Inesthétique et Mimêsis* lays out the foundations of a new thought of the links that *originarily* tie Transgression to Parody, in the era of the transgressive become auto-parodic. As with irony (see above), a seemingly "poor" age turns out to be much more interesting than it itself believes to be. Blindly, but it is to this blindness that philosophy always restores sight, the identity of the transgressive and the parodic *overplayed* by contemporary aesthetic "nihilism" is in fact a *find* [*trouvaille*].

It unconsciously formulates the following: Transgression is in fact *primary*, and is confused with scientific transcendentalization *as such*. The appropriation of the Laws of Nature and being are a transgression of those laws, a surpassing-preservation-excretion. This appropriation institutes a regime of new "laws," inexistent to Nature and being, which are the "rules" of civic life, what we generically gather together under the title of "politics." It is solely in this sphere of—literally *secondary*—rules that emerges a regime of "transgressions" precisely inexistent to Nature and animal life. These are all the phenomena brought together by metaphysics under Evil, and all our greatest artists since Sade have erected their paradoxical dithyramb. The great heroes of artistic Transgression are, from the onset, ironists. They were already *parodying* art, until then dictated by metaphysical solemnity, by handing their lyre over to what the latter considered as the most repugnant, by putting the Prostitute in the place of the Muse, the appalling and self-interested Crime in the place of the nobly sacrificial weapons, ugliness in the place of Platonic or Kantian beauty, etc.

We saw that ocular reflexivity was the animal proto-stage of mimetic appropriation. What singularizes technological *mimesis* whose artistic document has always been the critical commentary of "misfortunes" (as Sade would have said!) is that it doubles appropriation *by the void*. The simply animal, ocular *mimesis* is a "full" appropriation of that which is reflected. Whereas technological *mimesis* is an appropriation as it were *by the void*.

Then, in conclusion, the title of our little lexical book, *Transgression and the Inexistent*, becomes clear. In transgressing the material existent through the appropriation of its transcendental Laws, in transcendentalizing, in other words, purifying and voiding in eidetic forms, the material existent through appropriative transgression called Science, man *introduces the void into the world*. The appropriation of the transcendental Laws of the being [*l'étant*] is the transgressive appropriation of an Inexistent. The SoN does not seek to act original. It thereby, in its own manner and within its own capabilities, revisits a glorious backbone of metaphysical modernity since Kant and not before (that the latter should be the promoter of one of the most saturated adjectives of philosophical history that succeeded him, i.e. the "transcendental," has obviously nothing fortuitous about it). "Man introduces nothingness into the world"; this has already been said, and brilliantly, by Kant and by Heidegger, by Hegel and by Sartre, by Schelling and by Bataille, by Nietzsche and by Blanchot. The SoN says it again, its only pride consisting in saying it otherwise. The essence of my polemic with Badiou is that the latter, for the first time, says black is white, resurrecting Plato as he wishes, in a manner beyond all decency. Only the idea becomes real; the constituted, which is the *purely anthropological* intromission of the void in the world, the metaphysical invention par excellence, becomes the constituent. This philosophy acts *as if the void had always been there*. The sentence, "(O)ntology, therefore, can only count the void as existent"[1] entails the gravest consequences for the coming philosophy if it adopts it without further examination. The strictly "political" swerves of its author are nothing but a symptom—besides, superficial—of the manner in which his indubitable genius has recapitulated the criminality inchoative with respect to metaphysics as such. The whole question consists in knowing whether this vast recapitulation should be read as envisaged by its author, in the right way around; or completely in the wrong way. It is not difficult for honest readers to understand why I eventually ended up opting for this latter solution.

The Spirit of Nihilism: the deconstruction of this concept, in Nietzsche and Heidegger, consists in asking, especially, to Nietzsche: *what would become of us without the introduction of the* Nihil *on earth?* Nothing. Nothing of what Nietzsche promotes would survive a very hypothetical "interdiction of nothingness." There is no "nihilism" because, taken literally, the "nihil" is not a bad, but a good thing. We must admit, it is also a catastrophe, *the* catastrophe incumbent upon us with respect to what religion, better than philosophy, thought as "original sin." Nietzscheo-Heideggerian "nihilism" is a psychology of decadence that must be rejected once and for all. The only serious question that remains is all those phenomenological modes in which this void is *materialized* catastrophically. It is all those forms recognized as those of Evil. This question is old and serious, but in another way than the question of "nihilism" (see above).

Why did the modern artist, *including* its "postmodern" version, make a sarcastic, provocative, paradoxical praise of Evil? The transcendental laws appropriated by science are *empty*. The attestation of this void consists of the political "laws" that realize it: these are conventional laws, out-and-out empty, but this void is *chosen*, as Kant realized it first. The Laws of Science are the laws of a *necessary* void, whereas the Laws of civic life are those of an *arbitrary* void. The modern artist made praise of the criminal, the blasphemous, and the rascal, because the latter, through their transgressions, *reveal* the both transgressive *and* parodic essence of Law, *every* Law. Their "arbitrary" acts simply respond to the arbitrariness of civic Law itself. Whereas Science and the complicit metaphysical functionary sublimated this appropriation of Nothingness into "ontologies" in charge of the purging of singularities; the civic Transgressor, the criminal, the blasphemous, or the rascal constitutes the return of this singularity to the very inside of the metaphysical closure that is *literalized* as rules of civic coexistence:

originarily iniquitous politics. The artists told us that the *illegalities* committed by the "reject of humanity" are not *more* so than the legalities instituted by civic coexistence; the latter *eventally* necessitated by the devastating overpower with which technomimetic appropriation endows man. But then crime is not less of an event, which speaks volumes on the eventalness of science itself, and its consequences. Moreover, "legislation" could very well have been a term of the SoN's fundamental lexicon. To save it means to emphasize that Transgression, in what touches the "ontology" of the technomimetic animal, prevails by far over all Legislation, whether scientific or political; and in spite of the original metaphysician, it is art that has always seen this better than anything.

Ontologique de l'Histoire meant: how every event, in other words, a Transgression that is each time transformed into what is called a "transcendental" since Kant, *is phenomenalized*. Every event is a phenomenon that can be shown; its result, appropriation, is not so, and it is a new ontological and judicial Law; but this transcendental is phenomenalized in its turn, becoming something other than an ethereal transcendental. Take the most simple and solid example of original sin, the archi-transgression that founds man, and gives the absolute transcendental called Science.[2] This is what I called, perhaps somewhat too pedantically, "ontological," which I must admit is a contraction of the two moments of Badiouian metaphysics: being [*l'être*], the onto-, which becomes appearing, identified with pure logic. How does the scientific transcendental phenomenalize itself afterwards, how does the technomimetic approriation of a transcendental Law regulate itself? By definition, not in the form of the transcendental, but in the form of something which is no longer Science at all, but Politics: this is how the first of "our" events, archi-transgression, is phenomenalized.

On this point, the hostility towards Badiouian neo-Platonism cannot be more complete and more argued. *The Spirit of Nihilism* refutes that politics can be considered as independent from Science, which is the meta-autistic case with "modern" Platonism. Even Plato himself had the good taste of not thinking that way. Art, love, science, the Law, etc., are all regions that permanently communicate with each other. If psychoanalysis, but already libertinism and courtly love, today sexual liberation and pornography, discover new things on eros, and even and especially *create the new*, in Good as in Evil, in this domain, it is extremely easy to show that this is because of the tectonic slides in our ontological vision of the world, in the grip of the each time-specific scientific and technological upheavals. It is easy to see how the invention of photography turns the history of painting upside down, and a little bit later how the invention of cinema drastically changes the whole history of art, but already the invention of the camera obscura in the high time of the Great Masters, notably the Flemish. Piero della Francesca revolutionizes the entire history of painting *through* his properly *mathematical* work. However, "modern" Platonism claims, despite all evidence to the contary, that all these domains (science, art, politics, love) never interfere with each other. They idealize a given field, the Idea of Art, and they cook up from scratch a form of Sacred Invariance of this Idea throughout the ages—and *the* concrete arts. On the contrary, I call "philosophy" the one and only discipline of thought capable of thinking these interferences. It is perhaps nothing other than the description of the *play* of these interferences.

There is not an iota of reason to return to the Heideggerian diagnosis of a metaphysics accomplished definitively by the age of technological gigantism: the Nothingness appropriated by science and sublimated by metaphysics is *monstrously* literalized therein.[3] The crimes of civic right are literally *nothing* next to the automatic criminality perpetrated each second by the *parodic* automatism of the technological and technocratic, i.e. metaphysical, Leviathan. The transgressive appropriation of the Inexistent is accomplished in what it always was; the monstrous expropriation of the existent. Yet our age is the first to have the means of *knowing* it, through a knowing which is no longer that of metaphysical yes-manism, the eternal mimetic ancillary of transcendent positive science, the immanent result of which is political calamity.

Schürmann said there were two fundamental approaches to the philo-sophical vocation: either to see the other of the visible, or to see *otherwise* the visible. Ethically, the two kinds will never agree; to dramatize professional hostilities means it is never enough to insist on the gravity of the stakes philo-sophical work is *responsible for*—or blindly irresponsible, precisely for selling relentlessly a transcendent alterity to the visible. This age is, *to the naked eye*, the one where micro-transgressions rise to the surface on all sides of civic life, in order to blame the most originary and buried truth of the metaphysico-historical adventure: causing the edifice of "ontological" legislations to collapse before our eyes, the collapse of "civic" legislations being nothing but a derived case of the latter.

Such is the one and only challenge that lies ahead of the coming philosophies.

Appendix

Propreptic to *Being and Sexuation*[1]

What will lead Deleuze very quickly, well before his encounter with Felix Guattari, to take an interest in schizophrenia, which he endows with a quasi-ontological dignity, is his thought on masochism, a thought still very much marked by psychoanalysis. In *The Logic of Sense*, he will write, "In the beginning was schizophrenia."[2] Without a profound understanding of what Deleuze put forward on masochism in his *Masochism*, we cannot really understand his thought on schizophrenia. This is one of the things the present book, *Being and Sexuation,* gives account of: a discussion with Deleuzians about the root of Deleuzism, the root of schizophrenic ontology that is Deleuzism, the root that constitutes his reflection on masochism.

Deleuze, in his *Masochism*, does not yet have a polemical relation with psychoanalysis as he will have later, and he does not yet speak of schizophrenia. We might even say that this book is imbued entirely with psychoanalytic—in particular Lacanian—vocabulary and categories; to such an extent that Lacan will not hesitate to tell his students that the best book ever written on masochism is the one by Deleuze, and that no psychoanalyst has been able to match him on that. Therefore this book needs to be read exactly for what it is, that is to say, strictly as a book of psychoanalysis, *the* reference-book of psychoanalysis on the question of masochism. And without a profound understanding of what masochism signifies for Deleuze, we cannot truly understand the heart of the matter in his quasi-ontological thought of schizophrenia.

What is one of the clinical criteria used to qualify schizophrenia? Well, psychiatrists often say that the schizophrenic, who happens to be a woman most of the time, "suffers" libidinally from never being able to make a distinction between her desire and jouissance.

Now, what is Deleuze's theory on masochism in *Masochism*? Within the limited time of this lecture, it is impossible to entirely go through a book as subtle as *Masochism*. But let us try to summarize the broad lines, those that will lead me to my aim. Deleuze tells us that the operation carried out by the masochist is first of all essentially ironic. The fact of choosing a Mistress for himself is a trick, a construction. From the psychoanalytic point of view, and not insignificantly, the ironic operation of the masochist primarily consists in undermining the stereotyped *topos* of psychoanalysis, in other words, the super-egoistic predominance of the Father figure, by putting in its place the figure of the Mother. We can say that, in the masochistic imaginary theorized by Deleuze, and a few years before he defines his ontology as "crowned anarchy," the masochistic imaginary is somewhat the "crowned Matron." For the masochist, the Mother becomes the Superego, whereas for the average neurotic, it is always the Father.

To what end? To the end which Deleuze then needed in order to "ontol-ogize" what will later become the mainspring of his philosophy, which is a philosophy of desire, like that of his reference-Master, Spinoza. Unlike the sadist for instance, whom Deleuze analyzes at length and with a certain respect in this book, and who invests all his "libidinal economy" on the side of jouis-sance, the masochistic operation, says Deleuze, consists in leaving jouissance offside, deferring as much as possible jouissance—in the most trivial sense of ejaculation that ends the process—and getting settled in desire, that is to say, in phantasm.

At this point it should be noted that this is phantasm in the masculine sense of the word: the more a man gets settled in desire to the detriment of jouissance, the more he gets settled in phantasm: besides it is in his seminar *The Logic of the Phantasm* that Lacan will pay homage to Deleuze's theory of masochism. Lacan will say years later that to account for phantasm such as it functions in the woman is much more difficult, and that its logic is other than man's. This latter logic is in a way algebraic: the more a man gets settled in desire, the more phantasm grows. It is in this growth of phantasm that the Deleuzian masochist voluntarily places himself, for putting off for as long as possible the moment of jouissance. The libidinal economy of the sadist, for instance, by no means obeys a logic dominated by phantasm.

So we see here the production of what will become the ontological categories—in libidinal economy alone—of Deleuze's accomplished philosophy, for instance the category of the plane of consistency. The masochist is the one who makes his desire into a full desire, a desire that becomes more and more intense as he, with the help of his Dominatrix, manages to put off the moment of jouissance. The masochist is the one who, by putting off jouissance indefinitely, turns his desire into an intensive plane of consistency, a field that is intensively full, traversed by increasingly subtle, fantastical differences. This field cuts across two known terrains at the same time: the terrain of philosophy and the terrain of psychoanalysis. First, the masochist is the one who returns to chastity so often promoted by philosophers through other means. Spinoza, Deleuze's reference-philosopher and the philosopher of full desire par excellence, was the chastest of men. This detail is not without significance. Later, this will be one of Deleuze's leitmotifs against psychoanalysis: contrary to what psychoanalysis tells us, Desire lacks nothing; it is not affected by lack.

But there is a chiasmus here, in that Deleuze remains much closer than he would have liked to a certain psychoanalytical doxa: how come that, according to this doxa, Desire is affected by lack? Well the answer is, precisely, phallic jouissance. Thus Deleuze joins a certain contemporary discourse of psychoanalysis, which we shall call the discourse of right-wing psychoanalysis, and which is set up against certain supposed acquisitions of the May '68 movement, that is to say, the pornographic civilization of all-for-jouissance [*tout-à-la-jouissance*]. I cite below what Deleuze will say much later:

> There is nothing more revealing than the idea of a pleasure-discharge; once pleasure is attained, one would have a little calm before desire is rekindled: there is a lot of hatred, or fear, of desire, in the cult of pleasure. (…) Desire does not have pleasure as its norm, but this is not in the name of an internal Lack which could not be filled, but on the contrary by virtue of its positivity; that is, of the plane of consistence that it traces in the course of its process. It is the same error which relates desire to the Law of the lack and to the Norm of pleasure. It is when you keep relating desire to pleasure, to the attainment of pleasure, that you also notice that something fundamental is missing. (…) courtly love implies tests which postpone pleasure, or at least postpone the ending of the coitus. This is certainly not a method of deprivation. It is the constitution of a field of immanence, where desire constructs its own plane, and lacks nothing, any more than it allows itself to be interrupted by a discharge which would indicate that it is too heavy for it to bear. Courtly love has two enemies which merge into one: a religious transcendence of lack and a hedonistic interruption which introduces pleasure as discharge. It is the immanent process of desire which fills itself up, the continuum of intensities, the combination of fluxes, which replace both the law-authority, and the pleasure-interruption. (…) [in the masochist assemblage] the organization of humiliations and suffering in it appear less as a means of exorcizing anguish and so attaining a supposedly forbidden pleasure, than as a procedure, a particularly convoluted one, to constitute a body without organs and develop a continuous process of desire which pleasure, on the contrary, would come and interrupt.[3]

All this joins—only less unpleasantly—the discourse of those I call right-wing Lacanians against our post-pornographic civilization, and its push-to-jouis-sance [*pousse-à-la jouissance*] aspect which, to hear them, would have absolutely lethal effects. There is a book that came out a few years ago, which I do not like at all, and which was called *La pornographie ou l'extinction du désir*. If you experience too much jouissance, you put out desire, and hence you die spirit-ually. This is the secret affinity that links Deleuze to his supposed psychoanalytic enemy. But after all, this discourse which equates the compulsion of jouissance with death had existed for a long time, and it was the discourse of religion, notably monotheist and notably Christian religion.

I therefore pass over the fascinating and subtle details of the Deleuzian theory of masochism. Very quickly, after having given this lecture, I started asking myself a question: very well then, jouissance, pleasure-discharge is put off indefinitely by the masochist or the courtly lover in order to fill entirely his desire's plane of consistency. The less one experiences jouissance, the more one desires, and gets settled in the delights of phantasm, it seems coherent. But after all, is this not a matter of a *topos* confined to the masculine position? Such was the question that would put me on track. In fact can this *topos* of jouissance as the interruption of desire be applied to the losing side [*l'autre côté du manche*]—as Lacan would have said with his somewhat gangster-like cheeky humour—that is to say, to the woman's side? At first it is on a very trivial, empirical level that I asked myself this question, thinking about women I had known more or less in the biblical sense, it goes without saying. Let us ask women if for them jouis-sance represents the point of interruption of desire. The least one could say is that we will leave them, in their overwhelming majority, perplexed.

Contrary to the psychoanalytic snobbish contempt for empirical sexology surveys, I read quite a lot of sexology books, and, whatever the place or the time, the reported observation is as overwhelming as a secret of Polichinelle: at least a good third, and in certain surveys they say two-thirds, of women never attain this famous jouissance; what they call frigidity. Hence the problem of a great majority of women does not really seem to be to produce, according to Deleuze, a full Desire by putting off constantly the moment of jouissance, but much rather, to reach it in one way or another. The secret of Polichinelle says they do not always reach it, not even often. Then we can say just like that, very quickly, that woman would be the agency—pathological even—of desire, like the hysteric of psychoanalysis who is so often frigid too, whereas it is man who would articulate everything around jouissance, including in its suspension, as in the case of the masochist. But of course this simplistic dichotomy would not satisfy me.

The Deleuzian *topos* of a jouissance which would dialectically be the enemy of desire, for interrupting it automatically, is a masculine *topos*. On the woman's side, this *topos* seems to be ineffective. Then this reminded me of a rather nasty joke made by two very activist and militant lesbian friends of mine whom I am very fond of: "Heterosexual coitus. You know: when man tries not to come, and he cannot, and when woman tries to come, and she cannot either."

Such is Deleuze's so to speak "feminist" response: so that the man finally manages, in a way, not to come, well then, ironically he has to submit to the Woman, to the Mistress; and this is exactly the masochistic operation which, besides, leaves intact the question of knowing whether the Mistress, for her part, eventually manages to reach something, and in which mode. That she finds some satisfaction in it is indubitable, the entire question consisting in knowing what the nature of this satisfaction is. In all of Deleuze's philosophy of maturity, there would be much to say on the consequences of such a primary decision, but I remain on our aporia. The masochist reaches full desire by being slave no longer to his jouissance, but precisely to the one who should give it (jouissance) to him, and who opportunely prevents him from doing it: the woman becomes Dominatrix.

On the losing side, on the side of the woman, the mystery of it all does not remain less intact. Here after all we touch upon a problem psychoanalysis has stumbled over all its life, as Lacan summarized in the seminar *Encore*:

> The plausibility of what I am claiming here—namely, that woman knows nothing of this jouissance—is underscored by the fact that in all the time people have been begging them, begging them on their hands and knees—I spoke last time of women psychoanalysts—to try to tell us, not a word! We've never been able to get anything out of them. So we call this jouissance by whatever name we can come up with, "vaginal," and speak of the posterior pole of the uterine orifice and other such "cunt-torsions" (*conneries*)—that's the word for it! If she simply experienced it and knew nothing about it, that would allow us to cast myriad doubts on this notorious frigidity.[4]

"Experienced it *and knew nothing about it*." Psychoanalysis had started off from the mystery of hysterical symptoms, where it discovered the unconscious, only to end up in an absolute abyss concerning whatever could be known about feminine jouissance: from one unconscious to another, as a novelist would say. One thing is certain: Deleuze and his theory of full desire implicitly supposed the psychoanalytic theory of castration, that is to say, phallic jouissance as desire's point of interruption, as the sporadic hole of the lack, of the void, in masculine desire. Obviously, this was null and void in terms of the feminine position. The woman not only systematically fails to reach it, and therefore does not need to defer jouissance in order to produce a full desire for herself; but, moreover, it well seems that she does not know much of this jouissance, at least as far as Lacan is concerned. It is even probably why Freud discovered the unconscious not on the masculine, but on the feminine side. Even if only for this reason, psychoanalysis is not outdated, since it looks like we still do not know much of feminine jouissance, and in spite of all the outcomes of sexual liberation and mass pornography, we are still swimming, in this respect, in an ocean of ignorance [*inconscience*].

This is, very roughly summarized, where I was. How to get myself out of this mess? It is at this point that would intervene the Rousseauist dimension which has almost always determined the decisive turning points in my philosophical path. In the strict sense of Rousseauism: meaning, the text that founded our political as well as philosophical modernity, the *Discourse on the Origin and Basis of Inequality Between Men*, which caused so much babble and was so much caricatured, even while it would lead on, like a dark clinamen, to the French Revolution, as it would to Kant's transcendental or to Hegel's negativity. Philippe Lacoue-Labarthe will say straight out that in this text we witness the birth of something like *transcendental negativity*. Against the caricatures that have been made to this day of the state of nature in man, it must be kept in mind that Rousseau says extremely little about this state itself. "I ventured some conjectures," he says. What interests Rousseau is the caesura by means of which man "leaps" over the state of nature, through technological, or in other words linguistic, astuteness, in order to "found" all our political problems, in respect of the unnatural foundation of private property. It should never be forgotten that in Rousseau, the state of Nature is founded only negatively. What holds him back in this text is by no means the animality forsaken by the cultural caesura, of which we will have nevertheless kept the inexplicable image of the good savage merrily hopping about in the open air, doing no harm to anybody. The animal origin is scored out negatively, in order to explain positively how we pass to the state of culture, that is to say, to the *fact* of political expropriation, of the existence of private property in the one and only anthropological closure.

Lacoue-Labarthe: "Man's animality is not really what holds Rousseau's attention. In the order of the narrative, or the conjecture, the whole thing is quickly dispatched with."[5] The animal in man is simply defined by Rousseau as the animal of the satisfaction of need; what will interest him is this leap over need which will define, in a way, Culture. It is this trifling remark which will found very quickly Kant's transcendental reflection, as well as Hegel's dialectic of negative origin. Later, we will have recognized what will precisely differentiate the reflection of a Freud or a Lacan from the reflection of a contemporary of Rousseau's, namely Sade, who considered the worst possible sexual acts of violence as simple effects of Nature. Rousseau straightaway talks about what psychoanalysis will later talk about: namely, a sexuality detached from the sphere of need.

This is how I proceeded in order to get myself out of the mess caused by the aporia of desire/jouissance such as incompatibly applicable to the two respective sexuated positions of the state of mammalian nature on the one hand, and the state of culture on the other, where things will be, if I may say so, *queerified*.

Secondly, it is at this point that a slightly cruder and more literal Rousseauist aspect intervenes. I not only officiate outside the university, but I have also lived a long time in the country: so my Rousseauism has something of a little "art brut" about it, closer to the caricature it is so often made into, actually. Let us call this, "philosophy in the bousoir."

Being therefore accustomed to a peasant proximity with all sorts of mammals, with all my philosophical and psychoanalytical categories in my mind, as well as the aporia that kept on bothering me, I thought about what I had always observed of what is called "rutting" in animals. Like Rousseau, I began prudently, "I ventured some conjectures," a kind of hypothesis on the state of nature, on all these mammals such as I observed them, a hypothesis that gradually became the central "libidinal" thesis of my book: that, in the animal origin from which we are cleaved by language, what is called Culture, a pure negative assumption like Rousseau's, in that state to which we have access, precisely, only by virtue of being cleaved from it, in this animal origin, there is evidently no sort of difference whatsoever between jouissance and desire, on the—not feminine but—female side.

The adjective sounds violent. The thesis is itself violent in its initial formulation: the so-called "mystery" of feminine jouissance, upon which even Lacan threw in the towel, is explained all at once by the "Rousseauist" founding operation whereby we will lay down that at the origin, right at the pre-linguistic biological originarity, as to what concerns the rutting of mammals, that there is not the least difference between desire and jouissance on the "female" side. It is a matter of a one and the same libidinal "substance," as it were. This was the Rousseauist hypothesis. In the state of nature "ventured" by pure hypothesis, it really seemed that there was no difference of any kind between desire and jouissance, when such and such a female mammal is on heat.

So here is what happens, and the sort of concepts you come up with, when you pass your time milking cows rather than studying for master's degrees: you venture, at least hypothetically, that the "secret" of feminine jouissance that remained hermetic for so long is precisely something other than jouissance: it is a perfect identity of desire and jouissance.

I therefore dare use the adjective "female," which doubles the violence of the thesis by the violence of what can be called our semantic unconscious. Such is the violence my hypothesis—put in these terms—produced at the beginning, especially on my female interlocutors, but also on men gallant enough to ask me—for instance, that journalist from a famous fashion magazine—whether I did not in that case reduce woman to her animality, when it is a matter of the exact opposite; therefore, the violence of the hypothesis itself, which is doubled with the so to speak unconscious violence our vocabulary is charged with. A sort of semantic misogyny that historically weighs upon the entire idiom which serves us to speak of sexuality. If you say "male," nobody feels anything pejorative whatsoever. If you say "female," we see all the inappropriate connotations rush to the wicket. For instance, years ago, an advertisement said: "Whatsit Perfume: Very male. Very good." Let's imagine an advertisement that says: "Whatsit Perfume: Very female. Very good." An MLF lawsuit is assured.

For instance, it took me a year to explain this thesis to my companion, a phase which was not without violence because of all the semantic sedimentations that pejoratively connote our glossary on the subject and proves that we will need to make still more effort in order to really be feminists. But after forty-five minutes of violent abreaction she began to understand, and from then on everything went well for the best of couples in the world. Besides, it happened very close to here; it would appear that the place inspires me. Let us call this, the "clinamulm."

Not woman but female, since woman is precisely the animal of language cleaved from her situation of being animal. We also notice that—and it provides a sort of simple Rousseauist matrix to what psychoanalysis called castration—that it be after days of playing and chasing, when the male finally achieves his aim, that is to say jouissance, the rut is interrupted for both. In other words, the sort of trance that takes hold of the female for days on end is interrupted with the ejaculation of the male. As to the male, he does not display desire like the female does during the rutting period. Heat is a jouissance for the female, not for the male. Most often, as far as a good mujik like myself could observe, the female seems not to experience any pleasure during the coitus itself. On the other hand, it is for days on end, during what the behaviorists call being on heat, that she seems to experience a quasi-continuous jouissance. And besides it is hard for us to imagine adapting this situation to ourselves, namely to the anthropological closure, except in the imaginary, or this space of phantasm whose logic Lacan, as well as Deleuze, explained so well. And of course the whole point is there: There is no woman on heat, except precisely by way of the misogynist metaphor, inflated by the pornographic imaginary. Yet we find something of it here. How? At this point I take the liberty of making another citation, not from an accredited thinker, but from a very thinking writer, and someone Lacan appreciated tremendously, namely, Philippe Sollers:

> A friend of mine, she said to me: what is good with a woman is that it never stops. The negative aspect is that it is a matter of an exhausting and posses- sional activity, like a death which would live on. Rubbing is under censorship, very well, and it is not I who invented excision, the issue of vaginal jouissance still remaining an interrogation mark. As to the clitoris, we can be absolutely sure of what happens there, and as to the rest, a word to the wise is enough. There too, to me it seems indispensable not to lie anymore and to underline the enormity of simulation in these flusters. It is funny how very few men are aware of this. All this is passionately hidden. Utter confusion reigns. I yearn for a thinkable historical moment when we will be able to say things that have never been said, especially on simulation. On the other hand, what cannot be simulated is clitoral jouissance. That it should be a positive thing for a woman, there is no doubt about it; but that it should also be extremely worrying for the metaphysical surveillance whose object is women, there is no doubt about that either. Men in general are unaware of the simulacrum, which means that there are stakes of power that are never analyzed. They imagine they should get there, and get there quickly. Most women complain about this when you listen, they don't understand why men panic like that in order to penetrate them. I ask you, why should penetration be compulsory?[6]

It is precisely in order to avoid this supernumerary obligation of coitus or penetration that this "elegant solution" was invented, says Lacan: the solution of medieval courtly love, or masculine masochism, precisely those libidinal "forms of life" that will be promoted by Deleuze. And just as Deleuze, in his *Masochism*, interrupted a cliché which was common even in psychoanalysis, that is to say: the cliché of a sadomasochistic complementarity which, thanks to this book, we discovered—even in psychoanalysis—to be nothing but fiction; which is also to say: that the masochistic position should be considered for itself and not with complementary reference to the sadistic position, which should be considered in its autonomy as well; likewise, in my work, I myself have been insisting for a long time on the fact that we should separate, against a common "progressive" cliché, the gay and the lesbian, and do this precisely in light of the question of penetration. In the masculine homosexual universe, penetration happens to be practised statistically much more often compared to the average so-called male heterosexual; conversely, the bulk of the statistics on lesbian practices consists of an avoidance of penetration, except for very specific singulariza- tions—think about the joke made by my two friends. But this is precisely what singularization is. At the very heart of so-called sexual "minorities," there will be sub-minorities in which such and such gays will define themselves by the avoidance of penetration, and such and such lesbians by the outbidding of this with so many gadgets.

Within the same chain of reasoning, I will talk a little bit later about something I strongly emphasize in *Being and Sexuation* as well: the absolutely radical difference in nature that separates properly feminine masochism from the SM of masculine masochism. All this to say that, in this instance, there is something indubitably "Deleuzian" in my method, or in other words, Bergsonian: you take binary lines, differences in nature between man and woman, masochist and sadist, gay and lesbian, and you cross them, which gives the differences in degree that will singularize, irreducibly, each and every one of us. In his reading of Bergson, Deleuze will insist that in immanence there is nothing but mixtures. For instance, if you cross the masochist line with the feminine line, you will get something altogether different from when you cross the masochist line with the masculine line. Between the two masochists, there will be nothing but differ- ences in degree (the violence and the radicality of the practices, from a light stroke of the strap to fist-fucking, etc.); but if you add to this the qualitative- somatic line of "man" or "woman" you will again have a difference in nature: masculine and feminine masochism will be as disconnected, as irreducible one to the other, as what Deleuze would prove with Lacan's assent: there is no more "complementarity" between sadistic and masochistic positions than there is, in Lacanian theory, between castrated-phallic jouissance and feminine "jouis- sance." This is why it is not called complementary, but "supplementary."

In the given time of this lecture, neither will I have the time to talk duly about something that holds an essential place in my work, and which I owe to a brilliant discovery by Philippe Lacoue-Labarthe: Hegel's famous *aufhebung*, the operation of suppresion-preservation sustaining the dialectics of historical progress, is nothing but an unconscious translation—and which happens to come unconsciously, from Rousseau—of Aristotle's *catharsis*. Aristotle's *catharsis*, which qualifies the only aesthethic operation of Greek Tragedy, consists in suppressing while preserving, that is to say, in transforming, through dramaturgical imitation, the affects too painful to undergo in real life, Terror and Pity, into positive affects, not to say affects of jouissance. In Tragedy, the originarily painful affects of Terror and Pity become affects of jouissance: they are therefore suppressed in their "natural" painfulness, and yet remain preserved, since what we feel before the peripeteias of Oedipus or Antigone is still well and truly Terror and Pity. Suppression, preservation: we will have recognized Hegel's famous *aufhebung* here, and Lacoue-Labarthe shows that Hegel takes it from Rousseau, who took it from Aristotle's *catharsis*. Hegel extended Aristotle's uniquely aesthetic *catharsis* such as to encompass all sectors of human activity: technics, for instance. Yet Aristotle himself, who invented the concept of *techne* in the sense we understand it, had not thought of applying *catharsis* to it, whereas needless to say technics is that which suppresses nature while preserving it. Technics is nothing other than the *catharsis* of Nature. For example, the very well known Aristotelico-Hegelian schema, the more or less pertinent link between Aristotle and Hegel: the wood of this table is suppressed as the natural wood from a tree, and yet preserved as wood. Hegel extended this processuality such as to include all sectors of human activity, except for sexuality perhaps, which was not fitting at the time. For this we will need to wait for Freud. Now, what is Freud's unconscious? It is indeed something which suppresses while preserving. For instance, in my book I elaborate quite at length on the respective manners of the hysteric and the neurotic in the clinical cases enumerated by Freud in his *Five Lectures on Psychoanalysis*: the manner in which the hysteric suppresses the memory of the sexual trauma which she nevertheless preserves in its symptoms—a preservation which thus makes her what she is, that is, hysterical; and the manner in which the masculine neurotic suppresses a trauma and preserves it at the same time.

It is fascinating because Freud's talent for observation is exceptional: he shows you that the hysteric forgets everything about traumatism concerning its strict, empirical factuality; the only "memory" she has of the trauma is precisely the memory of the totality of the symptoms that mark her body, like a hieroglyphics that gives the account of the trauma in her stead. The analysis is precisely what will lead all this to reminiscence, what will draw the verbalized account of the trauma that is buried in amnesia by the threshold of hysterical consciousness, but that her unconscious spells out on the surface of her body through the uncontrolled violence of the symptoms. Freud is still more precise: he says that in the hysterical body, the only thing which truly "remembers" the trauma is its affect. She suppresses all conscious memory of the anecdote, but preserves it entirely as affect, and that is the unconscious; in any case, it is for this reason that Freud discovered it on the side of women rather than men, even if, once the discovery was made, he realized there was not less of an unconscious in men than in women, and we will see very soon how.

Thus Freud claims that in a way, as much as consciousness has forgotten everything about the crime scene, the hysterical affect remains *strictly the same* as in the moment that the traumatic events took place, precisely because the hysteric has forgotten the totality of those facts. Now, as regards the masculine neurotic whom Freud calls the obsessive-compulsive neurotic [*névrosé de contrainte*], it is exactly the opposite. A neurotic, even severe, almost dangerous, like the famous Rat Man, a masculine neurotic, is someone who remembers absolutely each and every fact that constitutes the trauma; he even remembers too much, and that is what makes him obsessive, but he has *emptied out the crime scene entirely of his affect*. What the masculine neurotic has suppressed entirely is the affect, and what he has preserved is all the rest, in other words, the cold verbalization, the falsely detached account of the trauma itself. For him, the work of analysis will consist in recovering the plenitude of the affect on the couch. That is why, when an obsessive neurotic starts crying in his analyst's office, it is rather a very good sign, a sign of recovery.

The "mystery" of feminine jouissance obeys the same logic of suppression-preservation. If my negative "Rousseauist" hypothesis is correct, and if we rethink about what Sollers' girlfriend said—"what is good with a woman is that it never stops"—we can say that woman is, libidinally, the one who suppresses her animality while preserving something of it. There again, we stumble upon the Hegelian *logion*: man is defined by the preservation of what he himself negated.

What is animal rutting? We know nothing about it, except through what a good mujik like myself can externally observe, certainly more often than urbanites like yourself. It is an identity of origin, as they say; and, as monotheism knows as well, we have no direct access to the origin, we have nothing but a myth, the myth of original sin, that is, the mysterious collusion of science and the libidinal: the tree of knowledge, the apple that Adam ate, at the double insti-gation of Eve and the mysterious serpent. Man is the mammal separated from his animal origin by science in its broad sense. That is why there is no way he can get back to this origin except by way of parody. Our whole sexuality, even and especially in its most extreme forms, is marked by the seal of parody, that is, the repetition of that which we have lost. That the talking mammal should also be the mammal of sexual compulsion, this is because in repetition we commemorate, we compulsively try to reach something we have lost for good. This is what monotheism called, with the well-known consequences, "original sin." If my bucolic-metaphysical hypothesis or what I call the "Rousseauist mujik's hypothesis" is correct, then the "mystery" of feminine jouissance is what preserves the originary animal identity of desire and jouissance, at the very point where and when it suppresses this identity. In our view, this preservation-suppression is almost always done in the form of parody.

Now this is what is shown, in every possible way and from every possible angle, in pornography for example, in so-called standard, hetero-normal pornography, the sort of films they show on Canal + on Saturdays at midnight. What is it that we see in these shows? Well, precisely, women who come [*jouir*] = desire constantly, waiting for what constitutes the principal jouissance in these sorts of films, the phallic jouissance that puts an end to the man's desire. Yet we know very well that this jouissance overacted by the professionals of the sex industry, as dear Marcela Iacub would say, is not a true jouissance, and neither is the desire with which this jouissance is mimetically identified. However it is this masquarade itself, this semblance, which gives us millions and millions of images showing the same thing: women paid to act out, right in the middle of real coitus, the ecstatic identity of desire and jouissance, which is the truth. And, as in the natural matrix of mammalian mating, everything ends up with phallic jouissance, on both sides. At the heart of pornographic imagery, we find glorious phallic achievement. This is psychoanalytic theory become literal, just as in the artistic domain, mass pornography is Sade becoming literal.

As Lacan said in a crucial speech he made in Rome in 1975, it is always semblance that runs the show. Semblance does not dissimulate truth, as a commonplace philosophical trend would have it, for instance the "Platonism" reactivated by one of your eminent elders. Semblance is not truth itself either, as a more recent platitude of an anti-Platonic postmodernity would have it. Semblance is the inalienable condition of truth, precisely of the truth we have lost. The talking mammal that has lost all possible comprehension of what rutting could be finds it again precisely by parodying it. There is a commemorative aspect to all parody because initially, in the sixteenth century if I remember correctly, parody was a musical, that is to say, religious genre. Semblance produces the anthropological truth by compulsively commemorating what it has lost. For instance, the truth of our sexuality: pure cultural, voluntarist, supernumerary artifact of the supposed "natural" sexuality that we have lost. We do not know what animal rutting is, but it is by repeating it to no avail that we produce the entirety of our sexuality, for better or for worse.

And this is the case for both the scoring and the losing side [*des deux côtés du manche*], as dear Lacan would say.

What I am saying here will indeed end up disrupting [*mettre à mal, ou à mâle*] the primacy of phallic jouissance, something Lacan bravely reminds us as well in a passage from his 17th seminar:

> So then, let us try here to give body to this notion by another abrupt statement that I would ask you to note is central to Freudian theory: there is no happiness except from the phallus (*il n'y a de bonheur que du phallus*). Freud writes this in all sorts of ways, and even writes it in the naïve fashion which consists in saying that there is no more perfect way of approaching enjoyment than the masculine orgasm. Only what the Freudian theory puts the accent on, is that it is only the phallus that is happy and not its bearer, even when, not out of oblativity, but out of desperation, he brings it to a partner who is supposed to be in desolation at not being herself the bearer of it. Here is what psychoanalytic experience positively teaches us. The aforesaid bearer, as I express it, struggles to get his partner to accept this privation, in the face of which all his loving efforts, his little attentions and tender services are in vain, because they reawaken the aforesaid wound of privation. (…) This is very exactly what is revealed to us by what Freud was able to extract from the discourse of the Hysteric. It is starting from there that it can be conceived that the hysteric symbolises this primary dissatisfaction.[7]

This is what we can start to question, despite the respect we still maintain for the courage of truth showed by people like Freud and Lacan. For, if what psychoanalysis calls castration complex, a sort of metonymic ressentiment of the hysterical woman, this repetitive centrality of phallic jouissance, evidently exists, it would still need to be explained why it is on the side of what Deleuze calls becoming-woman—and not only in masochism—that so many men seek a sort of supplementary jouissance, an intensity, which the classic virile position, mere phallic jouissance, does not seem to be able to provide them. We can see a sort of object testimony in the fact that there are a lot more transsexuals who start from a biologically masculine origin to end up as woman than there are cases in the opposite direction; even in phenomena of transvestism—without insisting on masochism—the trend is, statistically speaking, very clearly in this sense, and not in the other.

For psychoanalysts, especially Lacan, the hypothesis on the subject oscillates between the following: there exists an other, supplementary jouissance, the feminine jouissance which we do not know much about but which we can surround [*cerner*][8] by a kind of asymptote; and then there is the pure and simple nihilistic assumption of the inexistence of any feminine jouissance, which would be in any case the equivalent in intensity of phallic jouissance. This is what, in his pessimistic moments, Lacan gives us to understand anyway: feminine jouissance, all things considered, is a matter of hysterical semblance alone. If we provisionally accept this extremist but not entirely incredible hypothesis, if we remain on this object lexicon, well then we would still have to explain why so many men so willingly renounce the all-risks-insurance of phallic, virile, indefinitely repeatable jouissance, and go looking for an exit permit on the side of this other, supplementary jouissance—Lacan insists on the adjective "supplementary" and not "complementary"—that is, the supposed feminine jouissance surrounded by mystery.

This is the dark zone my thesis perhaps helps to shed light on, re-examine. For instance, Lacan thus assumes that we cannot say much about this jouissance, but that we can at least surround it, approach it: we will see that, somewhat unlike the object lexicon, being not exactly a matter of "jouissance" in the sense imported by phallogocentrism, this metaphor of "surrounding" [*le cerne*] is fitting: in other words, the form of feminine libido—feminine, in the sense of the animal of the second sex, as Simone said, affected by language, namely woman—is structurally *asymptotic*. It is on this point that my book concludes. In mathematical terms, feminine libido is topological, whereas masculine libido, modeled on the clear and distinct cleavage between desire and jouissance, is an algebraic libido. Feminine libido is the infinite approximation of a forever lost identity of desire and jouissance. Masculine libido is the ever-renewed repetition of a finite algebra that leads from desire to jouissance which interrupts and empties out everything, before setting off again for a tour around on both sides. Besides, this is the logic of the sadist: compulsive algebraic repetition which gives us—rather than the heroes delighted with their crimes as depicted by Sade—the obsessive-compulsive neurotics crawling on the couches. This is also why the masochist like Deleuze, who perverts the virile algebra by placing himself in the asymptote of a desire which defers jouissance infinitely, at the same time places himself in the topology of what Deleuze will call: the becoming-woman.

Now, as I mentioned above: feminine masochism, once again, has strictly nothing to do with such a *topos*. Here too, perhaps even more than anywhere else, the stake involved for the feminine masochist is not to defer as much as possible this jouissance which would interrupt everything, but rather to the contrary, *to reach it*: with bondage, for instance, a sophisticated manner of being tied up and subtly beaten in order to reach orgasm, or else by other, more brutal means. This is why in SM there is a fundamental notion of "forced orgasm" which, as if by the greatest coincidence, is ever only applied to feminine somatic subjects. So there too we see a radical disjunction in the "nature" of feminine and masculine masochism. And it is through the de jure infinite crossing of the diverse para-Bergsonian "lines in kind," man/woman, gay/lesbian, sadist/ masochist, etc., that we arrive precisely at this "proper," irreducible, unique, unexchangeable nature which is the nature of each singularity resulting from these combinatorics.

For, one of the consequences of all this is a question of fundamental importance to my entire undertaking: the question of singularization. Feminine libido, literally and in every sense, is singularized according to a range of possible differentiations much broader than man's, at least of man in what he assumes as "normality." Lacan said that the "normal" in sexuality, especially concerning the animal of language, meant strictly nothing, except for the phantasm of the "nor-male" [*nor-mâle*].

The range of singularizations related to the becoming-woman is therefore much broader than that of the "nor-male." As we know by memory of Polichinelle, this goes from frigidity to the most extreme and uncontrolled jouissances, passing through many intermediary stages. One day, needless to say in which circumstances, a woman said to me something which had really struck me then: "Just now, I'm half-coming" [*je mi-jouis*]. We cannot really imagine a man saying something like this, say, in an adult movie at the moment of ejaculation. This is why much later Deleuze will say that no becoming is possible on the side of what he calls the empty transcendental of white, western, heterosexual man. Singularization is always on the woman's side, because the summit, nirvana, or all the synonyms you like, is exactly the opposite of singularization: it is the identity desire=jouissance such as we lost because of language, because of semblance in which we commemorate all this. And all this to such an extent that even when a man wants to singularize himself, it is to the side of becoming-woman that he turns, like Deleuze himself through masochism. The identity desire=jouissance, for being lost with the caesura of language, is diffracted so to speak, beyond this caesura, in the literalized parody that constitutes the entirety of our sexual practices. This originary identity forever lost as such, turns all "feminine" libido—whether one be man or woman—into an infinite asymptote towards the recovery of this originary identity. [And it is precisely because this asymptote goes towards an identity, although it is condemned to being an asymptote, that it is always singularizing. Conversely, it is because masculine processuality is always aligned on the repetition of the simple difference of desire and jouissance, that it always leads back to the *empty* principle of identity.]

Here we have a possible formulation of the libidinal thesis developed in my book. Where masculine libido, originarily, before accessing language and for instance the libidinal economy of a masochist ascetic according to Deleuze (masochist ascetic is perhaps a pleonasm for "philosopher": Lacan said historical Stoicism was a politicized masochism), follows the teleological and therefore algebraic *topos* of a desire oriented towards an outcome, that is, phallic jouissance, well then the originary form of feminine libido would rather be an intensive asymptote, which approaches more or less the supposed originary state of pre-linguistic animality, which is also the state of a perfect identity of desire and jouissance. Moreover I am so very convinced by this point that, to talk like Derrida, my whole intention is burdened by the "phallogocentricism" of metaphysical language, meaning: even the act of writing the equality of desire and jouissance is uncalled-for; we would need another word. I mark this sign of equality in order to say that, in my eyes, there is only one libidinal "substance" in the feminine position, and not two. In the end it is as simple, that is to say, as complicated, as that.

The becoming-man, for its part, always ends in what psychoanalysis calls castration. This can be verified very easily by examples of queer sexualities lived by women of biological origin who undertake a becoming-man. Of course, there too we find fascinating processes of singularization, but always much more limited, less colorful, if I may say so, than the becomings-woman. This is, without a doubt, what was meant by one of Lacan's most controversial statements: everyone, man or woman, who loves women is heterosexual.

This is what my thesis could actually help to shed light on. If feminine libido is really what I say it is, the topological approach, the intensive asymptote of the negatively assumed state of nature—drawing inspiration from Rousseau's method—we understand why Sollers, who is well-versed in the subject, might give away the secret of Polichinelle: "with a woman, it never stops." If her libido originates in a state of nature where it is during rutting that she desires and comes [*jouir*] indistinctly, and if it is coitus that happens to end this supplementary "jouissance" of psychoanalysis, whereas this same coitus is, conversely, a kind of "consecration" of jouissance for the man, then Sollers' precious remarks are doubly relevant. This is moreover confirmed by all sexology books: the overwhelming majority of women reach orgasm by solitary or "assisted" masturbation, and often—here too the secret is very well kept—by "rubbing" which, Sollers tells us, is "under censorship." I remember a woman who confessed that she had the most intense orgasm she ever had by rubbing herself against a chair. This in no way means that women never take pleasure in coitus; but that, here as elsewhere, this pleasure is learned, that it is a cultural construction. Woman, being originarily topological, learns to enjoy something that belongs to the domain of algebra, all this depending also very often on what is called the "partner." Just as on the other side, on the side of becoming-woman, for instance masculine masochism, or courtly love already a millenium ago, proceeds in the opposite direction: there man experiments with a topological economy of sexuality. Whatever they say about it, it is actually because of our situation as talking animals, our ability to pass virtually from one sex to the other, that it is only amongst us—and precisely owing to science—that there can ultimately be transsexuals, literally. Being the good mujik that I am, I have never seen a bull become cow for instance, no more than the other way around. It will happen perhaps, and it is even sure to happen one day, but precisely thanks to, or because of, our scalpels and our hormones.

II

So this is how it goes for the libidinal thesis, resumed too quickly. It was already complicated enough like this, even if enriching in terms of the very numerous phenomenological results that can be obtained by the application of my thesis.

Yet here I am feeling the need to complicate things once more, by importing them to the domain of metaphysics. This time it all began far away from the rue d'Ulm, in a posh contemporary art gallery in Switzerland, owing to another invitation in 2006, which dragged me out of my retreat and my manure baths in Perigord. The theme was "acceleration," the somewhat—I must say—cheesy theme of the technological acceleration of all things, and therefore of obsolescence, of the age of the precarious which constitutes the somewhat nihilistic obsession of a certain contemporary art. Yet, after all, as it was relatively well-paid—unlike at the Normale Supérieure—I wanted to find a way to get on with it; that is to say, to avoid the question, not to get sucked in by the post-Heideggerian or Virilionian or Baudrillardian theme of technical acceleration which devastates everything and especially art, good manners, respect, and I don't know what else.

I soon enough found an Idea which would get me out of this trap. It happened like a eureka moment, which can be stated simply at first: since Heidegger, modern philosophy is a thought of the co-belonging of being and event. You see where I am going with this. At the same time as Heidegger—by reassigning our field of study to its originary question, to the question of being—dominated the philosophical twentieth century, he doubled this innovative *revival*[9] by introducing a theme itself entirely novel in philosophy: the theme of the event, or of what is an event. It could be possible to show—but it is beyond my aim here—that the question of the event is a question that could have arisen only after the Nietzschean diagnosis of the death of God. I mention this only on the account of this death, on which I will quickly return, but in the sole light of our singular aim.

Being and event: this is the title of a contemporary classic in philosophy, written by a somewhat controversial (one cannot help asking why) fellow, who happens to be a colleague of yours, and a *caiman* not so long ago. But the envoi is Heideggerian, in the *Contributions to Philosophy*, a text still not yet translated into French because it was written in Germany between 1936 and 1938, and because it contains stuff that is rather compromising for the white-washing operation whereby devout French Heideggerians try to clear their Master's name of all collusion with Hitlerism. [Any resemblance …] It is in this text, which is as brilliant as it is awful, as innovative as it is unaccomplished, that appears with all its initial might the thematic of the event, the event in being, being as "distributor" of events, event as "influx" [*influx*] of being—the more event there is, the more there is being—and finally being itself as event. In this somewhat insane text, which is a long draft disrupted and choked by the historical circumstances surrounding it, we thus find all the seeds of what post-war French philosophers will explore in their singular way, especially from the sixties onwards up to this day, with us included.

I realize there is something almost mathematical, thermodynamical about all philosophies which would take up the subject, up to Alain Badiou and the eponymous title of his *magnum opus*. It is that by comparing the various economies which link being and event in the respective philosophies, we notice a kind of unthought but absolutely self-evident Law at work in all these conceptual creations: the slower is being, the faster goes event. The faster goes being, the slower is event. So here was my little idea, the idea which assured me a way out of this business for the said contribution (and I was very proud of what I had found, but I think the Swiss audience, consisting uniquely of professionals, did not get my enthusiasm at all). I could then talk of acceleration while avoiding the all-sweeping empirical description of technology. I was placing myself within the perspective of the condition of technology, which is our initiatory exclusive domain, metaphysics.

If being is slow, event goes fast. If being is fast, event goes slowly. Let us take two particularly striking examples—and I am not the first to take them as the two antagonistic "poles" of contemporary metaphysics: Deleuze and Badiou. For Deleuze, being is called the virtual, and the virtual goes very fast. Deleuze says: an infinite speed of appearance and disappearance. So in the Deleuzian system the event will be, it will always be a slowing down, a gaining of consistency [*mise-en-consistence*], a kind of eternalized interception of this infinite speed of being. On the other hand, for Badiou, the self-enthroned hyper-Platonist, being is identified by mathematics. Ontology is mathematics, and therefore being, in the Platonico-archaic mode, is that which is eternal and immobile, like Aristotle's prime mover, even if the comparison would not be particularly pleasing for the person principally concerned. There would be a lot to say about the presuppositions of this purely noumenal vision of being, but it is a matter of fixing the thing, not to point out the obvious: in a so to speak fixist, frozen ontology like Badiou's, well, we see that event itself goes extremely fast, at the speed of lightning even. While for Deleuze it is being that is an infinite speed of appearance and disappearance, for Badiou it is event that is even a speed so infinite of appearance and disappearance that you ask yourself if it ever existed, like thunder you can only recognize by the claps. This is what his metaphysics tells us: event is extra-being; it does not belong to being. It is even this quasi-theology of the event that led me to make a lengthy deconstruction of this somewhat aberrant postulate of an event which would not belong to being, a deconstruction which puts forward extremely precise arguments.

For Badiou, on the one hand, being is immobile and eternal, and on the other, event is of a precarious and infinite speed; in such a way that if you take an ontology slightly slower than his, like Heidegger's, where being is not eternal but slow—what Heidegger revisits about the Greek aletheia, that is, the pulsation of veiling and unveiling whereby being reveals itself to us historically—then the only thing which speeds things up a little is, opportunely, the event. It is the only moment where the somewhat placid slowness of Heideggerian being, the veiling-unveiling of being, unveils itself a little bit faster. But it still goes a little bit slower than in Badiou. So you see, there is a sort of proportional mathematics, a dialectics of speed and slowness in the event: being is immobile for Badiou, slow for Heidegger, fast for Deleuze. As a result, event is very fast for Badiou, a little less so for Heidegger, altogether slow for Deleuze. We shall finally add that it is not by chance that all this will coincide with the respective libidinal economies of the three authors. In *Being and Sexuation*, I call Badiou's vision of sexuality, "transcendental machismo." It truly is a kind of philosophy of pure virility. There is a virile heroism in Heidegger as well, but even so it is somewhat thwarted by his Nazi adventure which will lead him to become something of a better fellow, slightly more of an ecological hippie, and therefore almost feminine in what concerns his questioning of being (the rediscovered proximity to *physis*, etc.). Whereas for Deleuze, we have seen what it was all about: becoming-woman, therefore, probably, an ontology itself more "feminine."

Finally, let us add that "feminine" ontologies always grant a privileged place to what may be called the metaphysical pathic, the affectual in philosophy. And besides, if the primitive scene of the division of ontology into masculine and feminine dates back to Plato and Aristotle, we see clearly that the latter grants much greater importance to the affect than his philosophical Master and Father, to the point where he turns it into the historically most influential concept, the one contained in his opuscule *On the Soul*. The soul is the body of the affect, of pure sensation; this will be exactly—even if he was not aware of it—the concept of what Deleuze will call the Body without Organs, which he often illustrates by the example of the masochist precisely. This is something I point out often, but after all Deleuze's famous Body without Organs is nothing other than Aristotle's soul. Finally, if the Plato/Aristotle couple can be considered as the primitive scene of the ontological division of sexes, we can say that all masculine ontology has a strong propensity for verticality, and feminine ontology for horizontality. Moreover, I quite simply would not have written one line of *Being and Sexuation* without the precious remark of a friend, a great writer and essayist, a great academic like yourselves, Tiphaine Samoyault, who one day told me that for her Platonism was untenable, especially in the form it is given by an eminent colleague of yours, a Platonism which she felt like a violence, like the very matrix of common anthropological violence itself, for the simple fact that she was a woman. A woman could only be Aristotelian.

The question of horizontality versus verticality is also the question of the void in philosophy. Vertical, "masculine" ontologies are "voiding" [*évidantes*] ontologies; horizontal, "feminine" ontologies, from Aristotle to Spinoza, which are for that very reason almost always philosophies of Nature, are ontologies where the void is most often foreclosed. This question of a discontinuous ontology, caesured by the void as masculine desire through the castration of phallic jouissance, opens up to a crucial question in philosophy: the question of the transcendental. On the contrary, feminine ontologies, as Deleuze formulates, are philosophies that fight against diehard transcendentalization; they are philosophies of "full" immanence, of the "foreclosure of the void," as Badiou says—as if by the greatest coincidence—on the subject of Aristotle and Spinoza.

Speaking of the latter, Deleuze will say that he is the "prince of philosophers," the only one "never to have compromised with transcendence." Which is not far from being, on the contrary, the principal charge brandished by Badiou against an antagonist philosophy: all excessive, or even moderate, proximity to immanence and empiricity will be considered suspect.

To this we can add another striking law that runs through all this unconsciously. It is that, as we move towards more "virile" ontologies, of which Badiou constitutes the unsurpassable limit, we move towards a *separation*—as clear-cut as possible—between being and event, to such an extent that event would not even belong to being. The separation of being and event is less clear-cut in Heidegger, since sometimes he does happen to write "being: event." The reason is that, unlike Badiou and unlike Deleuze, Heidegger—even more radically than Kant—wanted to be done with all philosophical dogmatism, which is an effort I share retroactively, since it is Badiou's somewhat peremptory apodicticity of logico-mathematical universalism which would lead me to reject violently, somewhat hysterically, his "philosophy." It would have to be studied at length, everything he utters on the difference of sexes, and the manner in which all this ends up running into what someone who knew him well, Jean-Claude Milner, calls "facile universalism." Moreover this is what the book I present you with had begun doing, courteously, as regards "transcendental machismo." And eventually, the rejection this philosophy inspired in me comes full circle to what Deleuze said: white, heterosexual, western man is the empty universal. That in philosophy the restored promotion of such a unilateral universalism should precisely come from such a cast-iron subjective typology, such is the irony of the bar-room philosophizing which is also always, in part, what philosophy is. Because, in Deleuze, being and event are identified much more closely than in Badiou and even Heidegger. It is also often a commonplace of philosophical debate: Spinoza's ontology is the most feminine ontology there is. There are lots of Spinozist women. "Whyyyyyyy?", would have asked Deleuze with his old witch's voice. In other words, if he—Spinoza—had been a modern philosopher: an ontology where being and event are strictly and everywhere the same thing. A chapter of my book is called: "being=event in Deleuze."

So this is the other Law, which comes after the Law of perfect proportion of speed and slowness in the event: it is that, the more an ontology "were feminized," the more being and event would be identified. So you see where I have been heading, and you see the somewhat heretical riddle that results from the speculative domain opened up by this book—my book: the masculinization of ontology, which would separate being and event as it goes along, and the feminization of ontology, which would bring closer being and event as it goes along until they are identified, would disturbingly coincide with my strictly libidinal thesis—that is to say, with the libidos of their respective authors, the said libidos themselves often made explicit in their philosophies. In feminine libido there would be an originary, perfect identity of desire and jouissance, which all actual libido would like to join asymptotically; just as, asymptotically, a feminization of ontology would tend to come always closer to an identity of being and event. It is for this reason that once again I mention at length another philosopher who happens to be a biological woman, Catherine Malabou, and her important book called *The Heidegger Change* where, as I demonstrate, she attempts a sort of heretical appropriation of Heidegger. For her, being and event are definitively the same thing. Unlike Badiou, whom I label with "transcendental machismo" which consists of a separation as radical as possible of being and event, since man is the imposition of the radical semantic break between desire and jouissance that all becoming-woman comes to disrupt, I call "transcendental hysteria" this speculative manner in which being and event are constantly identified, which is superlatively the case with Malabou. In each page of her book, so to speak, being changes, being *is* absolutely incessant change, becoming and metamorphosis, permanent event, which can be, after all, just as tenable as an ontology of "transcendental machismo"—Badiou's— where, because of the absolute segregation between being and event, we think, quite conversely, that it occurs almost never anything that matters and that being is most often atonic and identical to itself, etc. Deleuze liked to compare his philosophy to a witch's philosophy, and besides it is not by chance that he physically looked like an old Carabosse, yet after all if there is one person who beat him on his home ground, it is no other than Malabou: each page of her book is full of event-expressions such as: "beingness stands for the being which stands for being" [*l'étantité vaut pour l'étant qui vaut pour l'être*], "the absolute exchangeability of the originary deal," "the economy of an originary ontological substitutability," "everything is exchanged against itself, against the other, being [*l'être*] on account of the being [*l'étant*], the being [*l'étant*] on account of its essence, essence on account of being [*l'être*],"[10] etc.

The least one could say is that in this hotchpotch the only truly by-no-means-feminine, not-the-least-bit-queer ontologist is Alain Badiou. In all the others, there is always a moment when being is confused with event. In Malabou, this is absolutely. In the book, I suggest quite convincing—I think—avenues on the isomorphism of a certain libidinal functioning of "classic virility"; and what Badiou transcendentally draws from it as to the dialectics of a perfectly discriminated being and event, in a brilliant manner—I must admit—in terms of metaphysics, is not the problem. It is even for this reason that it is so interesting. If, as a perfect progressive beautiful soul, I just wanted to cut my teeth on the macho on duty, I would have made do with Alain Soral.

Doubtless, all that is somewhat sacrilegious about my endeavour lies therein. Indeed, if we agree on the fact that it is phallic jouissance that empties masculine desire in its repetitive, if not sadistic, compulsion (Milner, thinking of Badiou, once said that Platonism was meant to be fulfilled in sadism); if the Deleuzian masochist is this masculine figure whose phallic jouissance sanctions desire, and who tries to ward off the void by way of full phantasmatics whose ritual of foreclosure of jouissance fills his Body without Organs; and finally, if this phallocentric dialectic of void and fullness is null and void in the feminine position, and the dialectic of void and fullness entirely inappropriate in relation to a masculine libidinal economy, well then there is a disturbing coincidence with the fact that "virile" ontologies from Plato to Kant should lead to vertical transcendentalism, whereas horizontal, "feminine" ontologies, from Aristotle to Spinoza, should be ontologies of the plane of consistency, of the fullness of immanence. And the least one could say is that the Badiou/Deleuze antagonism provides us with precious innovative tools to revisit something which will have traversed, unknowingly, the entire history of metaphysics.

In yet other words: what separates a hetero-centered ontology and a more "feminine" ontology is the economy which links therein the empirical and the transcendental. The more we move towards a vertical, "virile" ontology—a "scoring thought" [*pensée du manche*], as Lacan says in his accent like Tony Montana—from Plato to Kant to Badiou, the more we move, as it were, towards a transcendentalization devoid of empirical content. As someone I like a lot, a great philosopher still not well known, Reiner Schürmann says:

> (…) reason prescribing objective realities to the world knows what is essential even before experience. Here lies its violence. Such contents possessed in advance have been made into the weapons of every dogmatism. The Cartesian version of material autonomy leads directly to projects like Condorcet's "mathematizable society".[11]

For instance, in *Logics of Worlds*, anyone who can read will see that the possible libidinal economies whereby the human animal singularizes itself are all led back by Badiou to the same archetypal transcendental of the good old hetero-heroic couple. Even in this respect—and so you see that it is all profoundly coherent—Badiou cannot keep himself from bringing everything back to the same empty transcendental. It is even what remains fascinating for so long in this philosophy: the manner in which it maximizes metaphysical violence par excellence, or transcendentalism up to a level never attained before, even by Kant or Husserl. And this is just as well what eventually deceives us when we have explored it all, but that is another story.

Conversely, an ontology which would "feminize" itself, like the ontology of Deleuze, will proportionally bring together the transcendental and the empirical. This is what Deleuze, according to a formula still debated today, called transcendental empiricism. We would also have to talk about the empirico-transcendental doublet in Foucault, whose libidinal economy was at the very least singularized; or about the manner in which Derrida, the deconstructionist of phallogocentrism, deconstructs the empirico-transcendental doublet by a *mise-en-abyme*. It is nothing less than this site that is opened up—still groping a little here and there—by *Being and Sexuation*. In Malabou's work for instance, the fascinating thing about her book is the extent to which the ontological transcendental seems to coincide on every page with the crudest empiricity. Really, we often get the impression that she talks about herself, even whilst her book remains throughout a book of pure metaphysics, which was after all the case of Heraclitus, or Parmenides, with whom all our troubles began. We again see that these "feminine" metaphysics, Deleuze or Malabou, are always asymptotic, like what I said about feminine libido itself.

Then, on that level too, *catharsis*, that is to say, Hegelian *aufhebung*: what is suppressed is all the same always preserved; not only is the hypothetical state of nature preserved in the indubitable state of culture, planetary technological unification of the human species, but metaphysical transcendentalization, be it closest to the empirical and precisely because of that, always preserves something of the libido which produced it.

Yes, all metaphysics is always sexuated, because all thought is always differentially, singularly, sexuated. It is even for this reason that, in the end, there is no longer metaphysics except in its turn singular; which does not mean non-universal, but means most certainly—and this is excellent news—that the time of metaphysical univocity is bygone. Which is also to say: God [*Dieu*]— or Diou, as the poet Pierre Guyotat wrote ten years ago—is dead. And so it also means that philosophy, and the philosopher who produces it at any rate coincide in the most perfect, that is to say, the most singular manner.

This is why, against the overhanging dogmatic of a Badiou, but also against a certain Deleuzian systematic which can too verge on dogmatism, we have to return to philosophy as the plural critique of philosophy. That is why I put forth Heidegger's attempt to pluralize, to plurivocize the question of being, by drawing a definitive line on all doctrinal and unilateral conceptions of philosophy. Neither feminine nor masculine, but rather traveling constantly between the diverse shades of the specter spread out between the two, it is metaphysics itself which becomes in a way *queer*—taking over the critical envoi of modern philosophy—and thus fights against all prescriptive, apodictic, dogmatic, subsuming, neo-normative determinations of philosophy. After all, we can just as well reckon, in a somewhat bi-polar manner—and this is the becoming-queer of metaphysics—that with the meta-virile position of metaphysics, event is extremely rare, precarious, fleeting, and that, with the meta-feminine position, we can say the opposite, that is to say, that there is event a little bit everywhere and all the time, in a sort of pathic immanence. Just as phallic jouissance is at the same time the center, the "voiding" [*évidant*] heart of masculine libido, even while its taking-place as such has indeed something extremely precarious and fleeting about it, like the meta-virile conception of the event, this on the one hand; and on the other, the pathic and even protopathic identity of desire and jouissance is the both omnipresent, immanent nucleus of feminine libido, which it attemps to reach asymptotically at each and every moment, and which, in the meta-feminine metaphysical projection, results in a proportional proximity of being and event, of the empirical and the transcendental, etc.

With means certainly humbler than Heidegger's, by shifting every philosophy on the ground of its so to speak psychoanalytic overdeterminations, by psycho-analyzing as it were each philosopher from the point of what he or she puts forth—or not—on the sexual question, one gives oneself just as well the means of philosophizing psychoanalysis, of pointing out that all questions concerning sexuation always assume, whether one is aware of it or not, an ontological discourse. The time of a dogmatic philosophy which would overhang the entire content subsumed by the facilities of the transcendental—for instance, logico-mathematical—in order to deliver always and everywhere its unilateral truth, in other words, a philosophy that happens to be neo-normative, nor-male-izing [*normâlisante*] is over, well over. All philosophy of the twentieth century, the philosophy that succeeded Nietzsche, with very few exceptions like Léo Strauss, Habermas, Rawls, or Badiou, has tolled the knell of any possibility of thinking being [*l'être*], and therefore the being [*l'étant*] normatively. This is what Reiner Schürmann called: principle of an-archy, in the strictly philosophical sense of the impossibility of an *arche* from which all the rest could be inferred—in particular norms to set it in motion—by tearing down the order of reasons on the basis of a first principle that is beyond discussion. The profound novelty of our age is ultimately the definitive relinquishment of such a principle.

This will allow me to conclude in a slightly elliptical manner, by talking a little bit of myself: if I spoke from the sole point of libidinal economies, of singularization, it is perhaps because herein lies the way to think beyond the great, henceforth saturated philosophies of Difference, without throwing ourselves, out of spite, into the arms of a philosophy where the principle of apodictic universalism, identifying concept and subsuming transcendentalism, triumphs anew. Singularity is no longer exactly Deleuze's or Derrida's difference, even if it is perhaps already that of Foucault's or Schürmann's: it is the manner in which difference is *monstrously* caesured by the positive universal of science. It is this caesura which means that the coming philosophical universality will be anything but easy. And it will be much to its credit.

Notes

Foreword

1   Translator's note: L'EsdN [*l'Esprit du Nihilisme*]: the SoN [*the Spirit of Nihilism*]. When in abbreviated form and not in italics, it is used by the author to refer to the system as a whole. When it is not abbreviated, the book will henceforth be referred to as *The Spirit of Nihilism*.

2   New York: Continuum Publishing Group, 2009.

3   Without the shadow of a doubt, the predominant contemporary influence on my work (*Broken Hegemonies,* trans. Reginald Lilly, Bloomington: Indiana University Press, 2003). In *Algèbre de la Tragédie*, even more than anywhere else, one can notice the extent to which I attempted the impossible, that is to say, the conciliation of the two most ambitious and also most opposite and irreconcilable contemporary philosophies not only of today but that have ever been: Schürmann's and Badiou's. This great disparity, which could lead me to nothing but an agonizing struggle and a kind of speculative suicide, pushed me to the point where I finally had to decide: it was the one *or* the other, with no possible compromise nor settlement.

4   Translator's note: *"la femme mi-existe, ou m'existe."* Alberto Toscano, in his translation of the *Logics of Worlds*, translates this phrase as "a woman (semi-)exists or exists for me." I did not entirely adopt his translation, in an attempt to replicate the forced grammatical structure of the original.

5   Because we are dealing with the squaring of a vicious circle: the *modern* (post-Kantian) philosopher, being inalienably academic, cannot but foreclose the state-dependent condition that conditions his practice. A double foreclosure even, when he prides himself on being beyond shame to profess (literally and in every sense …) a great lord's contempt, and even a bellicose hostility which thinks itself as "heroic," for the State that feeds him. And since everyone considers, implicitly, that being a functionary is consubstantial with the *Figure* of the philosopher, no one even imagines laughing at the tragi-comic aspect of such a performative contradiction. On the other hand, the independent author who lays claim to the concept, who is non-academic, and therefore *by definition* does not know the first thing about philosophy, the "anti-philosopher," being unable to say anything sensible on the conditioned, cannot but bitterly point the finger at the naked king of state allegiance.

6　Rousseau, after his fifties, spent the rest of his life persecuted in all of Europe; Kierkegaard too, precociously became paranoid (he no longer went out of his house so to speak), and having exhausted the resources of his paternal inheritance, he died at the age of forty-two; Marx spent all his life in the darkest of miseries, "Christlikely" identifying himself with the people whose theory he was making; Nietzsche also lived in utter destitution, and became mad at the age of forty-eight; Benjamin lived in material and moral destitution which became unbearable at the end of his life, and he committed suicide at the age of forty-eight; Bataille lived in a precarious state and chaos all his life, and at the age of sixty, he was still asking for money from his friends; Blanchot, in his sixties, spent ten years in an isolated place, with neither hot water nor electricity … The history of non-academic thinkers has been nothing but an uninterrupted martyrology for two centuries. The strangest thing about it is that it has *never* been noticed: it is impossible not to see a professional, that is to say, professorial deformation here, yet another one …

Affect

1　Edgar Allan Poe, *The Essential Tales and Poems of Edgar Allan Poe,* ed. Benjamin F. Fisher (New York: Barnes and Noble Classics, 2004).

2　Theodor W. Adorno, *Minima Moralia: Reflections on a Damaged Life*, trans. E. F. N. Jephcott (London: Verso, 2005), 150.

3　Pascal Taranto in *Le ressentiment, passion sociale,* ed. Antoine Grandjean and Florent Guénard (Rennes: Presses Universitaires Rennes, 2012; my translation).

4　Reiner Schürmann, *Broken Hegemonies*, trans. Reginald Lilly (Bloomington: Indiana University Press, 2003), 400.

Appropriation

1　We will have recognized the difference between herbivore and carnivore animals, to which I will come back later.

2　Heidegger in Reiner Schürmann, *Broken Hegemonies*, 548.

3　We owe the present remark to Quentin Meillassoux's unpublished dissertation, *L'inexistence divine* (see the note below), where he says: "(…) hylozoism is the only irreligious way of thinking the emergence of life, in the sense that all immanentist thought (…) finds itself constrained to assume a minimal common point between matter and the qualitativity of life. This is why it is a matter of a fundamental option of thought, and not of a historically dated theory, confined to the materialism of the eighteenth century for instance. Sometimes Deleuzian immanentism itself presents striking hylozoic consonances, such as the following passage from *What is Philosophy*: "Of course, plants and rocks do not posess a nervous system. But, if nerve connections and cerebral integrations presuppose a brainforce as faculty of feeling coexistent with the tissues, it is reasonable to suppose also a faculty of feeling that coexists with embryonic tissues and that appears in the Species as a collective brain (…). Chemical affinities and physical causalities themselves refer to primary forces capable of preserving their long chains by contracting their elements and by making them resonate: no causality is intelligible without this subjective instance. Not every organism has a brain, and not all life is organic, but everywhere there are forces that constitute microbrains, or an inorganic life of things" (Gilles Deleuze and Félix Guattari, *What is Philosophy?*, trans. Graham Burchell and Hugh Tomlison, London: Verso, 1994, 212–13). I completely agree with Meillassoux's anti-hylozoism, although with entirely different conceptual means and ethical motivations. Again, see the note immediately below.

4   One of the two unpublished books mentioned in the foreword will include a great discussion with a philosopher of our generation, as important as he is little known in his own country: Quentin Meillassoux. The book will consist of a presentation (Meillassoux publishes very rarely, indeed being a largely "unpublished" author …), a critical discussion, a confrontation, and a book "around" things, all at the same time (the influence of this young philosopher on international academic production is already huge). As to the confrontation: it will consist of a very elaborate technical critique of what he calls "event," in comparison with my own conception, which will shed light on some aporias of his.

5   This is one of the questions not only asked but also answered by the SoN. Right from its originary envoi, philosophy has dreamed of "taking power," literally and in every sense; but historically it is religion that fulfilled this dream to its detriment. Why? A convincing answer came from Nietzsche: Christianity is a vulgarized Platonism, that is to say, a Platonism brought to the reach of the plebs. Yet this is far from being enough: after all, Nazism too, which was a modern *religion*, shamelessly vulgarized Nietzscheanism. We will have only shifted the question from its real center of gravity. A religion is always an applied conjunction of a politics, an aesthetics, and a metaphysics. Where has metaphysics always failed in its successive diagnoses—from Plato to Nietzsche—concerning the desirable suture between an art and a politics? The SoN answers: in the underestimation of the aesthetico-political question of *play* (see below), which it moreover shares with all religion.

6   In other words, an event, period; a pathology with respect to the apparently stable Laws of nature. The carnivorous plant does to the animal what the animal does to the plants: becoming-animal, in a sense which is not exactly Deleuzian … Here, we need to understand the oxymoron of a "transgressive Law," which is inchoative

with respect to the event and strictly *statistical*, that is to say, trans-statistical, as
I often say. That technomimetic event should have "fallen" on the animal that I
am egoically has the structure of a pure and simple miracle: I could have been
born a chair (but the chair would never know anything about it; it would never
suffer from not having been an appropriative being [*étant*], animal or human) or
a battery chicken (the harrowing injustice—globally dominant because of us—of
an animal who will never know the reasons why all its "life" was made into hell).
What do beavers and their bridges, or birds, and their sophisticated language and
their nests lack to achieve a technological hegemony that would be equivalent
to ours? Not much: a few million years. This is what the ecological turning
point of our History means; its speed, which all the same pushes the question of
communism not to the background, but at the very least to the appendix of the
ecological question and to the dependency thereon: the ontologico-historical of
the suicide of the species which led the subtle *physis/techne* dialectic, i.e. technics
as *originary supplementarity* of Nature itself, in what it regionalizes of itself as
living. Historical appropriation is the extreme precarious end of an appropriation
itself precarious: life on earth. The SoN asks: life, as event, would it not be the
cosmological equivalent, the macrocosm, of what sexual jouissance, in our
somatic microcosms, is to life itself? Statistically, from the millions of sperm
trying to conquer the egg, only one of them has a small chance of achieving its
aim, and often enough, all of them fail. The "ground" [*fonds*] of things is that all of
them could have failed for good, and Nature could have not been stabilized into
the statistic Law of fertilization; like this Nature itself could have not come about,
and differentiated itself in the indifference of mineral infinity.

7   Catherine Malabou, *The Heidegger Change: On the Fantastic in Philosophy*
     (Albany: State University. of New York Press, 2011).

8   We will see how the SoN as well entirely refutes the contemporary philosophical
     pose of anti-anthropologism.

9   This school of philosophy, currently the most lively, is the result of ten years
     of Badiouian domination over the international university, but also of "The
     Meillassoux Effect."

10   My unpublished book concerning Meillassoux will elaborate on the issue, showing
     that the emergence of matter cannot be taken as an event. Why? Because of
     something which is by itself absolutely demonstrable: matter has never emerged
     from anything; it has always been there. It is "eternal," if you like, but only itself
     is eternal, and not what it blends with. A fine example of the subsuming spell of
     our metaphysical idiom, and a fine example of linguistic ethics, for why we must
     always remain vigilant against the ever steadfast grip of this spell over us.

Art

1   Translator's note: in English in the original.

2   Matthew Barney, in his film *Cremaster 3*, stages horse races where the horses are decomposed like living carcasses as they run.

3   In the book *Controverse* (Paris: Seuil, 2012), which is a brilliant dialogue of the deaf between Alain Badiou and Jean-Claude Milner, the latter recapitulates an obvious fact about which his interlocutor wants to know nothing: the age of revolutionary overbidding as the only reality of emancipatory politics was buried with the atrocities of China's Great Proletarian Cultural Revolution. He says: "… the fundamental given we should remember is that the Revolution has failed (…) it is an internal failure, because it is not true (…) that a people can be dissolved in order to be replaced by another; it is not true that, to install any social form whatsoever, a people can massacre itself in the name of the people in order to put as it were another people in its place. All this constitutes a failure inscribed within the very terms of the project. (…) As it went on to destroy all forms inherited from Chinese history, it destroyed itself as historical form" (Alain Badiou, Jean-Claude Milner and Philippe Petit, *Controverse: Dialogue sur la politique et la philosophie de notre temps*, Paris: Seuil, 2012; my translation). Badiou still does not manage to see the obvious, and answers according to the classic logic of *mimetic* surpassing: of course, China's Cultural Revolution is a failure, but it is a failure "like" the Bolshevik Revolution was a failure, or "like" the Paris Commune, or "like" the Springtime of the Peoples of 1848, or "like" the Jacobin Terror was a failure. Therefore this failure must be thought "like" for instance Marx and the communists thought the failure of 1871. Last but not least, Badiou cannot help letting out the real story: Mao or Pol Pot are today treated by reactionary propaganda "like" Robespierre and Saint-Just were treated in the early nineteenth century. That in the meantime a regrettable anomaly of accounting occurred, that while the Jacobin guillotine cut off only three thousand heads, dead bodies in Cambodia were counted by the millions, and in China by the tens of millions, are only details for "modern Platonism." Hence the respective diagnosis developed in my *Inesthétique et mimêsis* (cited above), in a still "benevolent" fashion: Badiouian philosophy is a *generalized mimetology*, a monstrous parody of classico-dogmatic philosophy, like Wagner was a gigantic parody of "great art," with the mouth-watering political outcomes we all know, which will in no way keep Badiou from being willing to pair Wagner with Mao (and Žižek, with Stalin …), for all practical purposes. The last great philosophers of surpassing have therefore nothing more to offer—in terms of future surpassings—than gigantic *parodic regressions*: sanguinary in politics, pompous in art, and if possible, the ones in exact proportion to the others. For the exact same reason which I will only

indirectly elaborate in these pages, it is precisely because May '68 had something of a *parody* of Revolution or of *play* in its notion, that today it remains much more interesting—and bears a veritable political future for our century—than the atrocious Sino-Cambodian revolutions. In politics as elsewhere, the ideology of surpassing is *really surpassed*. It is no longer a question of surpassing the surpassing; our historical task is to *think surpassing otherwise*. The SoN assumes no other task; but the present book is the most striking recapitulation I ever wrote in order to explain how and why.

4   Mehdi Belhaj Kacem, *La chute de la démocratie médiatico-parlementaire* (Paris: Sens et Tonka, 2002).

5   Translator's note: in English in the original.

Aufhebung

1   See above, *Inesthétique et mimêsis*.

2   A particularly original contemporary artist, who is also "ethical" in his approach to violence, is Michael Haneke. He is the only one to wrong-foot the "aestheticization" of the most horrible violence, most often made by art, and particularly by modern audio-visual arts: in short, *catharsis* in its vulgarized sense. He is the only one to try and show violence hyperrealistically, and therefore to produce a counter-*cathartic* effect: an almost insomniac, sickly uneasiness that makes us "touch" the absolutely unlivable aspect of human violence, which is "sublimated" by most other artists, although without success. Yet it could easily be shown that this cinematographic "Brechtism," like already in Brecht himself, this applied critique of *catharsis* could become ordinary, is *ever more* "cathartic." It is exceptionally so, like in Brecht, because it rediscovers the initial secret of Attic Tragedy, which was not only its "therapeutic," but also *pedagogical* function. The violence of most "mass contemporary arts" is notoriously "therapeutic" ("to relieve" [*défouler*] is the word by which the modern idiom translates ancient *catharsis*), but it is practically never didactic.

3   This is one of the reasons why the terminal philosopher of ultra-terminal surpassing that is Badiou had to strive in a thousand ways to "prove" to us that death is ... nothing.

Desire

1   Philippe Lacoue-Labarthe, "The Poetics of History," trans. Hector Kollias, *Pli* 10 (2000): 16.

2   Lacoue-Labarthe, "The Poetics of History," 16–17.

3   Ibid., 17.

4   My concept of parody is to its common understanding what Hegelian *aufhebung* is to Aristotelian *catharsis*: an exhaustive extension of the application of the drawn concept. *Catharsis* was a processuality, an operation applied conceptually to the sole domain of art; *aufhebung* is the same operation such as it holds sway in *all* dimensions of human activity. In the same way, the parodic is usually understood as a certain kind of aesthetic practice or entertainment; in the system of the SoN, it concerns *all* of human activity, including the most derisory aspect of daily life.

5   Jacques Lacan, *The Seminar of Jacques Lacan: The Four Fundamental Concepts of Psychoanalysis (Book XI)*, ed. Jacques-Alain Miller, trans. Alan Sheridan (New York: W. W. Norton & Company, 1998), 189.

6   *Being and Sexuation*, the only as yet unpublished volume of the SoN cycle, performs its exhaustive demonstration.

7   Duchamp's gesture and his "nihilism" however can be summarized in passing, and in the particular perspective of the SoN, in a simple as well as decisive manner: well before Heidegger and Lacoue-Labarthe, he showed that art, being basically *techne*, henceforth could no longer assert its autonomy which was never challenged within the long artisanal tradition to which it belongs. When industralization completed the circle of technological appropriation, Duchamp made big news by marking the dramatic expropriation which would strike the "propriatory" [*propriatoires*] criteria of art, which until then clearly defined its inside and outside, precisely by an each time singular (pictural, musical …) set of inviolable artisanal and therefore technical competences.

8   The Catholic and reactionary novelist Richard Millet, in an interview, summarizes this point as follows: "As soon as the satisfaction of sexual drives becomes an order-word, we are in absolute nihilism" (Richard Millet and Romaric Sangars, "Maestro en Crise," *Chronic'art*, May 6, 2007, http://www.chronicart.com/digital/richard-millet-maestro-en-crise/ [accessed February 7, 2014]; my translation).

9   Valentin Husson, *La poétique de Rousseau*, unpublished.

10   Translator's note: masculine masturbation.

11   Jean-Clet Martin, *Plurivers* (Paris: P.U.F., 2010).

Ontological Differend

1   Nihilism.

2   In one of his seminars, he made a slip of the tongue: "I *believe* in the existence of principles." In other words, Badiou unwittingly rhymes with Schürmann, since, even though one self-proclaims himself a hyper-philosopher, the principal choice

henceforth concerns the fideist act, and principles are not more demonstrable than the existence of God since Kant.

Event

1   It would be impossible to sum up here the sophisticated details of this strictly ontological dialectic. I refer here to the whole of *Ontologique de l'Histoire*.

2   Translator's note: *esthéthique* in French: term coined by Lacoue-Labarthe.

3   At this point, I must mention the subversive greatness of Reiner Schürmann's deconstructive construction, which the SoN merely completes without altering it in any way. Metaphysics would be defined by the maximization of the two ultimate phenomenological traits of everyday existence: natality and mortality, which are not biological birth and death. Natality is what leads us towards the common, the universal, the love; hence the fact that metaphysics has always recognized Good in it (still today, with Badiou alone). Mortality is what subtracts us from the common, the universal, the love: that which isolates, breaks, makes suffers, singularizes, and it is therein that classico-dogmatic metaphysics has always recognized Evil. We can no longer fail to acknowledge (apart from Badiou ...) that natality, maximized by metaphysics into Universal, into eternal Communism and Good that applies to all, is what has produced, as if "under its command," the most terrifying evils: by subsuming the singular as a particular case of the universal, it inflicts on it enslavement, denial, torture, and death. Once again in Badiou's work, what he calls "singularity" is yet and again never envisaged except in accordance with its possible contribution to the positive universality of truths: as in the whole classico-dogmatic tradition, "pure" singularity is considered for this very reason either as a nothing, or as an incongruous Evil. Schürmann, without *simply* overturning the old schema (surpassing it ...), deconstructs it *pragmatically*. It is not at once a matter of saying that mortality is the source of all good, and the impetus of natality, that is to say, life maximized by metaphysics and technology, quite simply an Evil. The fact *is* that the mortality that subtracts me, removes me from metaphysical subsumption, is what singularizes me, and therefore the source of a possible "Good," just as the unifying and universalizing Good, because of its always renewed denial of the trait of mortality, aggravates the latter in the singularity to which it applies the subsumption: it enslaves, tortures, and kills it *infinitely*.

4   For me the brilliant guiding sentence comes once again from Reiner Schürmann: "Evil is born when I affirm and desire *in the face* of the law that which I automatically do *prior to* it" (Schürmann, *Broken Hegemonies*, 412).

5   All considerations which, I must say, make me extremely skeptical about the

cosy Marxist-"Platonist" dream of the end of the division of labor—the ideal of total and polyvalent man. I have elsewhere opened up about this. But in short, always for the same reasons: the fact of having "surpassed" our animal finitude traumatizes the latter, precisely because of the trans-natural obligation to work, to exhaust one's strictly physical powers for a task meant mostly for survival and expropriation in exchange for a poor parody of "appropriation": salary—what Marx, however, brilliantly conceptualized as "surplus value." To demand that this finitude make itself *furthermore* capable of "doing everything" is the proto-fascism congenital to the originary surge of philosophy, forgivable in the innocence of its beginning, but unforgivable in the frame of two and a half thousand years of horrors, and at the end of a century which has been the unrivaled apotheosis of all atrocities, in the very, Platonic, name of always "total" man. To surpass humanity, by enslaving its overwhelming majority, that is to say, by making them work, has already cost dearly; to surpass this surpassing will only increase the cost of atrocities exponentially. This should be the implacable lesson of the twentieth century. Yet philosophical infantilism, comfortably paid and at the pulpit, will never hesitate to send us back for another round: it is not itself that will pay for it. Despite all its roaring leftist *petitio principii*, I have always seen the function of professorial stardom as the exact equivalent of the factory boss: a metaphysical sublimation of a relentless division of labor which admits being all the less so, since it claims to program the exact opposite. Plato's *Republic* is, after all, just like a huge enterprise where the boss alone holds a somewhat pleasant place—others can go on sweating blood, waiting on him hand and foot. As for me, I have always seen myself at the lowest end of the managerial ladder of professional philosophers: something like the sweeper, or the cleaner of toilets ...

Expropriation

1   Louis Scutenaire, *Mes inscriptions (1943–1944)* (Paris: Allia, 1982); my translation.

2   Schürmann, *Broken Hegemonies*, 3.

3   The question of Right, although not explicitly dealt with in my philosophy, is crucial for me, on the same account as other great "truth processes." The novel dialectic of Transgression/legislation lays the basis of a new philosophy of Right; but for the time being, I leave it, with admiration, up to the later Hegel, as well as to Kojève's little-known masterpiece, *Outline of a Phenomenology of Right* (ed. Bryan-Paul Frost, trans. Bryan-Paul Frost and Robert Howse, Maryland: Rowman & Littlefield Publishers, Inc., 2007).

4   Translator's note: in English in the original.

5   Not more than it does in the superficially good-natured and profoundly

cynico-chauvinist hagiography of "Subject-love" which tells us that, literally, woman is made *only* for love, and therefore for man whom she seconds, and that in short it matters not that all Didos should be destined to die for Aeneas.

6   And, to add even more emphasis to our speculative "delirium," we know that the process of industrial farming of these animals has them feed on the recycled remains and excrements of their own sort—the comparison with Auschwitz is entirely justified here, and even is exceeded in certain respects. Is this not the matrix of the event's "negativity," the impossibility of *material* self-belonging, the "forcing" of which, equally as foreclosure of being, produces "Evil?" The human being, in symbolizing the taboos of incest and cannibalism, does he not have a deep consciousness of the fact that the "positive" event gives itself in the *intelligible* form of a "self-belonging" barred from the real, and yet whose entire "Evil," crime, etc., consists in the Will to the impossible?

History

1   Translator's note: in most cases, with the consent of MBK, I rendered *l'être-historique,* and its variants such as *l'être-communautaire,* by "the being-historical," and "the being-communitarian," in order to put the emphasis on "being." However, in some cases such as the above, I adopted the viable alternative, "the historical being," in order to put the emphasis on the first term.

2   Translator's note: in English in the original.

3   Schürmann, *Broken Hegemonies,* 570.

4   What is more, "algebra" comes from the Arabic word "al-jabr," which means: constraint and reduction. To brush one's teeth or to fill out one's tax forms does not basically come from another essence than the practice of "pure" sciences.

5   Translator's note: in English in the original.

Irony

1   Translator's note: Lacan's wordplay is a play on the similar sounds between "les non-dupes errent" ("the non-dupes err"), "le nom du père" ("the name of the father") and "le non du père" ("the no of the father").

2   I want to spice things up here with a personal anecdote. What Guyotat captures in an extraordinary manner in this book considered by many as his most hermetic—which says a lot—is the essence of the *dialects* spoken in the streets of the Maghreb, and which are always literally *monstrous* blends of literary Arabic with countless parasitic neologisms from western languages. These dialects, most

often too obscene (blasphemous) to be transcribed anywhere in Arabic writing, display an often astonishing coprolalic creativity: when two children insult each other, it can go on for hours, and it is a poetry which by definition escapes all memory. It is Guyotat's genius to have managed, in my eyes and especially my ears, to "convey" something of these by-definition-doubly-accursed postcolonial languages: banned from official use in the relevant countries, and inaccessible to western countries. Here is the anecdote: knowing Arabic and having grown up in the streets of Tunisia, I happen to read aloud very well this text deemed unreadable. Perhaps even too well: I recall having read about ten pages to a friend, who happened to be slightly tipsy, and the cruel obscenity of the language moved her so much that she had to go and be sick. I offer myself without reservation for a public lecture of this great forgotten text. This is a genuine call for tenders.

3 Jean Baudrillard, *The Conspiracy of Art*, ed. Sylvère Lotringer, trans. Ames Hodges (New York: Semiotext(e), 2005), 27.

4 Philippe Lacoue-Labarthe, *Poétique de l'histoire* (Paris: Galilée, 2002); my translation.

5 Jean Baudrillard, *Simulacra and Simulation*, trans. Sheila Faria Glaser (Michigan: University of Michigan Press, 1994), 3.

6 It is hard for me not to mention the admirable thesis of the young Kierkegaard, which still held onto the time when irony was an aristocratic prerogative: *The Concept of Irony*. In this book, Kierkegaard brilliantly shows that the master ironist is also the *mythical* tutelary figure of philosophers, namely, Socrates. Does the latter pretend to be ignorant? Not at all! He puts his ignorance on display, cards on the table, and this is what differentiates him from his interlocutors, who all think they *know* something, without pretending at all. By pretending to pretend that he does not know, by playing himself, he leads his interlocutors to self-refute themselves, one milestone after another, each marked by a question of the spiritual acupuncturist. What comes out of this knowledge soon collapsing like a house of cards by the ironist's unctuous attack? The fundamental category of philosophy, which is truth, and which is always a de-composition of all established knowledge. There would be a lot to say here, but the concept of Ontological Differend (see above) painfully opens up the "wound of truth," by blaming the *abîme* for its inadequacy in principle to all, especially scientific knowledge. The "conflictuality without agreement" that is truth, says Schürmann, and perhaps my work only serves to dramatize all its intuitions—when I systematize those of Lacoue-Labarthe.

7 Pierre Carlet de Chamb Marivaux, "The Constant Players," in *Marivaux Plays*, trans. John Bowen et al. (London: Methuen Publishing, 1988); my translation.

8 For me the reference *philosophical* book on the transsexual question is Pierre-Henri Castel's *La Métamorphose impensable* (Paris: Gallimard, 2003).

9 I'm thinking namely of Agamben—both the tutelary figure and empirical friend of *Tiqqun*.

Play

1   Schürmann, *Broken Hegemonies*, 3.

2   I do this in *Ontologique de l'Histoire*, as well as in *Inesthétique et mimêsis*.

3   Translator's note: in English in the original.

4   *Controverse*, ibid.

5   Mehdi Belhaj Kacem, *Society*, Auch: Tristram, 2001.

6   See the foreword.

7   Serge Daney aptly remarks somewhere that Americans substitute the value of "sincerity" for the value of "truth." Quite simply, they confuse the two.

8   These "Hegelian" reflections came to me under the impact of the Tunisian Revolution, which was an ideological "shock" of the utmost importance, to such an extent that I am still reluctant to gather together all I wrote on the subject.

9   Translator's note: in English in the original.

10 For me, Serge Daney's work is equal, in depth and in intelligence, in *soundness* [*justesse*] and in altruistic emotion, to Blanchot's. His genius for film-criticism-which-became-much-more-than-that—a writer and a thinker of the first rank—could be summarized as follows: in giving equal standing on whatever "cultural" pedestal to the slightest intelligent B movie, not to mention the great masters of the art of cinema, which will however never cease to be "vulgar" or "plebeian" art, Daney created a spiritual attitude which could go without saying, but which is, quietly, so exceptional that we must pay it tribute by naming it: *democratic aristocratism*. In short, I think today, along with Blanchot and Debord, Daney is the last of the great thinkers to have appeared outside the university: a thought which is certainly not "philosophical" in the professional sense of the term, a thought nevertheless, which I predict future philosophers will benefit from exploring.

11 Tranlator's Note: "*inégaux en puissance*," in the French version.

12 Edgar Allan Poe, *The Complete Tales and Poems of Edgar Allan Poe* (London: Penguin Books, 1982), 141–3.

13 Poe, *The Complete Tales and Poems of Edgar Allan Poe*, 215–16.

14 Having explained all this, Philippe Nassif pointed out to me that I metaphorized here, perhaps unconsciously, the same type of difference as between a non-cumulative practice—mine—of philosophy and academic "compulsivism," where you have to push your way through a jungle of rhetorical conventions. When I come to think of it, it is hard to say he is wrong.

15 David Sklansky and Alan N. Schoonmaker, "Poker is Good For You," *Two Plus Two Internet Magazine*, Vol. 3, No. 9, 2009, http://www.twoplustwo.com/magazine/issue33/sklansky-schoonmaker-poker-good-for-you.php (accessed February 7, 2014).

16 Translator's note: in English in the original.

17 This collective published two reviews in France, then for a while was associated with the neo-Situationist collective *Tiqqun*, translated for the most part into English, and mentioned above (see *Irony*).

18 Which, in my humble opinion, should not jeopardize the hot nights following the confrontations …

19 Translator's note: in English in the original.

20 With the greatest Stu Ungar, this relationship even took the form of the most demented infantilism. That is why he was called the "Mozart of poker."

21 Samuel Beckett, *Endgame*, trans. Samuel Beckett (New York: Grove, 1958), 24.

22 John Cale and David Owens, "John Cale: 'I might be exhausted but at least I know my brain is working,'" *WalesOnline*, September 29, 2012, http://www.walesonline. co.uk/lifestyle/showbiz/john-cale-i-might-exhausted-2024872 (accessed January 31, 2014).

23 We should note that this land coincides, in an immanentist mode, with the theologico-political pattern of the end of History, from St. Augustine to Hegelo-Marxism. I prefer once again to leave it to Lacoue-Labarthe: "It is well known: the scheme set up by Rousseau on the question of the origin (i.e. the condition of possibility) of culture does not simply open the space of transcendental reflection; it is strictly governed, even though lacking any formalization, by a dialectical logic, in the sense of so-called speculative dialectics. (…) teleologically thought, history can be deciphered as the putting-to-work of a design of nature's which would end, through the conflict or opposition between nature and culture (freedom, for Kant) (…), with their final reconciliation in an art that, reaching its perfection, would become nature again. This is the sense of history" (Philippe Lacoue-Labarthe, "Traduction et histoire," *L'animal* 19-20 [Winter 2008]: 142; my translation). In other words, *if* a political teleology of the Kantian, or Hegelian, or Marxist kind, were still possible, *then* play would represent in my work the ultimate finality of humanity. Let us be clear: where politics (see below) represents the reign of the *obeyed* rule, play represents the reign of the *freely consented* rule. A humanity which no longer does anything but play will be a humanity that has completely gone out of politics, and therefore History. You will tell me: "You talk to us about thinking otherwise the act of surpassing; but are you not falling, surreptitiously, in the good old trap, in imagining in play this "terminal surpassing" that you so carefully beware of everywhere else?" Answer: no, on the contrary, here as elsewhere, I am putting into practice what I am saying. It is a matter of a regulating idea. Alas, I do not dare imagine *really* that play replaces politics entirely, this on the one hand (therefore, no historical teleology); but on the other hand, *if such a full advent of play became realizable* (and, *de jure*, i.e. materially, such an event is already of the order of the possible), it would illustrate

marvelously this "shift of surpassing": full play would be the accomplished *catharsis* of the political, that is, what all art always already is locally; but it would not suppress politics *without preserving anything of it*. On the contrary, it would preserve its essential part: the pleonectic fury, its full energy. The impasse of "real communism," yesterday's as well as tomorrow's, will always be this calamitous illusion, in itself always pleonectic, of suppressing man's every pleonectic tendency, without preserving anything of it. And we saw that this suppression without preservation was literalized as mass graves; and was sublimated, in Badiou's classico-dogmatic revival, in a Sophistic irrealization of Death.

Catharsis

1   Translator's note: in English in the original.
2   "News Real," *River Front Times*, December 9, 1998, http://www.riverfronttimes.com/1998-12-09/news/news-real/full/ (accessed March 20, 2014).
3   *Courrier international*, special issue (July–August 2009); my translation.
4   Fabrice Soulier, "Le poker français dans la tourmente," *Fabrice Soulier*, February 2, 2013, http://www.fabricesoulier.com; my translation (accessed January 1, 2014).

Logic

1   Poe, *The Complete Tales and Poems of Edgar Allan Poe*, 217–18.
2   Mehdi Belhaj Kacem, *Esthétique du Chaos* (Auch: Tristram, 2000).
3   Ibid.
4   This philosophical Logic of being as event will completely unfold in my as yet unpublished book on Meillassoux.

Evil

1   I think this is something Badiou as well as Meillassoux could maintain, and it is one of the apples of discord.
2   Wrongfully, in my opinion, as you will have guessed. On that subject too, one of my hitherto unpublished books cited in the foreword will elaborate in depth, along with Meillassoux's "theory of immanent immortality."
3   Translator's note: the term *bousoir* is a pun with reference to Marquis de Sade's "philosophy in the boudoir," *bouse* meaning "cow dung."
4   Schürmann, *Broken Hegemonies*, 412.

5   This will be one of the essential discussions in my unpublished book on
      Meillassoux, which obviously continues the *dispute* with Badiou's "inhumanism"
      as well. One of Meillassoux's great "discoveries" is to launch an attack upon
      the "correlational" age of thought; and every school of "Speculative Realism"
      that Meillassoux's work has sparked in the entire world, consists in a war that
      some would describe as a pre-critical and therefore dogmatic regression against
      the philosophical "correlationism" since Kant. "Correlationism," in its most
      preliminary definition, consists in saying that there is nothing that can be thought
      that is not a correlate of the thought that thinks it. From Kant to Deleuze,
      including Hegel and phenomenology, not to mention Wittgenstein and Heidegger,
      thought always "contaminates" that which is thought [*la pensée « contamine »*
      toujours le pensé]. Driven by Meillassoux's very brilliant demonstrations, the
      postulate of "Speculative Realism" is henceforth that thought can think that
      which is radically outside all thought, for instance, the accretion of the earth
      or the Big Bang of billions of years ago, or the disappearance of the earth, or
      even of the entire cosmos at a time when by definition there will no longer be
      any thought. Not that I exactly deny the validity of this statement. I am simply
      drawing attention to something entirely absent from this philosophical trend as
      a whole, and which is quite obviously at the heart of a philosophy of the event,
      as what Meillassoux's philosophy *should* be: every event of appropriation *creates*
      correlates. Every event, whether vital or scientific, introduces to the world a
      set of correlations that did not exist before. Therefore, what I propose as the
      "speculative turning point" of philosophy is, rather than wearing itself out going
      against the new windmill of "philosophical correlationism," and thus refusing
      somewhat abreactively every correlational postulate wherever it may be, to *change*
      paradigm with respect to the correlate. In order to do this, we must think being as
      event. Moreover, with the exception of Meillassoux himself, the philosophies of
      "Speculative Realism" that propose "inhuman and anti-correlational ontologies,"
      each one more so than the next, are remarkable, as it happens, for *never* proposing
      any theory of the event. The ontologies of "Speculative Realism" could join
      together under the banner of "Being without event."

Mathematics

1   In mathematics, the axiom of foundation invented by Zermelo-Fraenkel
      demonstrates, transcendentally, that in order to "posit" [*poser*] a being [*un étant*],
      you always have to presuppose an *other* being. This is expressed, among others,
      by the absolute transcendental law which says there *cannot* be any "smallest
      member" in any region of the being, because you always have to presuppose, for

the presumed "smallest" member, *at least* one other smaller member composing it, as well as another, bigger member whose composition it enters.

2   Not so much on the margins of the SoN's general thematic, but implicit in this book alone, this is one of the other possible canonical definitions of art, including and perhaps *especially* "contemporary" art: the approach, the exposition, the capturing of the *pure* singularity, unexchangeable with any other, which science by definition leaves out of its field. Contemporary art *picks up the leftovers* of metaphysics.

3   It is owing to a rather ironic remark I made to him, and which he copied as is in his *Second Manifesto for Philosophy* (trans. Louise Burchill, Cambridge: Polity Press, 2001) that Badiou claims to have "resolved" the Kantian problem of the impenetrability of the in-itself. And for me such was the unique power of *Being and Event*, when I discovered it passionately in 2000–1: all of a sudden, a *contemporary* philosopher claimed, and convincingly, to have resolved the ontological problem on an equal footing with my two previous "champions" on the subject: none other than Spinoza and Hegel. Such was the power of the Badiou "impact" on me: a living philosopher had managed to assert a *thesis* on being which really seemed capable of reviving all the prerogatives of the most classico-dogmatic metaphysics: the most immemorial. One day someone asked me to say something on Badiou's ontology. I replied that there was *no* ontology-of-Badiou's. There was something much more powerful: the identification of ontology with mathematics. Where Reiner Schürmann tried to destroy every possibility philosophy could have to hold on to what he calls "thetism," Badiou had found the ultimate Holy Grail of a non-critical philosophy: the *thesis* of an identity of being in the mathematical statement. And it is actually this *thesis* that eventually crumbled before my eyes, like a magnificent cathedral reduced to ashes. It is this collapse that explains afterwards my complete apostasy: the general calamity of the principial *theses* which Badiou, with new consequences, thought himself entitled to pronounce on the ethico-political, the aesthetical, the erotic, and of course the epistemological. Badiou is the Wagner of philosophy: all at once, his apogee, his recapitulation, and his kitsch-decadent parody.

4   Which led him, once more, to *theses* each more aberrant than the other. For instance, in 1988 at the *Collège de Philosophie*, he declared: "As animals, we are eternal!"

5   We must understand well that the principle of identity is something other than the principle of equality. Yet precisely the mathematico-metaphysical error par excellence consists in the "deadly transfer" between the same, identity and equality.

Mimesis

1   The first two chapters of *Ontologique de l'Histoire*, as well as a hitherto
    unpublished text, *L'être=l'événement selon Deleuze*, are the two works where I
    explain myself fully on the subject.

2   Jacques Derrida, *The Margins of Philosophy*, trans. Alan Bass (Chicago: Chicago
    University Press, 1982), 135.

3   In very broad terms: it is from the event of appropriation that proceeds all
    differences, i.e. post-evental *singularizations*, starting with the decisive evental
    difference that overdetermines all the others: that of *physis* and *techne*. Take the
    difference man/woman, which the Derridean front of *Gender Studies* is striving
    to "deconstruct": here as elsewhere, the risk of affirming a difference always
    "more profound" than the simple "metaphysical" sexuated difference is not only
    to undifferentiate a *real*, pre-metaphysical difference (native of *physis*, and not of
    techne); it is above all to miss the real movement of the *queer* differentiation (and
    beyond, with the "accursed" singularities of zoophiles, coprophiles, necrophiles,
    pedophiles ... severely reppressed by the "Law"), which *properly* defines humanity.
    The Appendix, in fact the entire volume of the as yet unpublished *Being and
    Sexuation*, is no doubt my most "clairvoyant" attempt at description of this
    immanent mechanics of differentiation, which we obtain *thanks to* "metaphysics"
    (that is, technomimetic astuteness), and not "against it," which to me looks like
    the hypertrophied Achilles' heel of Derridean deconstruction. In fact, the infinite
    process of libidinal singularizations is explained by the *appropriation* of the male/
    female difference, then by its diffraction into ever wider networks of legislative-
    transgressive *games*. In the same way, the transcendental is the differentiating
    appropriation of the empirical; and being, the differentiating appropriation of
    nothingness, etc.

4   Metaphysical moment we owe to Badiou, without the shadow of a doubt. The
    only, but unforgivable, mistake of the latter is to have understood nothing of the
    metaphysical upheaval of difference in the twentieth century, and thus to try to
    maintain identitarian hegemony within the scope of the explosion of the Whole
    and the One. Even the term "Multiple," the central name of the being [*l'étant*] in
    his metaphysics, is nothing other than a way of *identifying* difference. It is on this
    point and on this point only that not only Badiou's *philosophy* is a wreck, but also
    half of his metaphysics: the half which identifies ontology with mathematics; that
    is, *identifies being*. But we had to go through this gigantic historical patch in order
    to, inopportunely, blame the "victory" of the Heideggerian intuition: it has become
    impossible for us to *identify being*.

Nihilism

1   Tristan Garcia.

2   Pierre-Henri Castel, "Les perversions, la sexologie et le mal" (5th session, unpublished seminar), March 27, 2003, http://pierrehenri.castel.free. fr/S%E9minaires%20ALI/perversion270303.htm; my translation (accessed February 2, 2014).

3   Jean-Claude Milner, *Le Triple du plaisir* (Lagrasse: Verdier, 1997).

4   Castel, "Les perversions, la sexologie et le mal"; my translation.

5   Furthermore, it is important that the meaning of my "deconstruction of deconstruction" be clear: it is in virtue of the very great proximity—not to even mention my admiration for the magnitude of his work—with Derrida that I take the critical responsibility *of going further than the thought of différance*: Hölderlin's "faithful infidelity," the necessity to betray in order to be faithful more profoundly than a "forthright" faithfulness. In particular, in what concerns the ethico-political consequences, such as attested to by the following excerpt from *The Animal That Therefore I Am* (the title of my foreword being an obvious allusion to it): "No one can deny seriously any more, or for very long, that men do all they can in order to dissimulate this cruelty or to hide it from themselves; in order to organize on a global scale the forgetting or misunderstanding of this violence, which some would compare to the worst cases of genocide (there are also animal genocides: the number of species endangered because of man takes one's breath away). One should neither abuse the figure of genocide nor too quickly consider it explained away. It gets more complicated: the annihilation of certain species is indeed in process, but it is occuring through the organization and exploitation of an artificial, infernal, virtually interminable survival, in conditions that previous generations would have judged monstrous, outside of every presumed norm of a life proper to animals that are thus exterminated by means of their continued existence or even their overpopulation. As if, for example, instead of throwing a people into ovens and gas chambers (let us say Nazi) doctors and geneticists had decided to organize the overproduction and overgeneration of Jews, gypsies, and homosexuals by means of artificial insemination, so that, being continually more numerous and better fed, they could be destined in always increasing numbers for the same hell, that of the imposition of genetic experimentation, or extermination by gas or by fire" (Jacques Derrida, *The Animal That Therefore I Am*, ed. Marie-Louise Mallet, trans. David Wills, Bronx: Fordham University Press, 2009). *No one … apart from the classico-dogmatic neo-metaphysician.*

6   Pierre-Henri Castel, "Les perversions, la sexologie et le mal" (4th session, unpublished seminar), January 30, 2003, http://pierrehenri.castel.free. fr/S%E9minaires%20ALI/perversion300103.htm; my translation (accessed February 2, 2014).

7 Translator's note: in English in the original.

8 And Philippe Lacoue-Labarthe's just as brilliant readings of Hölderlin. Where my general philosophico-ethical project places itself in the shadow of Schürmann's historial phenomenology, all the decisive *concepts* which led to my break with Badiou, for instance, proceed from the latent philosophy that Lacoue drew from Hölderlin's work: if "my" event is different from Badiou's, I owe it to Lacoue. The Hölderlinian concept of transgressive event is not *exactly* the same as mine, but mine would not have existed without the access Lacoue provided me to Hölderlin's philosophy of latent History. *Idem* also for the extension of the concept of an archi-transgressive event so as to include the Hegelian *aufhebung*, understood as a monumental reprise of the Aristotelian *catharsis-mimesis-techne* complex.

9 Reiner Schürmann's *Heidegger on Being and Acting: From Principles to Anarchy* (trans. Christine-Marie Gros, Bloomington: Indiana University Press, 1987) is the most extensive and profound commentary ever written on Heidegger, the decisive book on the question. Once you close this book, the last classico-prescriptive projects of modern philosophy, from Habermas to Rawls, from Leo Strauss to Badiou, appear as what they are: null and void.

10 A short introduction for Anglo-Saxon readers: a terribly mediocre philosopher, yet one who enjoys a public success worthy of a rock-star in France. This author, bolstered with a supermarket "Nietzscheanism" and "Epicureanism," actually practises a kind of ressentimental demagogy by taking on opponents always stronger than himself in the name of vague libertarian-democratic and "hedonistic" values.

11 Translator's note: in her translator's preface to Badiou's *Plato's Republic* (New York: Columbia University Press, 2013), Susan Spitzer gives the reason why she translates *L'Idée du Vrai* as the Idea of the True (whereas it might have been rendered as the Idea of Truth), explaining that Badiou instructed her to maintain a clear distinction between *le vrai* and *la vérité*.

12 But not fascisms, mind you …

13 Translator' note: in English in the original.

14 In *Being and Sexuation*, I push the speculative temerity to the point of asking whether this typically "phallogocentric" faculty of division of material homogeneity in representational butchering is not only the condition of possibility of all the slaughters in History, but also of the oppression of the feminine physical homogeneity as its division into detachable "parts." What psychoanalysis called "fetishism," and what I call "archi-pornography," in other words, cutting up woman's whole body into literally detached pieces, as we see in the crudest examples of pornography. And thus whether, incidentally, what psychoanalysis recognized as woman's "ontological" hysteria did not proceed from this dividing, metaphorically butchering violence to which masculine libidinal pleonexia subjects the woman, who is with good reason is called man's "object."

15   In "Plato," or what is left of it, everything is by definition stereotyped.

16   In *Après Badiou*, I already show that this sense, the only correct one, in the
end can only be the one and same thing as "communism," that is to say, the
gigantomachich being-in-common allowed solely and always by technological
facticity. This is illustrated well enough by the fact that, save for the Hitlerian
Reich or Benalist Tunisia, it is in countries with an experience of real communism
that, today still, state monstrosity is the most effectively tentacule and
omnipotence. I cannot repeat the demonstration here. Let us simply say that if,
as I said above, the practical destination of metaphysical deconstruction is the
dismantling of the technological, then what is at stake is nothing short of the
dismantling of our "being-in-common" as well: the Platonico-Marxist-Badiouian
"eternal communism." If the ethico-political teleology of classico-dogmatic
metaphysics is what deconstructed itself by itself, and for me this is Schürmann's
indisputable diagnosis, then "communism" is historically the very last name
of the History of teleologies: it is this remainder [*reliquat*] that Badiou tries to
save painstakingly, by putting forth nothing but patent antiphrases, as we see.
Remainder, because we are done with the simple determination of Good as
everything that leads to the common, unification, mathematizable organization.
Determination which the communist utopia *de facto* brought to its self-refuting
saturation: *by definition, the more humanity goes towards the common, the more
it goes towards the State.* To me, two destinies seem possible for the coming
humanity: either an assumed strengthening of the State, hence a factual
"communism," independent of the still constantly growing economic model
that will prevail therein: hence the becoming-play I wish for humanity will be
accomplished in the form of "play," every bit as gigantic and probably terrifying:
more totalitarian than all the totalitarianisms we have ever known. Or the
dismantling of technology—probably under the shock of a few big catastrophes—
begins to take effect, and along with it, the dismantling of the being-in-common:
then the decline of States will take effect as well, and humanity will learn again
to disseminate into increasingly restrained and elective groups, to live outside of
teleology ("without whys"), and the games will become once again as multiple
as the micro-communities themselves, by definition freely chosen (Marx's
"free association"). It is obvious that this "program," if it is one, coincides with
what would be the equivalent of an anarcho-ecologism, which would draw its
historical inspirations more from the Spanish Republicans or the Situationnists
than from the spectacular reversal of Marxism-Leninism into Stalinist or Maoist
super-statism.

17   Translator's note: in English in the original.

18   For example: I am sympathetic to the vegetarian cause. However, vegetarian
puritanism should not lose sight of the fact that had we not been ferociously
carnivorous hunters, we would have survived neither the ice age nor prehistory.

Yes, every "Good" is preceded by a Wrong [*Tort*], an Evil more originary than itself.

19 Friedrich Nietzsche, *Basic Writings of Nietzsche*, trans. and ed. Walter Kaufmann (New York: Modern Library, 2000).

20 In the sense of the *dialectical* definition Lacan gave of psychosis: what was foreclosed from the symbolic returns in the real. Chase away Evil from speculative discursivity, and it will come back in overdriven form in the real: from Plato to Wagner and Mao, the result would be deemed excellent.

21 It is in my unpublished book on Meillassoux that I will show that, among other brilliant anachronisms, Badiou's philosophy is the last metaphysics, because in placing itself under the supposedly "unassailable" ontico-ontological invocation of the logico-mathematical, it subjects every being [*étant*], with new consequences, to the yoke of real necessity. Suffice it to say here: this is why it reproduces, so pompously, the originary error of metaphysics: Evil, not falling under any "ontological" necessity, is nothing. Religion, even if only on this point, is a more lucid *thought* than philosophy, because it shows absolutely the fact that Evil arises from a contingency, an accident. It is precisely this "freedom of choice" of original sin that Rousseau and Schelling will undertake to "laicize," that is, *philosophize*.

22 This remark is of course a very personal interpretation, to draw Schelling a bit towards me: for him, freedom to do Good and Evil are actually co-originary. For me, Evil precedes Good, unless "Good" is understood in the simply pleonectic sense of *supplementary* appropriation allowed by *techne*, in relation to the appropriations of *physis*. But in that case, the "Good" itself, in the ethico-moral sense, would never have seen the light of day. Good is born, *only after* man becomes aware—on top of the "Goods" that technological existence endows him with—of the new sufferings he self-inflicts because of it. It indicates all the conceivable means to repair the damage.

23 Philippe Descola, *Beyond Nature and Culture*, trans. Janet Lloyd, foreword Marshall Sahlins (Chicago: University of Chicago Press, 2013).

Parody

1 Jean-Jacques Schuhl, *Rose poussière* (Paris: Gallimard, 1972); my translation.

Politics

1 In fact, it is almost never a question of pure and simple *abolition* of the old Laws: I will demonstrate this point in the book devoted to Meillassoux.

2   Theodor W. Adorno, *Aesthetic Theory*, ed. Gretel Adorno and Rolf Tiedemann, trans. and ed. Robert Hullot-Kentor (London: Bloomsbury Academic, 2013), 139.

Representation

1   Philippe Lacoue-Labarthe in *Voyage à Tibüngen: un portrait de Philippe Lacoue-Labarthe*, telefilm by Michel Deutsch, Sepia/France 3 Alsace, 2008, http://www. filmsdocumentaires.com/films/434-philippe-lacoue-labarthe; my translation (accessed February 4, 2014).

Science

1   About his *Forme et Objet. Un traité des choses* (Paris: P.U.F., 2011), I have intensely mixed feelings of extreme closeness and extreme distance towards this great philosophy book. To sum it up, influenced by the aforesaid trend of "Speculative Realism," Garcia starts somewhat too blindly from the "anti-Correlational" postulate, like all philosophers of this allegiance, and hence "equalizes" all the beings [*étants*] in an assumed anti-humanist absoluteness. Still at the same cost: the lack of a theory of the event, something somewhat "frozen" in the ontological (more or less Euclidean) flattening. However, paradoxically, in the brilliantly "encylopedic" dimension of this book, I end up recognizing myself in quite a few analyses and conclusions. I confided about it in "Lettre ouverte à Tristan Garcia," published in *La Revue Littéraire* (Paris: Léo Scheer, 2012).

2   Theodor W. Adorno, *Minima Moralia: Reflections on a Damaged Life*, 150.

3   I will elaborate this point fully in the unpublished book on Meillassoux. One of the most striking outcomes of the demonstration is that, in terms of critical epistemology, Nietzsche is infinitely more Rousseauist than he would have liked, and thus Heidegger as well. Once again digging the furrow opened up first by Lacoue-Labarthe, I show that Nietzsche and Heidegger, in the ultra-critical discourse they make for the first time in the history of philosophy on the subject of Science, no longer placing themselves under his invocation and fiduciary tutelage, purely and simply *paraphrase* Rousseau without even knowing it.

Techne

1   Jean-Clet Martin, *Une intrigue criminelle de la philosophie* (Paris: La Découverte, 2009). I owe to this admirable reading of Hegel infinitely more than I explicitly said out loud until now. It is done.
2   Martin, *Une intrigue criminelle de la philosophie;* my translation.
3   Ibid., my translation.
4   Still today, maybe even more than ever: Badiou, Žižek, Jean-Clet Martin, Meillassoux, Garcia or myself are all "defrocked Hegelians," as Meillassoux said publicly himself.

Transgression

1   Alain Badiou, *Being and Event*, trans. Oliver Feltham (London: Continuum, 2005), 58.
2   Badiou/Kant.
3   Besides, if metaphysics is well and truly accomplished in technology, does not the deconstruction of the former announce the practical dismantling of the latter? It would be political ecology become intelligent... The philosophies of one century are always literalized in the following century, or in the century after that. The philosophical teleologies of the nineteeth century have shaped the twentieth. Then it is to be hoped that the deconstruction of metaphysics has this future sense that I accord it, i.e. the dismantling of global technological totalitarianism, rather than its destruction (in the amphibolic sense of "*the* destructing (*it*)" [le *détruire*], which would run the sole risk of turning back against our simple survival, and the total destruction it is henceforth capable of carrying out).

Appendix: Propreptic to *Being and Sexuation*

1   The present text is the virtually untouched version of a lecture given at the École Normale Supérieure in rue d'Ulm on May 14, 2011. I include it here so that this recapitulation can be complete, because this dimension of *The Spirit of Nihilism* that is essential to this book is also the most speculative, especially in its "metaphysical" conclusions. All the rest is solidly demonstrative; this dimension, no doubt owing to its very subject, has something rather "floating" and—as it is the only adjective that so strongly asserts itself, I repeat—speculative about it. And yet it is not the one I am least proud of, and this little book would not have been a complete overview without it.

2   Gilles Deleuze, *The Logic of Sense*, ed. Constantin V. Boundas, trans. Mark Lester
    with Charles Stivale (London: Continuum, 2004), 147.

3   Gilles Deleuze and Claire Parnet, *Dialogues II*, trans. Hugh Tomlison and Barbara
    Habberjam ("The Actual and the Virtual" trans. by Eliot Ross Albert) (London:
    Continuum, 2006), 74–5.

4   Jacques Lacan, *The Seminar of Jacques Lacan: On Feminine Sexuality, The Limits
    of Love and Knowledge (Encore) (Book XX)*, ed. Jacques-Alain Miller, trans. Bruce
    Fink (New York: W. W. Norton & Company, 1999), 75.

5   Philippe Lacoue-Labarthe, "The Poetics of History," 16.

6   Philippe Sollers, *Éloge de l'infini* (Paris: Gallimard, 2001); my translation.

7   Jacques Lacan, *The Seminar of Jacques Lacan: Psychoanalysis upside down/The
    reverse side of psychoanalysis 1969–1970 (Book XVII)*, trans. Cormac Gallagher
    (from unedited French manuscripts with an eye to the official published version),
    VI 5–VI 6, www.lacaninireland.com (accessed February 4, 2014).

8   Use of the verb *cerner* (meaning "to delimit," "to outline," "to define," "to figure
    out," as well as "to surround") will be echoed a little bit later in the text by
    the term *le cerne*, meaning "a ring or circle that demarcates something"; for
    consistency, I translated *cerner* as "to surround" and *le cerne* as "surrounding," but
    the above meanings should also be kept in mind.

9   Translator' note: in English in the original.

10 Translator's note: "*tout s'échange contre soi, contre l'autre, l'être en faveur de l'étant,
    l'étant en faveur de son essence, l'essence en faveur de l'être.*"

11 Schürmann, *Broken Hegemonies*, 425.

Bibliography

Adorno, Theodor W. *Minima Moralia: Reflections on a Damaged Life*. Translated by E. F. N. Jephcott. London: Verso, 2005.

—*Aesthetic Theory*. Edited by Gretel Adorno and Rolf Tiedemann. Translated and edited by Robert Hullot-Kentor. London: Bloomsbury Academic, 2013.

Badiou, Alain. *Second Manifesto for Philosophy*. Translated by Louise Burchill. Cambridge: Polity Press, 2001.

—*Being and Event*. Translated by Oliver Feltham. London: Continuum, 2005.

—*Plato's Republic*. Translated by Susan Spitzer. New York: Columbia University Press, 2013.

Badiou, Alain, Jean-Claude Milner, and Philippe Petit. *Controverse: Dialogue sur la politique et la philosophie de notre temps*. Paris: Seuil, 2012.

Baudrillard, Jean. *Simulacra and Simulation*. Translated by Sheila Faria Glaser. Michigan: University of Michigan Press, 1994.

—*The Conspiracy of Art*. Edited by Sylvère Lotringer. Translated by Ames Hodges. New York: Semiotext(e), 2005.

Beckett, Samuel. *Endgame*. Translated by Samuel Beckett. New York: Grove, 1958.

Cale, John, and David Owens. "John Cale: 'I might be exhausted but at least I know my brain is working.'" *WalesOnline*, September 29, 2012. Accessed January 31, 2014. http://www.walesonline.co.uk/lifestyle/showbiz/john-cale-i-might-exhausted-2024872.

Castel, Pierre-Henri. *La métamorphose impensable*. Paris: Gallimard, 2003.

—"Les perversions, la sexologie et le mal" (5th session, unpublished seminar). March 27, 2003. http://pierrehenri.castel.free.fr/S%E9minaires%20ALI/perversion270303.htm (accessed February 2, 2014).

—"Les perversions, la sexologie et le mal" (4th session, unpublished seminar). January 30, 2003. http://pierrehenri.castel.free.fr/S%E9minaires%20ALI/perversion300103.htm (accessed February 2, 2014).

Deleuze, Gilles. *The Logic of Sense*. Edited by Constantin V. Boundas. Translated by Mark Lester with Charles Stivale. London: Continuum, 2004.

Deleuze, Gilles, and Félix Guattari. *What is Philosophy?*. Translated by Graham Burchell and Hugh Tomlison. London: Verso, 1994.

Deleuze, Gilles, and Claire Parnet. *Dialogues II*. Translated by Hugh Tomlison and Barbara Habberjam ("The Actual and the Virtual" translated by Eliot Ross Albert). London: Continuum, 2006.

Derrida, Jacques. *The Margins of Philosophy*. Translated by Alan Bass. Chicago: Chicago University Press, 1982.

—*The Animal That Therefore I Am.* Edited by Marie-Louise Mallet. Translated by David Wills. Bronx: Fordham University Press, 2009.

Descola, Philippe. *Beyond Nature and Culture.* Translated by Janet Lloyd. Foreword by Marshall Sahlins. Chicago: University of Chicago Press, 2013.

Garcia, Tristan. *Forme et Objet. Un traité des choses.* Paris: P.U.F., 2011.

Husson, Valentin. *La poétique de Rousseau.* Unpublished.

Kacem, Mehdi Belhaj. *Esthétique du Chaos.* Auch: Tristram, 2000.

—*Society.* Auch: Tristram, 2001.

—*La chute de la démocratie médiatico-parlementaire.* Paris: Sens et Tonka, 2002.

—"Lettre ouverte à Tristan Garcia." In *La Revue Littéraire.* Paris: Léo Scheer, 2012.

Kojève, Alexandre. *Outline of a Phenomenology of Right.* Edited by Bryan-Paul Frost. Translated by Bryan-Paul Frost and Robert Howse. Maryland: Rowman & Littlefield Publishers, Inc., 2007.

Lacan, Jacques. *The Seminar of Jacques Lacan: The Four Fundamental Concepts of Psychoanalysis (Vol. Book XI).* Edited by Jacques-Alain Miller. Translated by Alan Sheridan. New York: W. W. Norton & Company, 1998.

—*The Seminar of Jacques Lacan: On Feminine Sexuality, The Limits of Love and Knowledge (Encore) (Vol. Book XX).* Edited by Jacques-Alain Miller. Translated by Bruce Fink. New York: W. W. Norton & Company, 1999.

—*The Seminar of Jacques Lacan: Psychoanalysis upside down/The reverse side of psychoanalysis 1969–1970, (Book XVII).* Translated by Cormac Gallagher (from unpublished French manuscripts with an eye to the official published version). Accessed February 4, 2014. www.lacaninireland.com.

Lacoue-Labarthe, Philippe. "The Poetics of History." Translated by Hector Kollias. *Pli* 10 (2000): 1–23.

—*Poétique de l'histoire.* Paris: Galilée, 2002.

—"Traduction et histoire." *L'animal* 19–20 (Winter 2008): 141–8.

—*Voyage à Tibüngen: un portrait de Philippe Lacoue-Labarthe.* Telefilm by Michel Deutsch. Sepia/France 3 Alsace (2008). http://www.filmsdocumentaires. com/films/434-philippe-lacoue-labarthe (accessed February 4, 2014).

Malabou, Catherine. *The Heidegger Change: On the Fantastic in Philosophy.* Albany: State University of New York Press, 2011.

Marivaux, Pierre Carlet de Chamb. "The Constant Players." In *Marivaux Plays.* Translated by John Bowen, Michael Sadler, John Walters, Donald Watson, and Nicholas Wright. London: Methuen Publishing, 1988.

Martin, Jean-Clet. *Une intrigue criminelle de la philosophie.* Paris: La Découverte, 2009.

—*Plurivers.* Paris: P.U.F., 2010.

Millet, Richard, and Romaric Sangars. "Maestro en Crise." *Chronic'art*, May 6, 2007. http://www.chronicart.com/digital/richard-millet-maestro-en-crise/ (accessed February 7, 2014).

Milner, Jean-Claude. *Le Triple du plaisir.* Lagrasse: Verdier, 1997.

Nietzsche, Friedrich. *Basic Writings of Nietzsche*. Translated and edited by Walter Kaufmann. New York: Modern Library, 2000.

Schuhl, Jean-Jacques. *Rose poussière*. Paris: Gallimard, 1972.

Schürmann, Reiner. *Heidegger on Being and Acting: From Principles to Anarchy*. Translated by Christine-Marie Gros. Bloomington: Indiana University Press, 1987.

—*Broken Hegemonies*. Translated by Reginald Lilly. Bloomington: Indiana University Press, 2003.

Scutenaire, Louis. *Mes inscriptions (1943–1944)*. Paris: Allia, 1982.

Sklansky, David, and Alan N. Schoonmaker. "Poker is Good For You." *Two Plus Two Internet Magazine*, Vol. 3, No. 9, 2009. http://www.twoplustwo.com/magazine/issue33/sklansky-schoonmaker-poker-good-for-you.php (accessed February 7, 2014).

Sollers, Philippe. *Éloge de l'infini*. Paris: Gallimard, 2001.

Soulier, Fabrice. "Le poker français dans la tourmente." *Fabrice Soulier*, February 2, 2013. http://www.fabricesoulier.com (accessed January 1, 2014).

Taranto, Pascal. In *Le ressentiment, passion sociale*. Edited by Antoine Grandjean and Florent Guénard. Rennes: Presses Universitaires Rennes, 2012.

Poe, Edgar Allan. *The Complete Tales and Poems of Edgar Allan Poe*. London: Penguin Books, 1982.

—*The Essential Tales and Poems of Edgar Allan Poe*. Edited by Benjamin F. Fisher. New York: Barnes and Noble Classics, 2004.

Index